W9-CON-487

The

Final Station: Umschlagplatz

The Final Station: Umschlagplatz

Jarosław M. Rymkiewicz

Translated by Nina Taylor

Farrar Straus Giroux

New York

Originally published in Polish in 1988 under the title *Umschlagplatz*
by Instytut Literacki, Paris
Printed in the United States of America
Designed by Fritz Metsch
First edition, 1994

LIBRARY OF CONGRESS CATALOGING-IN-PUBLICATION DATA
Rymkiewiz, Jarosław Marek.
[Umschlagplatz. English]
The final station : Umschlagplatz / Jarosław M. Rymkiewicz;
translated by Nina Taylor.
p. cm.
1. Jews—Poland—Warsaw—Persecutions. 2. Holocaust, Jewish (1939–1945)—Poland—Warsaw. 3. World War, 1939–1945—Personal narratives, Polish.
4. World War, 1939–1945—Poland—Warsaw.
5. Rymkiewicz, Jarosław Marek. 6. Warsaw (Poland—Ethnic relations. 7. Holocaust, Jewish (1939–1945)—Poland—Warsaw—Fiction. I. Title.
DS135.P62W3363 1994
940.53′18′09438—dc20 93-39631 CIP

Gdańsk Station
Umschlagplatz
Cemetery
The Little Ghetto
BONIFRATERSKA
POKORNA
STAWKI
MURANOWSKA
NISKA
MIŁA
KUPIECKA
FRANCISZKANSKA
KOŻLA
NALEWKI
ŚWIĘTOJERSKA
WOŁYŃSKA
ZAMENHOF
KRASIŃSKI GARDEN
OKOPOWA
GLINIAKA
SMOCZA
GĘSIA
PAWIA
DZIELNA
NOWOLIPKI
KARMELICKA
LESZNO
NOWOLIPIE
KAROLKOWA
ORLA
SOWIA
ELEKTORALNA
KROCHMALNA
GRZYBOWSKA
WALICÓW
CEGLANA
TWARDA
PROSTA
PAŃSKA
ŚLISKA
SIENNA
WIELKA
ŻELAZNA
MARSZAŁKOWSKA
JERUSALEM ALLEY

The Final Station: Umschlagplatz

I SPENT a long time looking for a plan of Umschlagplatz. The numerous maps of the Warsaw ghetto show Umschlagplatz as a small rectangle. The more detailed ones have a second, smaller square inset in the first, representing the buildings, with four or five lines to denote the railroad sidings. The lines and rectangles tell us next to nothing, as they provide no basis for reconstructing the appearance of what, forty-five years ago, was known as Umschlagplatz. I read neither Hebrew nor Yiddish, but I have scanned many Hebrew and Yiddish books about events in the Warsaw ghetto, and none of them contained the plan I was looking for.

I was, in fact I still am, quite convinced that a Jewish historian specializing in the history of the ghetto must have drawn up a plan. It is on Umschlagplatz that the history of Polish Jews came to an end, was arrested and seemingly terminated. When history began again, as it did for a limited period, it assumed a form and direction quite unlike its previous incarnation. Places marked by such events are usually described by historians in minute detail, hence my hypothesis, my certainty even, that a plan of Umschlagplatz was drawn up long ago, in Tel Aviv or New York, and published in some compendium dealing with the history of Polish Jewry. This compendium, I am sure, is unknown and unobtainable in Warsaw. It is certainly not available in any library, which strikes me as odd, seeing that Umschlagplatz was situated in Warsaw.

After long and fruitless searches, when I was about halfway through writing this book, I appealed to Michal X. for help. I knew some of his friends had been through Umschlagplatz, and thought one of them might like to draw me a plan. Michal promised to do his best, but later said he couldn't help, and nothing came of it. My request must have struck his friends as a trifle bizarre. I can imagine their reaction: "What on earth does he want that for?" For forty-five years the Poles living near Umschlagplatz have evinced no interest in the place. When walking through or around the Square they may think of its history with a feeling of dread. They may spare a compassionate thought for the victims. It may cross their minds that the events marking this site belong not only to Jewish but also to Polish history. But even if they think along these lines, there is no evidence that Umschlagplatz has ever had any significance in the intellectual life of the Poles. I have no idea of its meaning for Jewish thought and spirituality. What concerns me here is the spiritual heritage of the Poles. They watered the potted flowers that had been secured to the old brick wall—all that survived of Umschlagplatz. They sensed the horror of it. Nothing more. The wariness of Michal's friends is perfectly legitimate. Why, forty-five years after the events, should a Pole, a goy, suddenly get excited about Umschlagplatz? Why should he want a plan?

I shall presently explain why. But first a few words about the plan. I finally succeeded in unearthing one. It was drawn up in 1946, or before, by Henryk Rudnicki, and published in his *Martyrology and Extermination of the Warsaw Jews* (Łódź, 1946), a book that is virtually unobtainable today. Rudnicki's work is not a reliable source. It contains many peculiar mistakes, to which I shall later return. As for the plan, whatever its faults, it is a document that cannot be lightly dismissed. So here it is, arguably the only extant plan of Umschlagplatz in Warsaw.

Various points of Rudnicki's plan are open to debate. None of the sources I have read mentions SS Headquarters, which Rudnicki locates on Niska Street. Befehlstelle SS, the headquarters of Einsatz Reinhard, was situated at 103 Żelazna Street. Above the entry to Umschlagplatz the plan shows an exit, to which no reference is made in any of the published texts. The same goes for the double wall on Zamenhof Street and Dzika Street: Rudnicki's sketch suggests that the columns of Jews entering Umschlagplatz were escorted between two walls. The position of a building identified by Rudnicki as a hospital is also open to doubt: it seems fairly unlikely that a hospital would stand in the middle of a street—intersecting it, as it were—with its gable wall overlooking Stawki Street.

The plan also fails to show buildings that, to the best of my knowledge, ought to be there. During the great extermination in July 1942, a building close to Umschlagplatz housed a Werterfassungsstelle agency. This institution

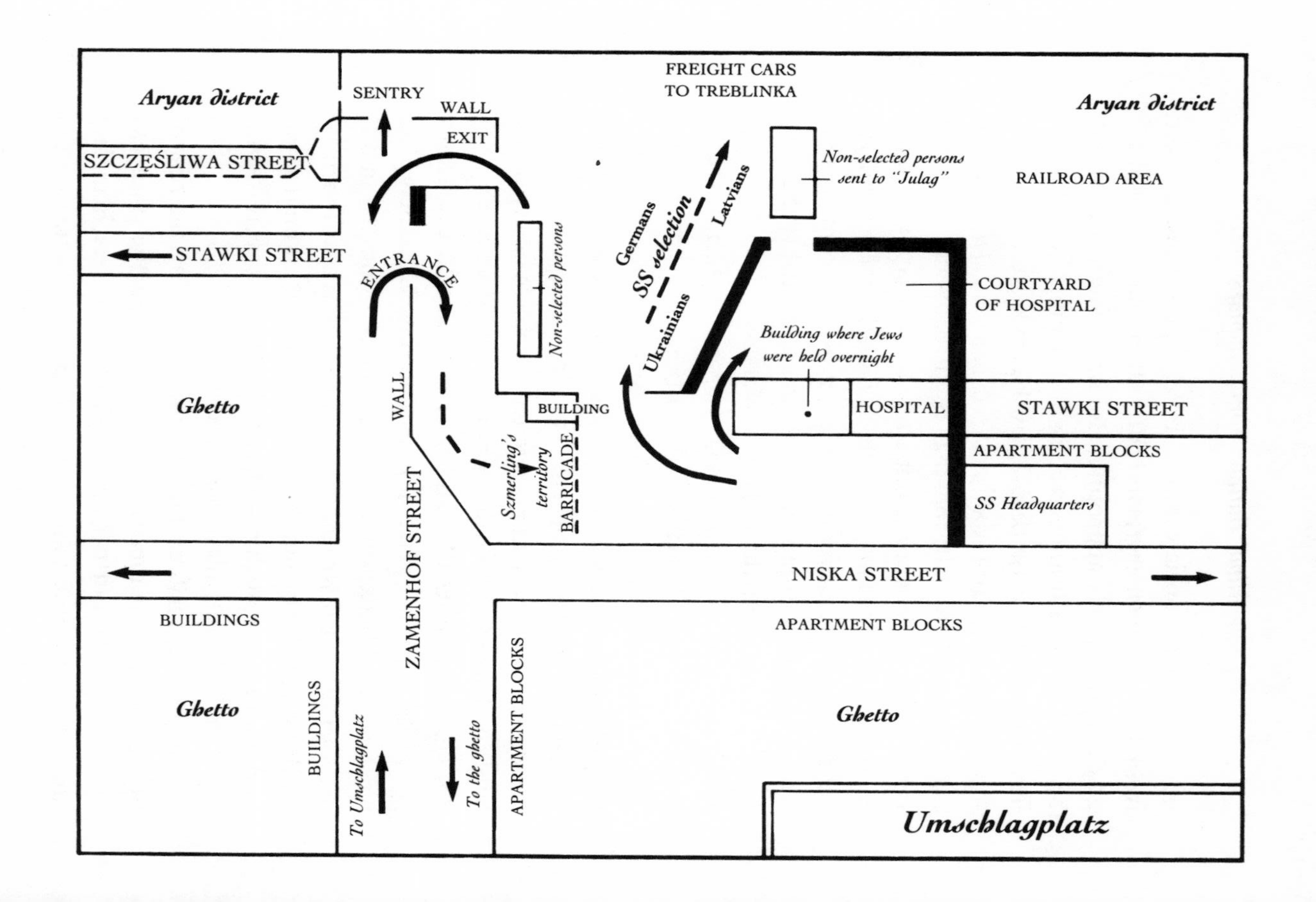
Aryan district
SENTRY
WALL
EXIT
SZCZĘŚLIWA STREET
STAWKI STREET
ENTRANCE
Non-selected persons
FREIGHT CARS
TO TREBLINKA
Germans
SS selection
Latvians
Ukrainians
Non-selected persons
sent to "Julag"
Aryan district
RAILROAD AREA
COURTYARD
OF HOSPITAL
Building where Jews
were held overnight
HOSPITAL
STAWKI STREET
APARTMENT BLOCKS
SS Headquarters
Ghetto
WALL
BUILDING
Szmerling's
territory
BARRICADE
ZAMENHOF STREET
NISKA STREET
BUILDINGS
APARTMENT BLOCKS
Ghetto
BUILDINGS
To Umschlagplatz
To the ghetto
APARTMENT BLOCKS
Ghetto
Umschlagplatz

(hardly the appropriate word, but what else can one call it: a commercial enterprise? a business concern?) sorted the goods and chattels appropriated from Jewish homes—to be precise, from homes that had once belonged to Jews. This building does not figure on Rudnicki's plan. Nor do the warehouses, presumably huts, of the Transferstelle bureau, the unit that delivered supplies to the workshops and transported their wares from the ghetto. I am not saying that Rudnicki made a mistake. He may have considered some sections of Umschlagplatz, such as the Transferstelle huts, to be too insignificant to be included on the plan. As he paid three visits there, he may well have noticed things that others failed to observe or jot down. The stories of survivors from Umschlagplatz tend on the whole to be frenzied and chaotic.

In *Polish Jews: The Final Chapter* (New York, 1977) the author writes that Umschlagplatz is *infamous*. I understand his intentions. He meant that atrocities were committed on Umschlagplatz. That is patently true. But he failed to see that the epithet is equivocal. *Infamous* Umschlagplatz. This could mean a place of ignominious death. Or a place desecrated by ignominious death. Equivocal terms should be avoided when writing about Umschlagplatz. The place where 310,000 people awaited their death is not *infamous*.

There are few such places on this planet. In fact, it may well be the only place of its kind. We who live in its immediate vicinity, in the very heart of Warsaw, ought to reflect on what it means for us, not in terms of the past, but in terms of our own reaction to what once happened there. Though the past is obviously important, as it has made us what we are now. Someone I know lived on Grzybowska Street, between Wronia Street and Żelazna Street, during the great extermination. From his windows he could see the small ghetto and the barbed wire, and Jewish children burrowing through to the Aryan side, pursued by Latvians in black uniforms. My informant, who is now over sixty, told me that what he saw and experienced then changed his whole life: he is what he is now because of what he saw. But I am chiefly interested in the future. What does Umschlagplatz signify in Polish life and Polish spirituality, and what does it portend for posterity? We live within the orbit of their death. That is why I needed a plan of Umschlagplatz.

JAKUB Wurzel removes his pince-nez and wipes it with a handkerchief, a green handkerchief with a purple border, then takes it by the gold wire between the lenses and examines it against the light, as though to determine if it might be used as a field glass and whether an object observed through this device held at arm's length would be magnified or reduced.

"Read that," he says, and pushes the newspaper lying on the wicker table—it is *The Illustrated Weekly*—toward Icyk Mandelbaum, who sits on the opposite side of the table in a wicker chair identical to the one in which Jakub Wurzel is ensconced. "It is very funny."

"I don't feel like reading," says Icyk, and he unfolds

The Illustrated Weekly. Page three, next to the photograph of Colonel Koc with Marshal Edward Rydz-Śmigły, is stained with tea or chicken broth—hardly surprising since the paper has been lying on the veranda for the last two or three months. "What is it you want me to read?"

"The column on page five," says Jakub Wurzel. "It's unsigned, unfortunately. It is a sort of futuristic novel in the manner of H. G. Wells or our own Antoni Słonimski, only it's column length. In Moscow, in 1941, Joseph Stalin is put on trial. When cross-examined by the prosecutor, Vyshinsky, he confesses he has been an English spy and has promised to sell Archangel and half of Siberia to the English. Whereupon Comrade Stalin is executed by firing squad and Comrade Budenny assumes power. Very funny."

"It may be funny," says Icyk. The sun at this time of the day—it will soon be midday and Mrs. Sara Fliegeltaub will appear on the veranda to announce the lunch menu—the sun is everywhere, on the veranda, in the dining room, in the kitchen, in the upstairs rooms. Icyk shifts his wicker armchair to avoid being blinded as he gazes at Lilka's beautiful long legs, while Lilka, with two jasmine leaves on her eyelids, lies in a deck chair beneath the bush from which the leaves were plucked. "It may be funny, but pretty unlikely if you ask me. I presume that Stalin, who knows what he is about, gives orders to shoot anyone who might want to shoot him."

"Do you think he shot our Radek?" asks Jakub Wurzel.

"I can't say," Icyk replies, having now calculated that if Lilka shifts just once more in her deck chair, her dress, a short flowery dressing-gown affair with buttons in front, will come still wider apart. Then he, Icyk, will be able to observe both her beautiful legs and her no less beautiful thighs. Come on, move. Icyk focuses hard. Please, please move, I will you to move this instant, since it is intolerable that your Szymon should have sole rights to gaze at your thighs. If God created such magnificent legs and thighs, He surely intended that they should be admired by all. Unless God, which again is not to be precluded, created those thighs for His own exclusive benefit and enjoyment. As though in obedience to Icyk's powerful though mute appeal, Lilka shifts in her deck chair, stretches her arms above her head, and grips the gray cloth of the crosspiece with her palms. Thereupon the flowery dressing gown drifts further apart, just as Icyk had willed it, to exhibit her magnificent thighs, and her sleeve slips from her outstretched arm to reveal the blond bush of hairs caked with perspiration in her armpits. But Icyk is unable to survey the blond bush or thighs for more than a second. Lilka adjusts her flowery dressing gown, crosses her legs, and pulls the hem over her knees, withdrawing her thighs and the hairy bush under her armpits from our vision, perhaps forever.

"It is not impossible," says Jakub Wurzel, "that Stalin is keeping Radek in prison so as to use him later for his own ends."

"Sooner or later," says Icyk, and he shifts his wicker chair again so that Szymon Warszawski, who is lying in the deck chair next to Lilka, won't notice that he, Icyk, is studying Lilka much too obtrusively. For if Szymon found out, he would sit through lunch with a sullen and injured air, glowering at Icyk to make him understand that Icyk has no right to stare so brazenly at a woman who belongs to him, Szymon. "Sooner or later, don't kid yourself, he'll have him shot."

"I feel sorry for Radek," says Jakub Wurzel. "Say what you like, he's very intelligent."

"If he were intelligent, he'd never have gotten involved in the first place," says Icyk, wondering if Lilka will move again, and with what outcome. But he promptly abandons that topic as another, infinitely more important thought occurs to him. Did God, in the moment He created that magnificent goy's magnificent legs, make any decision regarding their ultimate mission? In other words, did He decide who was to gaze at them in the future and who, be he Jew or Christian, would in due course become their proprietor? Or to put it yet another way, is the destiny of created matter contained in the creation process, and does God, in conceiving a given form, also conceptualize the form of its existence. Unless, quite the reverse, the act of creation is separate from the act of existence, and the history of created matter is merely the result of God's subsequent endeavors, or latter-day creative acts. If indeed God is interested in what He has once created, for it may well be that the whole thing leaves Him stone-cold. "I'm not impressed by the intelligence of your Radek. A Jew with his wits about him ought to anticipate consequences."

"But what if he really was a German spy?" says Jakub Wurzel. "Who can say? The Germans might have bribed him and then, you know, informed Stalin. Obviously with a view to undermining the Soviets, which must be a major point on their agenda."

"I really don't think it would be in Germany's interests to undermine the Soviets," says Icyk. "Germany needs a strong Russia with whom to forge an alliance when she strikes at England."

"It would be sheer madness for Germany to declare war on England," says Jakub Wurzel. "The English and the French would occupy the Ruhr within twenty-four hours, and within a week they'd be in Berlin. But coming back to Radek . . ." Jakub Wurzel wipes his pince-nez again and holds it up to peer at the jasmine bush and Lilka lying in her deck chair, as though to determine if the glasses might be used to observe in enlargement or reduced format all manner of future events—namely, the ambivalent plans of Stalin, Hitler, Mussolini, and other dictators regarding Jews. "It is not impossible that Stalin's aim is simply to get rid of all Jews. Which does not mean I consider him to be an anti-Semite. Such an outstanding politician, and he is undoubtedly an outstanding politician, cannot be swayed by personal prejudices. But he may have resolved that it is in the interests of Soviet Russia to remove all the Jews who staged the Russians' revolution for them and are still in positions of power today. Notice who gets sentenced in those disagreeable trials of theirs. Mainly Jews."

"But why should Stalin," asks Icyk, searching for the concept regarding the split or rift between creation and existence which he has mislaid through the blatant fault of Stalin, Radek, and other Jews in control of the Soviet Union, though it still lurks somewhere in the back of his mind. "Why should Stalin need to get rid of the Jews? If he is not, as you claim, an anti-Semite, what would he stand to gain from it?"

"The Jewish communist mafia," says Jakub Wurzel. "That's the problem that interests me, or rather interests Stalin. He definitely reads the English and French newspapers. And if he doesn't, his secretaries do. And the papers carry on about how the Soviet state is ruled by a Jewish power clique. And that's what Europe is scared of. If Stalin wishes to come to an agreement with the Germans or the French, which strikes me as more than likely, then he must first convince them that Russia is ruled by Russians, and not by Jews. That he is not a Jewish flunky. For they are not prepared to talk to someone they regard as a Jewish flunky. You see my point. To come to terms with Hitler, Stalin must get rid of the Jews. Do you remember his secretary, Miss Kaganovich?"

"No, I don't," says Icyk, speculating on his chances of nonverbal communication with Lilka. Will his thoughts about her person be imparted to her now that she appears to have fallen asleep in her deck chair and, if he steers his thoughts in the right direction, will they penetrate the dream she is having beneath two jasmine leaves? Now that would be gratifying in the extreme. "Is she the daughter of the Kaganovich in Stalin's current government?"

"It might be more appropriate to say she *was* his daughter," says Jakub Wurzel. "My impression is she's dead. As far as I remember, Stalin fired her sometime in April or May, there was something about her in the papers. Before that, Miss Kaganovich was his secretary and she wielded supreme power in the Soviet Union. She was even thought to be his wife. When he removed her, our press reported that it was the beginning of an anti-Semitic campaign in the Soviet Union. But I think Stalin might have removed her, or even killed her, for quite a different reason. Can you imagine Hitler welcoming Stalin's Jewish secretary or Jewish wife at the station in Berlin? Hitler would never have agreed to Stalin's visiting him with a Jewish secretary-cum-wife in tow. So Stalin may have axed Miss Kaganovich in order to pave the way for negotiations with Hitler."

"But perhaps . . . ," says Icyk. He shuts his eyes so as to imagine his thoughts infiltrating the dream that Lilka is having beneath the jasmine leaves and unfurling in her jasmine-green sleep to caress her drowsy thoughts. "But perhaps Stalin was no longer interested in Miss K. and so he fired her or even, as you suggest, killed her. Wouldn't that explain the sad fate of poor Miss Kaganovich? Or maybe she was very ugly. So ugly that Stalin couldn't bear to look at her for one more moment."

"However," says Jakub Wurzel, disregarding Icyk's patently silly idea, "I admit yet another possibility. Namely, that Stalin kills his opponents because he wants to introduce parliamentary democracy in Russia. To achieve that goal he must first eliminate the opposition, as a guy like Trotsky, unquestionably a born dictator, would never agree to such a thing."

If the act of creation, Icyk reflects, having tracked down the thought previously mislaid through the fault of Stalin, Radek, Trotsky, and Miss Kaganovich—if the act of creation is divorced from the act of existence and contains no guarantees for the future, then my destiny, as well as that of Jakub Wurzel and Lilka and her lover, Szymon Warszawski, is totally unimaginable, and all we can predict is that our fate will be unexpected and unprecedented; for example, Lilka might one day become my mistress, but that is as far as it goes. The same applies to Mrs. Sara Fliegeltaub, the owner of the boardinghouse in Otwock, who has just this minute stepped onto the veranda.

"For lunch, ladies and gentlemen," she announces, "there will be cold borscht and minced cutlets with potatoes and carrots. As for the dessert, that is my sweet secret—it will be a lovely surprise for my dearest guests."

For dessert that day Mrs. Sara Fliegeltaub had made an apple pie with meringue which was meant to set in the oven, but either because the meringue had seeped into the pastry or because the apples had been too juicy, the dough had partly dissolved and been turned into a soggy lump. Now the question is, if Sara had foreseen the fate of her dessert—namely, that it would be a disaster fit only for the garbage—would she have gone to the trouble of making pastry, peeling apples, breaking eggs, and whipping up the whites? One thing is sure, she would have refrained from announcing her menu and alluding to the sweet secret and lovely surprise. In the end, the mess was eaten by two half-wild ginger-yellow cats, one of them blind, that lived in the cellar of the boardinghouse.

The act of creation, Icyk muses, is divorced from the act of existence. With no guarantees for the created object, which waits in fear and trembling for the next relevant act of creation. After which it may be partly dissolved and transformed into a sodden lump like the pastry.

I agree with Icyk Mandelbaum, although I really should say that he thinks the same way as I do. I obviously cannot know what Icyk was thinking fifty years ago, in July 1937, on the veranda of Sara Fliegeltaub's wooden house in Otwock, when he discussed the fate of Radek, a native of Tarnów, with Jakub Wurzel and gazed at Lilka's legs, and I am therefore with some sense of embarrassment putting my own thoughts into his head. A Jewish poet and prose writer, born on Krochmalna Street in 1907, Icyk Mandelbaum was then thirty years old, and the author of one volume of poetry, one novel, and over a dozen short stories. He saw himself as the heir to Isaac Loeb Peretz, whom he felt he would soon surpass, and that is indeed what happened. Now it seems pretty unlikely that anyone in July 1937 should think exactly the way I, a Polish poet and prose writer with several volumes of poetry and one novel to my credit, think in July 1987. So I must modify the thoughts I am putting into Icyk's head.

It's too late now, but if way back in the sixties or seventies we had asked Icyk what he was thinking in July 1937 in Otwock, he definitely wouldn't have been able to answer our question. At best he would have mumbled something like: "I thought I'd had enough, I even said to Szymon Warszawski at lunch, 'Szymon, sir, I've had enough of all that, I'm simply fed up.' To which Szymon, who had certainly not had enough, for he found sleeping with Lilka exceptionally pleasurable, made no reply, but gave me a glance of unconcealed aversion."

So if Icyk cannot remember his thoughts at the time, I have no option but to implant my own ideas in his brain. There is, however, one thing I should point out to my dear, or, to use Mrs. Sara Fliegeltaub's favorite expression, my dearest readers. Once modified and inserted in Icyk's head, my thoughts undergo a process of change to become the common property of Icyk and myself. In other words, they are still my thoughts, but they have been scrutinized and interpreted from a distance and from a different perspective, for me quite unprecedented, rather as though I had been using Jakub Wurzel or Icyk Mandelbaum's pince-nez as a field glass. For in the summer of 1937 Icyk also wore a pince-nez. Later, in the fifties, his glasses had thick horn rims. Later still, in the seventies, he sported a fine silver or gold wire frame, identical to the wire of his pince-nez half a century earlier. So much for Icyk's glasses and his thoughts. Let us now return to the dessert.

"Forgive me, Pani Sara," said Icyk with exquisite politeness when, soon after the minced cutlets and carrots, the dessert was brought in and placed on the table by nineteen-year-old Fejga. Also known to the lodgers as Fecia (Fecia, I'm off for a walk, you can do my room now), Fejga was a general housemaid at the Cozy Nook, but Mrs. Fliegeltaub was displeased with her services and considered that her real vocation in life lay somewhere best left to your imagination. The apple meringue pie that Fejga now placed on the table had ceased to be meringue and had turned into a repulsive mess. After tasting the delicacy Icyk said, "Forgive me, your dessert is hardly what I would call a success. In fact, it is quite simply inedible." And with less than exquisite politeness he shoved away his plate with the piece of half-baked dough from which he had first excavated a fairly sizable hole with his fork.

"Mr. Icyk," said Mrs. Fliegeltaub, less to Icyk than to the rest of the company—namely, Chaja Gelechter, Jakub Wurzel, Szymon Warszawski, Miss Lilka, the promiscuous Fejga, and the Jewish God who from His high heaven commanded a full view of the pie and of Icyk pecking away with his fork, "Mr. Icyk is what one might call choosy."

And Chaja Gelechter said, "Don't be so picky." She then added for Mrs. Fliegeltaub's benefit, "I give you my word of honor, he will eat that pie."

"No, I won't," said Icyk.

"What a lovely surprise," said Jakub Wurzel, stabbing his piece of pastry with his fork as though to test the accuracy of Icyk's claim concerning its total inedibility, or to tunnel his way through to some hidden sweetmeat. "Coming back to Stalin, you know, there's yet another scenario we should consider."

"Namely?" asked Icyk.

"Namely," Jakub Wurzel said, "that Stalin hasn't the remotest intention of introducing a parliamentary system. Quite the reverse, it could be that he has his potential opponents executed because he is obsessed with the idea of becoming tsar. In the manner of Ivan the Terrible. Once he has eliminated all opposition, he will convene the Holy Synod and have himself crowned in Leningrad. Now, Radek and Kamenev, who are Jews, would never consent to that. That would also explain the case of Miss Kaganovich. The tsar of all the Russias could never marry a Jew. The notion of Miss Kaganovich as tsaritsa is really rather preposterous."

"I think your friend Stalin is hatching some other scheme," said Icyk, "but I can't say what."

"What can I serve to my dear guests now?" said Mrs. Fliegeltaub. "I have no other dessert in the house. But if you like, you could have tea with jam. Fejga, go to the cellar and bring us a jar of strawberry preserve."

"What a lovely surprise," Jakub Wurzel said again, this time clearly referring to the jam, and not to the inedible pastry or the murky plans of Joseph Stalin.

If in the act of creation, Icyk thought, no created object receives any guarantee, then everything is possible. Every conceivable surprise—and he pushed his chair away from the table to enjoy a better view of Fejga's legs, and a handsome pair of legs they were, as she headed toward the small hallway from which steps led down into the cellar via a trapdoor with a metal ring.

"I WAS eleven or twelve at the time," my sister says, "so I doubt if I can help you. What little I remember is more like separate, disconnected images. Though I do recall Laton's Café and the white-jacketed waiter who served me ice cream. Laton's was only a stone's throw from here, roughly where that courtyard with the metal sculpture of the deer is. But I can't even tell you if it was in 1941 or 1942."

"You are three years older than me," I say. "So you're far more likely to remember than I am. My mind is a complete blank."

We are sitting in a room overlooking the small square at the junction of Górski Street and Julian Tuwim Street. There are three photo albums lying in front of us on my sister's desk. The trees in Tuwim Street are smothered in tiny leaves. It is May 1987, and in the blinding light of the young fronds, in the blinding light of the azure sky that circles above Górski Street and the Square of the Warsaw Insurgents just as it once circled above Hortensia Street and Napoleon Square, my sister and I are looking at family photographs from half a century ago.

In January or February 1945 my mother came back to Warsaw from Piaseczno and went down to the cellar of the burnt-out house on Koszykowa Street to retrieve what she had buried there in the first days of the Uprising. I do not know what she had deposited in the cellar when the Uprising broke out, but I assume it must have been the silver dinner service and some of the more valuable items from our third-floor apartment. When leaving Warsaw, my parents took all their dollars and *świnki* with them, and for those who were born after the war and remember even less than I do, I should perhaps explain that *świnki* were Russian twenty-ruble gold coins. When my mother went down to the cellar at the beginning of 1945, the silver from her dowry had obviously vanished and in the light of concurrent events I can hardly claim this was a grievous loss.

But I am still curious to know in which German home, be it in Hamburg or in Bremen, the knives and forks with my mother's maiden monogram, "H.B.," are being used today. The SS man or Lithuanian guard who unearthed and purloined our silver knives and forks was kind and well bred enough to leave our three photo albums behind. They were of no use to him, but he could always have destroyed them gratuitously. That is why I consider him to be kind and well bred, although in other respects he was no doubt a murderer. Those three albums are all that has survived of the apartment on Koszykowa Street. I see this as a sign to my mother and me, and perhaps to posterity: this is what survives, expect no more. The children of the SS man who stole our forks may rest assured that I am content with what I have and never banked on getting more. The albums are now at my sister's. Two contain photos of the interwar period: Pułtusk, 1929, and Warsaw, 1936 and 1937. The third has photos of the war years: Warsaw, Otwock, Świder, and Józefów, 1941 and 1942.

"Look," says my sister, "that photo was taken somewhere in Marszałkowska Street. At the time"—and my sister scrutinizes my bald patch—"you were really quite a cute little boy."

Taken in the spring of 1941, the photo shows two really pretty children, a boy and a girl; she is the taller, walking alongside an elegant gentleman. The children are well dressed. The boy wears a sailor shirt with a tie and white socks. The girl, who holds his hand, has a narrow-brimmed hat on her head and two large white bows to tie her braids. If one were to place that photo in another album with the caption "Spring in Warsaw, 1936" or "Spring in Warsaw, 1937," no one would guess at the substitution or realize that a mild form of forgery had been committed. The elegant gentleman—hat, pince-nez, walking stick, and a white handkerchief in his jacket pocket—who took his two children for a walk on that spring day and met a street photographer is my father, Władysław. Mother used to call him Władzio or Władeczku.

"I have a feeling," I say, "that we weren't doing too badly in 1941. Perhaps the horrors of occupied Warsaw are not what they are made out to be. Maybe our professional martyrologists are misleading us when they carry on about the dreadful atrocities of the occupation. And even if they don't actually deceive us, they forget to mention that in spite of all the atrocities one could still lead a tolerably pleasant life in Warsaw. And their oversight is obviously a form of deceit. That photo could figure just as well in the album of a French or Italian family with the caption 'Printemps à Paris, 1941' or 'Primavera a Roma, 1942,' don't you think?"

"You're talking nonsense," says my sister. "A photo like that gives only a tiny fragment of the truth. You and I, two happy children, go for a walk with our father. But two streets away there's a police roundup, or else the Germans stand someone against the wall ready to execute him. Just because it's not in the photo doesn't mean it wasn't happening."

"I'm not saying there were no roundups or executions," I say. "I'm only making the point that our mother looks quite contented with life as she sits in Laton's Café drinking coffee with her friends. And that is also a facet of the truth about those times."

"And any moment now, heaven forbid," says my sister, "the Germans will encircle New World Street and whisk Mother off in a police car. And look, you can see there was a war going on; there's a German standing just behind mother and the other lady, it must be Auntie Helenka."

"Three Germans, in fact," I say. "There's another two in the background. I wonder what unit. SS men, I guess, though I'm not sure if they had caps with soft visors. And here, look, you're in a white dress, making your first communion. Beneath the shop sign shaped like a watch—you'd better put your glasses on—with 'Uhrmacher—Watchmaker' written in small letters."

"Of course I remember my first communion," says my sister. "It was in May 1941. And I also remember the shop sign in German and Polish."

"I didn't know there were bilingual signs in Warsaw at the time," I say. "That house opposite, the neo-Gothic one, is still there. And that is the corner of Marszałkowska Street and Skorupka or Sadowa Street. Do you know what Skorupka Street was called during the occupation?"

"No," says my sister. "Probably something quite different."

"Those aren't the photos I wanted to ask you about," I say. "I'm interested in the ones here. Look, that is Świder, in the summer of 1942. That's you on the swing near the house. Here we are both standing on the beach by the river. And here I am on the platform at Otwock. Cap and tie. The same white socks. But I can't for the life of me remember the house where we spent our holidays that year."

"Nor can I," says my sister, reading the inscription our mother has made on the page with the photo that was taken of me complete with tie, cap, and white socks on the high platform at Otwock. "Church fair in Otwock, July 19, 1942."

"Did you know," I say, "that in the summer of 1942 there was still a ghetto in Otwock?"

"You must be wrong," says my sister. "I thought they were all transferred to Warsaw at a much earlier date."

"I've forgotten where I read it," I say. "Either in that book about the history of the Warsaw ghetto or in Szpilman's memoirs. Afterward I tried to gather some facts about the Otwock ghetto, but I found nothing. Presumably no one has ever described it. If so, the chances are that no one will ever describe it now and no one will ever discover what happened there. The great extermination of the Warsaw ghetto began on July 22. If the ghetto in Otwock still existed in the summer of 1942, it must have been exterminated a bit earlier, say a few days before the extermination of the Warsaw ghetto. And the church fair in Otwock at which Father or Mother took those snapshots was on July 19. Don't you feel that's sort of indecent?"

"Why?" my sister asks. "Just because there was a church fair or bazaar on at the same time?"

"No," I say, "what bothers me is the fact that we two pretty, well-dressed, smiling, contented Christian children are standing on a platform, on a beach, under the pine trees, you're on the swing, I'm holding a big balloon, when only a couple of miles away you know what was going on. I don't have to tell you what was done to those Jewish children. Yet we Christian children could laugh and play and enjoy life. That's what I feel is so very indecent. Father smiles to you and says, 'Stand over there, Alinka, beneath that pine tree.' Then he bends down on one knee and presses the Leica or whatever to his eye. And again you exchange smiles, Father smiles at you, you smile at Father, because you really are awfully fond of one another, and Father is thrilled to be taking another photo of you, and you are thrilled to have your photograph taken. How utterly sweet and pleasant it is to stand beneath the pine trees in Świder or Otwock and gaze into the enigmatic shiny black lens, the secret depths of the camera, which any moment now will reflect and record forever part of the fabulous, terrifying mystery of life itself. The sweetness of life, the sweetness of that July, of that summer. When just a couple of miles away . . ."

"When you think about it," my sister says, "it's rather like putting one's finger on life's inner essence. Such a balmy day, yet full of horror. That's how I feel about it now. But the thought would never have crossed my mind then."

"But what strikes me as obscene," I say, "is not only the fact that we Christian children enjoyed that marvelous sensation of sweetness and of horror. It is obscene that we survived at all, when those other children, the Jewish children, went to the gas chambers and the crematoria. It was a most obscene idea on the part of the Polish or the Jewish God."

"Don't involve God in all that," says my sister. "It was a quarrel between Germans and Jews. Between humans."

"I don't care about the Germans," I say. "The Germans will atone for their deeds until the end of time, but that's an issue for their conscience, not mine. For me the issue is between Poles and Jews. As for God, I agree with you up to a point. In trying to involve Him we are merely trying to shirk responsibility: because He devised it all and made the decisions, we could do nothing to prevent it and what happened is not our fault. Though I still reserve the right to question Him about His role in all this. From the theological point of view it may not be acceptable to query God's intentions. But I'm not asking from a theological angle, I'm asking from the point of view of the small boy standing in his white socks and a cap on the high platform in Otwock. So my question is not 'Why did You do that to them?' but 'Why did You do that to me, that small boy on the platform?' But there's one more photo I'd like to show you, it always intrigued me. Tell me what you think about this one."

"That's me," my sister says.

"I know it's you," I say. "But who is that child, the small girl next to you, do you have any idea?"

The photo shows my sister in a short striped summer dress, standing on a path amid dwarf pines, her braid arranged in a crown around her head. The sun shining through the branches casts patches of light on her face, shoulders, arms, and dress. It is 1942, July or August. The photo was taken in Świder, most likely in the vicinity of the wooden house where we used to spend our summer holidays. Next to my sister, more or less level with her elbow, there is a much smaller child, clad in a long dress that almost reaches the ground. So it must be a girl, though this is by no means certain, as the child's hair is shorn close to the skull. One thing, however, is beyond question: the child's hair is black, very black, alarmingly black. My sister smiles to the person taking the photo, but the child's cropped head is strangely tilted, almost tucked into its shoulder, and it stares at the lens with apparent distrust, as though it felt nervous or even downright scared.

"I don't know who that is," my sister says. "Probably some poor girl from the village, or from next door. Look how oddly her hand is twisted."

"Either way," I say, "with looks like that she ought to have gone into hiding. She could have been shot on the street on sight, without being asked if her parents were Poles or Jews. But is it conceivable that our father or mother photographed you in Świder in 1942 with a little Jewish girl? It strikes me as most unlikely. Little girls like that used to be kept hidden in the closet. Yet here she is standing on the path, in bright patches of sunlight."

"Mother was such an eager photographer. In fact, she still is," my sister says, "though she doesn't have any talent for it. I wouldn't put it past her to do such a mad and stupid thing."

"If that was a Jewish girl," I say, "we could all have been shot under the pine trees for taking that photo. In bright patches of July sunlight."

"But I don't remember her," my sister says.

"You mean you don't remember if she was hiding?" I ask. "Or who was hiding her?"

"No."

"How could you have forgotten?" I ask.

"Quite easily," Alinka says. "You don't remember that much yourself."

"Hardly a thing, I agree. I don't remember the pines or the patches of sunlight. Or even my white socks and the high platform."

At this moment I am in fact lying to my sister, for there is one thing I remember perfectly. I can even put a date to the event, though it is purely hypothetical, as I cannot be one hundred percent sure. But I am overstating the case; there was no event as such, nothing actually happened. What I recall is more like a sensation or a premonition, connected with the fact that on that day everyone had been exceptionally good and kind to the boy in the white socks, and had given him magnificent presents. So it could well have coincided with my birthday, July 13, 1942. A deeply personal perception or premonition, what else can I call it, a very private reminiscence, which I have never told anyone until now. If I describe it today, it is because what occurred only a couple of miles away was taking place at the same time, and my perception was somehow linked to those events, or at least it is now.

It was my seventh birthday and I was running along a

path between the pines, past a hedge, then along a sandy woodland road leading I know not where. I was screaming and yelling in a wild and uninhibited way. I was breathless, literally choked by my wild, demented running and screaming. I don't remember what I was shouting, but I guess it was pretty inarticulate, yoo-hoo-hoo, yo-ho-ho, ya-boo, it's me. All because for the first time in my life I had sensed what it was to be alive, to exist, to partake in the unbelievable miracle of our existence here on earth. That sensation filled me with a joy I could express or articulate only by shouting and running till I was out of breath. Then I fell down somewhere by the roadside between the pines, and lay there for quite some time, sensing the fragrance of the pine needles and the coarseness of the moss; the pine needles were close to my lips: I existed. What more can I say, Alinka. That must be when you know what was taking place only a couple of miles away.

I SHALL now attempt to describe Sara Fliegeltaub's boardinghouse. To use the terminology once favored by authors of introductions to histories of philosophy, this immediately raises the epistemological and ontological issue of what is it I propose to describe. The house no longer exists, but I recall its general appearance quite well, because it was not demolished until the end of the sixties. So I can refer to only what I have remembered and retained in my head. What I discuss will be no more than the waves discharged by my brain. Sara Fliegeltaub's house has no other existence; it is as though it never existed. It might be more appropriate to refer to the chemistry of my brain and the chemical processes taking place within it.

But let us stick to the first term. My brain intermittently discharges waves that are related to the house or may even be the house. My memory, like every other memory, stores up thousands, millions, perhaps even billions of items. It seldom has the opportunity or the leisure to worry about the place. So the ontological status of the house is at best ambiguous: sometimes it exists, sometimes it doesn't. It comes and it goes. More often than not it is in abeyance. And even when it surfaces in the form of waves, it exists for only a few seconds, or at best a few minutes. Then it vanishes again, and its ontological status is something I am incapable of explaining: how can a house exist in the memory if that memory then forgets it for a period? Is "existence" the appropriate term for such a state?

Hence my preference for such expressions as "it appears," "it seems," and "as though." It is as though Sara Fliegeltaub's house had no other existence. That is all my memory, or my knowledge of my memory, can tell me. Yet what my memory tells me is at odds with my presentiment or intuition—here I'm in a quandary, as I'm unable to define it—the knowledge given to me I know not by whom or from where about the existence of something that no longer exists.

The ontological status of the house I have described, if I can put it that way, does not exhaust the full potential of its present existence. In other words, that ambiguous status is not the only ontological status it enjoys. Demolished in the sixties, in 1968 or 1969, Sara Fliegeltaub's house does not exist solely in my head and memory, or in the form of waves which my memory intermittently discharges. It exists in a different dimension. How? It exists in reality; and here I'd obviously rather not be asked what I mean by that word. In reality means in reality. I want to make myself clear. I am not saying that the house was transferred by Supreme Dispensation or Decree into a sphere one might define as metaphysical, where it enjoys an existence about which we inhabitants of the earthly sphere have as yet no inkling. That is not what I am getting at. If some metaphysical sphere does exist, its truth is definitely unfathomable, and totally unlike our earthly truth. The house exists in reality, in the Otwock of here and now.

When you get out at the station in Otwock, you set out along Warsaw Street—it is quite a long walk—and then cross over the tracks, turn right, and proceed as far as the small square situated at November 11 Street. Here you should turn left and head in the direction of Andriolli Street. You could also get out at the station in Śródborów—it is a slightly shorter walk—and cut down Narutowicz Street as far as the elementary school, then follow November 11 Street or some other street in the direction of Andriolli Street.

It is in the vicinity of Andriolli Street that our difficulties begin. I assume that Sara Fliegeltaub's boardinghouse—I mean its ambiguous and fluctuating ontological status—exists not only for me or in my head. I am not alone in emitting the waves that constitute the house, however intermittently. Nearby the house someone who discharges identical or similar waves (there may be a few dozen, or even several hundred of us) could ask, "Can't you see the paving stones, the asphalt, the red Fiat 125 parked just where the veranda used to be? So what do you mean by saying that Sara Fliegeltaub's house exists in reality?" Or he might phrase his question differently: "Where is the house which you claim exists in reality? I can see a driveway leading to a garage, a patio paved with red Czech terra-cotta, a glazed staircase, and bars in the windows. Nothing like the original place in fact." All I can reply is that I do not know what I have in mind when I state that Sara Fliegeltaub's house exists in reality.

Probably I have nothing in mind, because it has nothing to do with thinking. That house stands on the same site as the driveway leading to the garage, the terra-cotta patio, and the red Fiat 125. For if the house existed only as waves discharged intermittently by my memory, my life here would lose all sense: I would be thrown out of the sphere of existence into a sphere of nonexistence, nonbeing, nothingness. But the sphere of nonexistence does not exist. So my intuition tells me, and the knowledge given to me, though I do not know by whom or from where.

I shall now attempt to describe Sara Fliegeltaub's boardinghouse. After the war I imagine it was inhabited by tenants who were on the waiting list for an apartment in Warsaw. The leaking roof and the dry rot in the cellar and ground-floor rooms did not unduly trouble them, for they rightly guessed that the sooner the house collapsed, the sooner they would be rehoused in one of the new blocks in Rakowiec or Wawrzyszew. I wonder what the provisional tenants of the rot-infested house would have said if questioned about Sara Fliegeltaub: "I always thought the Jews, you know what I mean, were awfully smart, but they did make a nuisance of themselves, so thank God they moved out." Or words to that effect.

By the time the last of the provisional tenants had moved to Rakowiec or Wawrzyszew, Sara Fliegeltaub's house was in a sadly derelict state, fit only for demolition. The section of tar paper covering the left side of the roof had caved in and was flapping above the room where Chaja Gelechter stayed in the summer of 1937. The balcony above the veranda that once boasted a small gable roof had ceased to exist altogether. It had lost its roof, its floor, and its wooden balustrades with their pseudo-highland carving effects. I was there in October 1968, as the last Polish Jews stood on the platforms at Gdańsk Station waiting for the trains to Vienna. All I recall is the collapsed section of roofing, the demised balcony, and empty macaroni cartons on the veranda, where the side balustrades were also broken or sawn off. In packing, someone had probably accumulated too many cardboard boxes and had left them behind on the veranda.

A description of the house's transitional state in the summer of 1937 seems virtually out of the question, in view of the historical whirlwind that wrenched away the tar-paper roof, the veranda, the balcony, shutters, balustrades, the flower boxes, staircases and steps, and hurled them out of one historical space into another. I shall nevertheless attempt it. And may the pince-nez of Jakub Wurzel or Icyk Mandelbaum serve me as a kind of binoculars or field glass with which to view the past or future in suitable reduction or enlargement and scan the proddings of my intuition.

It was a two-story house with, in front, a flower bed demarcated by broken pieces of roof tile. But before I reach the flower bed I'll pause for a moment by the gate. It was made of vertical boards joined above and below by two flat iron bars, and it was painted green all over, as was the short, stout spring that joined it to the post. On entering the garden you had to hold it open, for when you let go, the spring caused it to snap closed again. Even as the gate was opened a ringing could be heard. From which I infer that there must have been a bell somewhere. But I remember neither the bell nor its whereabouts. Some climbing plant crept up the gatepost and over the gate. It had tiny white or pale pink flowers, probably convolvulus—yes, definitely convolvulus.

Now about that bell: I can still hear it ringing. Every now and again something rings; it is that bell. In view of what I have said about the ontological status of the house, I could use the impersonal form: that ringing can still be heard. The gate shares the status of the house: may what has once existed long continue to exist. Now to the flower bed. The flower bed was neglected and overgrown with weeds, though surely not always, for I remember pansies, yellow and mauve pansies. Also Chaja Gelechter soaring above the pansies and the broken pieces of tile. Why has Chaja stepped into the flower bed and why is she levitating above the pansies? Is she looking for something? I do not know, but I remember her gray shoes just above the pansies.

Beyond the flower bed, slightly to the right, were two large trees, probably deciduous, a rare thing in Otwock. The trees are no longer there, just two stumps. An expert could certainly identify them. But I am not an expert. The high brickwork base reached the level of my elbow, a meter or so from the ground, and along it ran a wooden ledge or cornice, from which the rain dripped and drained straight into the sand. There is no front entrance, but if you turn left you will come to the covered side entrance into the kitchen, with three steps but no handrail.

Turn left again and the veranda comes into sight. Above the veranda is a balcony with a small roof. The house is built of wood, but it is habitable even in winter, as the pine needles inserted between the boards provide excellent insulation. On the right, the veranda is shaded by a tall, thick Virginia creeper. You can sit on the balustrade of the veranda with your back to the plant; if you tilt your head backward you'll be wreathed in the stuff. The deck chairs in front of the veranda are in pretty bad shape. Due precautions should be taken before sitting in one, as it could fold up and pinch the fingers of the prospective user. More about the Virginia creeper: it swarms up to the second floor and screens one of the windows in a leafy drape. But the window can be opened, in which case patches of light and shade form patterns on the face of the person standing inside.

If the window opens, Chaja Gelechter will appear from behind the leafy drape, Chaja Gelechter with whom I, Icyk, have been in love for well over a year, and that's a very long time. But Chaja takes neither my love nor my perseverance too seriously. The gutter between the window and the veranda is likewise smothered with creeper. When it rains and the gutter gurgles, the sound seems to come less from the gutter than from the creeper. Something seems to be gurgling in the depths of the foliage, in the vegetal gloom: the gloomy, leafy, vegetal world is all a-gurgle. The rain soaks swiftly into the sand, which is several meters deep in Otwock, and puddles never stand for more than an hour or two. And that glum and gurgly sound, which I find slightly unnerving, sinks with the rain into the sand. So that is what Sara Fliegeltaub's boardinghouse looked like. My muddled description, my anemic imagination, fade away. What has been imagined disintegrates. What once had the consistency of boards, tar paper, sheet metal, now has the consistency of waves discharged by my brain to God knows where. Someone out in the cosmos may intercept these signals. The question is whether he then sees what I see: a house in a pine forest, a veranda, and deck chairs. For I suspect that the signals issued by my brain may reassemble into a different image. The question is: do we ever understand one another or can we ever hope to understand one another—my God and I.

"ZBYSZEK Bujak was betrayed," says Hania. "And Grot Rowecki, forty years earlier. And what happened to Szymon Konarski? I forget the details, but I bet he was denounced too. A hundred and fifty years before. So it isn't as though they betrayed only Jews. They betrayed their own kind too. Poles betray Poles; they always will. Germans betray Germans; the French betray the French. Endlessly. Surely you don't think it's some local Polish specialty. I can't remember where I read about someone who escaped from the ghetto during the great extermination and hid in the Aryan district of Warsaw. He said that one of the extortionists operating in the vicinity of Union Square and Puławska Street was nicknamed Judas by his colleagues. Just think what that implies. Just think what a professional conscience they must have had, if that's not a misnomer. They knew what trade they were plying. They knew it was an age-old, worldwide, never-ending traffic—to fulfill an atavistic urge and earn hard cash by informing on their brethren."

"But I'm not interested in the eternal aspect of the problem right now," I say. "I simply want to know why Poles blackmailed and denounced Jews. Why Poles, why Jews, why then. I agree with you, there's nothing very odd about their betraying their own kind. There are always the traitors and the betrayed. But you can't explain the betrayal of Jews in terms of the intrinsic unchanging character of human nature, or by the fact that God created us the way He did—not much of a success if you ask me. Of course it explains some things, but it is not good enough. There must have been a special reason for the huge number of extortionists in Warsaw at the time. I would like to know just what was going on inside the head of one of those extortionists, what he was thinking about, when he led some Jewish man or woman in '41 or '42 to Ujazdów Avenue—I think that's where Kripo was—and started haggling: 'Twenty dollars is not enough, throw in another ten or a silver cigarette case, and you're free.' "

"Abominable," says Hania. "But what do you stand to gain from peering into that man's soul? If an extortionist has a soul. Must you really get mixed up in all this?"

"Yes, I must," I say. "If I had a Polish wife I could let the matter drop. But you're a Jew, so I ought to know what those Poles—what else can I call them, they were Poles after all—wanted from you forty years ago. What did they make of you, and of your red hair?"

"At the time," says Hania, "I wore a black kerchief with yellow and red flowers." I am slightly taken aback by her reply, because I know she prefers to avoid the subject of her magnificent crop of red hair and the trouble it once caused. "I was a peasant child from a burnt-out village. I even remember the name of the village: Podbory. So no one had ever seen my red hair. Apart from the ladies who rubbed Sabadilla into my scalp. You know, it was a lotion for killing lice."

"I know," I say. "My hair was rubbed with it too. After the Uprising, I think. But why did I have lice in my hair? Where did the lice come from? I don't remember that."

"That was later," says Hania.

"What was?"

"The ladies and the Sabadilla. Probably in 1944. Just after the great extermination I was at Gienia's. She was our servant before the war, but a cut above the others; we always called her my *bonne*. I remember her wearing a close-fitting white lace bonnet with a white bow behind; that was because my mother felt that a proper nanny ought to wear a white bonnet. She lived in Grochów, and after the extermination she took me to her place. A brave girl. Germans used to visit her—SS men, I think."

"Hunting for Jews?"

"Can't you understand?" says Hania. "She entertained Germans. They drank vodka with her while I huddled under the table. I had nowhere else to go. I remember their boots. A white tablecloth and their black boots protruding under it."

"One of them," I say, "could have bent down to look under the table."

"I can't figure it out," says Hania. "Maybe those Germans knew I was squatting under the table. Gienia might have told them she had a child that she didn't know what to do with when they came by, and that she didn't want it to witness anything unseemly, I mean her cavortings with the Germans. If so, the Germans wouldn't have objected to my huddling under the table while they had their fun with Gienia. They'd probably have felt a bit embarrassed if I'd suddenly emerged."

"How long did it go on for?"

"What, my sessions under the table?" asks Hania. "It depends, usually several hours. But sometimes Gienia forgot about me and I was stuck there till morning. Only don't ask me to tell you what emotions I experienced in that position; I don't remember much anyway. Apart from the boots. And Gienia's joyous squeals, probably when they started pawing her. You know why I'm telling you all this?"

"Of course," I say, "it's Gienia's duality that bugs you."

"She entertained Germans," says Hania, "and to judge by her squeals she enjoyed it. But she was hiding a Jewish child, a redhead. One of her lovers, displeased with her services, could easily have peeped under the table and then marched us both off to the police station."

"I can admire Gienia's duality," I say, "because she saved your life. But the extortionist is a completely different kettle of fish. Even if there was such a thing as a two-faced extortionist who blackmailed the Jews and at other times behaved quite decently, he doesn't interest me. All that intrigues me is his extortionistic nature, or the extortionistic side of his nature. You know exactly what I mean: did they do it solely for money or was there some other motivation, something in the climate or atmosphere—I don't know how to put it—that made them do it? Something hanging in the air. A foul stench. And they could smell it."

"That stench," says Hania, "hung all over Europe at the time. The first half of our century stinks to high heaven. Like a huge heap of foul meat. But I'm not sure if I have the right to speak like that. That judgment should probably be pronounced a hundred or even five hundred years from now."

"I was born here," I say, "my nose is attuned to local aromas. But how do you see it? What did an extortionist think? How did his brain work? Did he just want to earn five or ten thousand zlotys? Or did he have something else in mind?"

"Oh, for heaven's sake stop," says Hania. "Why do you have to know? What difference does their motivation make? I've already told you: it's a repellent, nauseating subject."

"You remember Danka's story?" I ask. "The one about the woman at the corner of Grzybowska Street and Żelazna Street?"

"At the time"—this is Danka's story verbatim—"we were living on Grzybowska Street, between Wronia Street and Żelazna Street. The windows of our apartment overlooked the small ghetto and barbed wire. There was no wall there, just barbed wire. I used to walk past several times a day; it was the only way to the city center. We used the other side of the street. I often saw Jewish children in rags scrambling under the wire to the Aryan side, ragged little skeletons aged about five to seven. Once they had slipped through, they would start begging in the street or go from house to house knocking on the doors. The Germans—well, not actually Germans in this case; they had black uniforms, so they must have been Latvians or Ukrainians—fired shots at the small fugitives.

"One boy, he must have been about eight, called on us several times on Grzybowska Street. His name was Gecelek. It's not a name I know, but that is what we called him: 'Gecelek, we know some ladies who could hide you.' 'But I must go back, ma'am, my dad is sick and I have a little brother and I can't leave them alone. Someone has to work.' So eight-year-old Gecelek worked on the Aryan side knocking on the doors of Christian apartments. The last time he came to us—I think it was in May—he told us his dad had died, but his little brother was still alive, so he had to go back to the ghetto to look after him.

"But I want to tell you about that woman. I was nineteen at the time, and everything that happened, everything that was done to them—how can I put it?—has made me what I am today. I was a witness, and nothing will ever change my nature now, because it was the most decisive thing in my life: I witnessed it. To come back to that woman, we were both walking down Grzybowska Street, just a few yards apart. Suddenly she began to scream. I don't recall exactly how it happened, I mean I don't remember who first noticed the child crawling under the barbed wire. I think she did. But I don't remember the child; all I remember is the woman shouting. She screamed: *Jude! Jude!*—urging the Germans or Ukrainians or Latvians to perform their duty and shoot a Jewish child. Listen, Jarek, that was not the only incident of its kind, I swear. No one knows how often it happened. But I was not the only one who heard. It went on and on. That scream: *Jude! Jude!*"

"That woman," I asked. "Do you remember what she looked like?"

"Quite ordinary," said Danka. "Between thirty and forty years old. Anyway, she was unlucky; no one heard her prayer. Most likely there was no German or Latvian within earshot. So it all ended happily, if one can talk of a happy ending in such a context. There was a man walking ahead of me. He went up to the woman and slapped her in the face. Then he dragged her into a doorway and I don't know what happened next. He probably just continued to hit her in the face. Not that it matters. What matters is that woman. There's something about it I couldn't understand at the time, and I still can't understand it now. It's easy enough to grasp why the extortionists did what they did: they made a living from it. I can also understand the Germans: they were out to murder all Jews. But why was that woman so anxious for the Germans to capture and kill a Jewish child? Did she want to watch a small child die? What was she after?"

"From Danka's story," says Hania, "we can only infer that some people remain totally incomprehensible to others, as though they had an inexplicable mechanism inside them. If it is both incomprehensible and inexplicable, it defies description. Though who knows. Anyway it is not a topic for you. What can you be expected to know about it? You were only ten when the war ended, a small boy from Nowogródzka Street, from Koszykowa Street. When did you see your first Jew? Probably in 1945."

"If I'm not to explore this topic," I say, "then I'd like to know who is. Do you know anyone willing to take it on? And I don't mean just what occurred here between Poles and Jews. Ultimately it may not even be the most important issue. The historians can deal with that; it's their job to document and judge our treatment of the Jewish nation, faults committed, services rendered, how many trees we have earned on Har Hazikaron, how many blackmailers we executed during the war. I'm interested in an aspect of Polish Jewish and Polish Christian relations that has not been fully thought over yet. How shall I put it? We do not know why the woman on Grzybowska Street screamed: *Jude! Jude!* It's no use calling them bastards, scoundrels, anti-Semitic scum, because that explains nothing. Though maybe I'm wrong; perhaps many an honest, pious Christian and many an honest pious Jew has thought it all over, but is too frightened or ashamed to discuss it."

"But it is not a topic for you," Hania repeats, and tiny sparks light up, then fade and light up again in her red hair. There is something quite mysterious about this phenomenon: either her red hair catches and reflects the ambient light, trapping and entangling it, or else a secret tension is generated between the red locks, so the hair itself is a source of light. The sparks that flare up and then fade are a sort of electrical discharge, minute flashes of lightning that fly through billowing clouds, in a tempest of red hair. "That is a topic for the Jews, so let them get on with it. You just drop it."

"Even if the Jews haven't exhausted the topic yet," I say, "nothing they might still have to say can replace what the Christians can and ought to say on the subject. I sympathize with the Jews, with their wartime history and their contemporary history. I don't mean sympathy as a kind of pity, I mean it in the etymological sense of shared suffering, though not being a Jew, I feel like a Christian, I sym-pathize as a Christian. It is only as a Christian that I can address the problem. And a Christian testimony, to my mind, is what we need."

"You can't possibly write a thing like that," says Hania. "It's an absolutely impossible task. And even if you did, they'd give you such a thrashing you'd never live it down."

"Who would?"

"The Jews," says Hania, "and the Poles too. And frankly they'd both be right."

"Well, let them," I say. "In writing what it is my duty to write I am not trying to please the Poles or the Jews. It was all a highly disagreeable business, I don't think even God particularly enjoyed it, so there is no reason why anyone should enjoy it now."

"But remember, I warned you," Hania says. "As a Jew and as a Pole."

"Please, Hania," I say, giving her a push and even slightly hustling her, though not too brutally, as she appears to resist. "Please turn your profile to the window and the daylight. I want to see those small sparks of lightning flying through your red hair."

"I love you," says Hania with her profile turned to the daylight. "And that is why I'd rather you got involved with something slightly more enjoyable for yourself and for others."

"I love you too," I say, "even though you're a Jew."

Whereupon Hania should have retorted: "You anti-Semite" or "You anti-Semite from Koszykowa Street," to intimate that my remark is quite intolerable. But Hania, standing with her profile to the light, makes no reply. She merely looks at me with a mild expression of surprise, as though to say, "You amaze me" or "You upset me" or

"You make me laugh." And red sparks light up and fade and flutter through her billowing clouds of hair.

An attempt to describe Umschlagplatz. I assume this name came into use during the war. Before the war, the Square at 4-8 Stawki Street, on the other side of which the railroad siding along Błońska Street and Dzika Street terminated, was called Transfer (Przeładunkowy) Square. But I am not at all sure about this. I have not been able to trace its Polish name in any of the newspapers of the time or in novels where the action takes place in the Northern District. The term "Transfer" defines its essential character in the days when it was an important center for the Jewish wholesale trade; hence my assumption.

It is hard to say who first introduced the name Umschlagplatz, but it was probably the Germans. It came into use at the beginning of the war, and certainly before the great extermination of July 1942. The diary of Adam Czerniakow has the following entry for April 1942: "Five a.m. on Umschlagplatz. At eight o'clock 1,025 deportees arrived from Berlin." So Umschlagplatz was also Debarkation Square: Jews from Western Europe were disembarked prior to resettlement in the Warsaw ghetto, likewise food supplies for the ghetto inhabitants. Just after the war, in 1945 and 1946, the Polish name still occurs quite often in the accounts of survivors. It was then ousted by the German name, sometimes in the abridged form: "I survived Umschlag." "I escaped from Umschlag."

Nowadays no one in Warsaw ever says "Transfer Square," perhaps because in time the territory and the word have both acquired a symbolic value. Umschlagplatz denotes not only a defined, tangible place near Stawki Street in Warsaw but also a special realm of the spirit or, more aptly, a specific human destiny. Umschlag signifies limbo, gate to the underworld, antechamber of death. Umschlag is what befell the Jews who found themselves there. From the Polish point of view, its symbolic value is best encapsulated in a foreign word. One may not know the German noun *der Umschlagplatz*, but one grasps the allusion. Vagueness here favors symbolization. The process of change and symbolization it has undergone had already begun by the time of the great extermination. In Abraham Lewin's *Diary of the Warsaw Ghetto*, written during this period, I found the following references: "Death in the guise of Umschlagplatz creeps slowly upon us" and "they have dispatched them to hell (on Umschlagplatz)." In a report that was probably written by the novelist Gustawa Jarecka, under the title "The Last Stage of Resettlement Is Death" (November 1942), a similar sentence occurs: "They marched alone to the depths of hell, which bore the strange, enigmatic name of Umschlagplatz."

My aim is nevertheless to describe a specific place. I shall now explain why. I do not know how many accounts exist of the events that took place on Umschlagplatz between July 22 and September 12, 1942, and in January, April, and

May 1943. I don't even know if there is a bibliography, though I assume someone from Yad Vashem must have compiled one. As I have already said, I know neither Hebrew nor Yiddish, and so I can only consult works written in, or translated into, Polish. I have read several dozen such accounts, though there are surely more, probably several hundred if we include the Yiddish and the Hebrew ones. All the ones I have read share one feature: they say next to nothing about the actual appearance of the buildings, gates, walls, sentry boxes. A specific place has not been concretized, as though its appearance signified nothing for those who passed through it.

That I can understand: survivors memorized and chose to narrate only the most relevant facts—namely, what befell themselves and others. The texts naturally all refer to the victims and their murderers, but the place where they met is seldom, if ever, mentioned. One example. In the relatively detailed account by Henryk Nowogródzki, over ten pages in all, entitled "Three Days on Umschlagplatz" (published by Józef Kermisz in the second volume of *Documents and Materials Concerning the History of the German Occupation in Poland*, Warsaw, 1946), I found a total of three references: "large rooms," "gray walls," "There is no furniture." The rest of the narrative deals with the story of how the author came to be on Umschlagplatz, his experiences there, and his escape. The scene of the action cannot be reconstructed simply on the basis of these few jottings. They therefore do not enable us to *see* the place.

Now, why should I want to see Umschlagplatz, and why have I decided to describe it? Anyone researching the history of Polish Jews during the last war will be familiar with the psychological side effects. After several weeks or months of reading one's way through the realms of death, one lapses into a kind of psychotic state. Curiosity, the urge to unearth something new that motivates every historian, soon gives way to apathy and the desire to drop the subject; yet for some obscure reason it clings. It is like being in the middle of a nightmare: you'd like to wake up, you try to wake up, but somehow you can't. A nightmare is by definition obsessional, repetitive; hence that psychotic state and a pervasive sense of indifference that is highly unpleasant and shaming. A few hundred corpses, a few thousand, tens of thousands . . . Just one more method of killing.

I cannot deny that initially a sort of curiosity prompted me to read about Umschlagplatz, to find out what it was like and how people reacted to it. Now, though, I'd much prefer not to have to report on my findings. But I'm still in the throes of the nightmare, I can't extricate myself. That is my first point. My second point is that I believe I can be of some use, and if this is so, I clearly have no right to shirk my duty. Compared with what my fellow countrymen know (I began to write this book four months ago), my knowledge of what the Germans did to the Jews in Poland is vast. Compared with the knowledge of Jewish historians, or Polish specialists such as Władysław Bartoszewski, it is negligible.

A description of Umschlagplatz may already have been compiled by someone from Yad Vashem. Yet I have one advantage over present and future historians in the field.

A literary historian by training, I have devoted many years to the interpretation of literary texts, which involves gouging out individual words and scrutinizing them from every conceivable angle. This could come in handy. Umschlagplatz no longer exists; all that survives is the words describing it. Future generations will ask what these words meant. I would be pleased to be of some use. The great debt we all owe must be shared, so let each man make his small contribution.

They used to go along Leszno Street to Karmelicka Street, then through Nowolipki Street and Zamenhof Street to Stawki Street, "where Umschlagplatz was situated." That is how Leokadia Schmidt describes the way to Umschlagplatz in her book *We Escaped Extermination by a Miracle* (Kraków, 1983). There was another route, and some groups were herded along Muranowska Street or Miła Street or Niska Street. The former recurs most often. In Stawki Street there was a gateway. According to Marek Edelman (*The Ghetto Fights*, Warsaw, 1945): "There is only one narrow gap in the surrounding walls, which are closely guarded by the military police. This is the entrance through which groups of distressed and helpless people are driven." This is also where the selection was carried out by the military policemen.

In Hanna Krall's book *To Outwit God*, published for the first time in the seventies, Marek Edelman states that the only gate leading into Umschlagplatz was made of wood. He also mentions the concrete post next to the gate, which was still standing at the time of their conversation. Marek Edelman was a messenger in the hospital situated on Umschlagplatz. He stood by that gate, and as the columns came flocking into the Square he picked out the "ailing"—in other words, those who had to be saved and whom his comrades from the Bund—the Jewish Socialist Workers' Party—had pointed out in the crowd. "I stood by that gate for six weeks." Marek Edelman's testimony is totally reliable, but I cannot decide how to classify Hanna Krall's book. Is it reportage or a novel? No doubt it is both. The fact that it may be a novel makes it a less reliable source. To quote from her text: "Besides, the gate no longer exists, and the old wall collapsed when the Inflancka estate was being built."

According to Władysław Szpilman's *Death of a City* (Warsaw, 1946), written down by Jerzy Waldorff, the Square was linked to the town by a number of streets and closed off "by gates where those streets entered the Square." Szpilman must have meant Stawki Street, Niska Street, Dzika Street, possibly also Inflancka Street, and even Konarski Street and Młocińska Street, which are all situated to the northwest of the railroad siding. It follows that there were several gateways. From Szpilman's rather vague account one might venture to infer that the gate or gates were part of an enclosure that shut off the railroad siding from the north.

To reconstruct the scene: Szpilman walks in the direction of the train; he has the freight cars on one side, a cordon of Jewish policemen on the other. One of the policemen recognizes him, grabs him by the collar, and shoves him outside the cordon. "I took a backward glance: I saw an open space with railroad tracks and platforms, and the outlets of streets beyond. I broke into a run, heading in that direction. . . . I joined a group of Jewish Commune workers who were leaving the Square, and in this way I slipped through the gate." This must surely refer to a gate located beyond the tracks and the platforms, on the northern side. If so, did the trains from Umschlagplatz pass through a gateway? None of the sources I have read supplies the answer to this question. But maybe Szpilman slipped through the same gate, the one and only gate, mentioned by Marek Edelman. Quite apart from this gate or gates, there must have been other outlets from Umschlagplatz. I shall return to this point when I attempt to describe the buildings.

Now, about the wall surrounding Umschlagplatz. To quote Hanna Krall: "When the district was being developed the old wall collapsed, but it was promptly replaced with a new wall made of sound white bricks." In *The Ghetto Fights*, Edelman refers to "high walls." According to Leokadia Schmidt, a wall enclosed Umschlagplatz on one side only, but she does not specify on which side. "On one side it was enclosed by a thick, high wall." Szpilman, though, seems to suggest that Umschlagplatz was surrounded not by a wall but a fence: "Surrounded partly by houses, partly by a fence." In other words, a barrier made of wooden planks. But when referring to a fence Szpilman may actually have had a wall in mind. Or Jerzy Waldorff, in transcribing his words, may have turned the wall into a fence.

There is a third possibility—namely, that Umschlagplatz was enclosed by a wall in some places and by a fence in others. And a fourth: one witness could have seen a wall around the Square, another witness could have seen a fence. Latter-day witnesses could have been there at different stages of the extermination. Marek Edelman stood by the gate for six weeks, in July and August 1942. But he was not standing there in September or in January 1943, and by then Umschlagplatz could have looked quite different. The Germans were constantly altering the Warsaw ghetto, erecting fences, walls, gates, and wire entanglements.

This may well explain at least some, though certainly not all, of the discrepancies among eyewitness accounts. Marek Edelman states that the walls were high. But not extremely high. According to Leokadia Schmidt, the one wall she mentions could be climbed: "Taking advantage of the darkness, people climbed over the wall that surrounded the Square." There were gaps in the wall. I cannot determine if these openings were made at night by the detainees waiting in the Square and then bricked up on order of the Germans or if there were more durable or even permanent breaches. In his *Notes from the Ghetto*, Emanuel Ringelblum merely mentions the shots fired at those who "attempted to escape through the gaps in the walls by night."

Behind the wall or fence was the Square. According to Władysław Szpilman, it was "of oval shape" and could accommodate "up to eight thousand people." Schmidt calls it a courtyard, and a large one at that. Henryk Nowogródzki likewise uses the word "courtyard": "A sentry is pacing about in the courtyard down below," though in this case we cannot be sure if he means Umschlagplatz or a courtyard on Niska Street. There were two buildings in or rather around or next to the Square. Leokadia Schmidt mentions being bundled into "a building," and also the fact that "the several-story building where we found ourselves and the hospital building beyond" were situated by the Square.

The first building is that of the Old Archives on Stawki Street, so that is how I shall refer to it, though both buildings could in fact be termed hospital buildings. There was a hospital for infectious diseases in the Old Archives building during the war. It was only during the great extermination that part of it was allocated—I quote Leokadia Schmidt—"for the temporary detainment of people pending their deportation." The second building accommodated the children's hospital that had been transferred from Śliska Street and, according to Marek Edelman in *The Ghetto Fights*, "a small dispensary for treating casualties." In Hanna Krall's book, Edelman also refers to this building as a technical school. But the school moved into the hospital building only in the postwar period.

The height of the two buildings remains unresolved, and we will probably never know how tall they were. Several sources mention that the upper stories were patrolled, that the Germans made their selection one floor at a time, and that people fled from one level to the next. Leokadia Schmidt mentions the upper stories of the children's hospital: "The police wouldn't let us upstairs in the hospital." In *A Short History of the Berson and Bauman Hospital (1939–1943)*, Adina Blady Szwajger writes: "All I remember is the hospital door, the stairs where people lay, and the terrible stench of pus and excrement." And again: "I went on up, trying not to tread on bodies; the living and the dead lay side by side. Finally I reached our third floor." In Władysław Szlengel's poetic reportage, *What I Read to the Dead*, based on the stories of people who escaped from Umschlagplatz in the second half of January 1943, we find the sentence: "They wander from one floor to the next in search of water."

It would appear from Hanna Krall's book that the Old Archives building, which Edelman calls the school building, had three stories: "Their energy and vitality terminated on the third floor, for one could go no higher." In *The Ghetto Fights*, Edelman mentions "three-story buildings that had once been a school." So perhaps the erstwhile Old Archives and the building that served as a children's hospital during the extermination had both been schools before the war. Edelman also mentions that one of the buildings had an attic where one could hide. When they began loading the trucks, the people ran upstairs and "hid in dark nooks in the attic." Edelman recalls that someone spent three days in the attic and that several skiffies (Skif was the Bund's scouting organization) hid there for five days. He must surely mean the attic above the children's hospital. According to Władysław Szlengel, people also hid in the cellars: "For the time being about a hundred people managed to hide in the cellar. Then two hundred . . ."

Three stories plus attics and cellars. In one building or

perhaps in both. But we cannot be sure. In Henryk Nowogródzki's story "Three Days on Umschlagplatz" we find the following: "By night a few brave souls take their chance. They flit along the corridors. From the fifth floor there is an overhead gangway onto the roof of the neighboring house on Niska Street. It is like walking several meters over a precipice." Three floors or five? And which of the buildings had three stories, which had five? In Edelman's 1945 book both buildings appear to have three stories. The overhead gangway figures only in Nowogródzki's account; it is not mentioned elsewhere. But, as I have said, I know only the sources written in Polish or translated into Polish. Nowogródzki gives no further information. Was the gangway constructed by those who planned to escape from Umschlagplatz? Or was it a permanent bridge, built before the war, linking Niska Street with Stawki Street?

Next question: were there only two buildings on Umschlagplatz, or three? Leokadia Schmidt clearly mentions two, the Old Archives and the hospital. But she also alludes to what may be a third, "in which the public bath was formerly situated." She adds that at present, in 1942, "it has been converted into a dispensary." But it is not altogether clear whether or not the baths or dispensary form a third building. In another fragment she locates the baths and dispensary in the children's hospital building. Marek Edelman corroborates this in *The Ghetto Fights*, where he writes about "a small dispensary for casualties" located in the children's hospital building. But I have already quoted his other reference to "three-story buildings that had once been a school." So were there two buildings or three? The issue is further complicated by a hut which Edelman mentions when telling Hanna Krall about the concrete post by the gate. The post is the same as before, so logically the hut is too. Is the hut the third or a fourth building? Probably the latter, as a hut cannot be three stories high.

And now a further difficulty. In his account "Muranowski Square 7" (*Bulletin of the Jewish Historical Institute*, 1974), Michał Jaworski, who was on Umschlagplatz in April 1943, writes that after entering the Square he found himself in a kind of hall: "We were escorted through a large hall." Was this hall the hut mentioned by Edelman? Probably not: a hut is a long, fairly narrow sort of building, on one level only. The hall was large, and wide. The hall from Jaworski's narrative could be identified with the ground-floor room in the Old Archives building. But Jaworski writes: "After leaving the hall we were herded into a building." In other words, the hall did not belong to any building, but stood apart, it was a separate entity. Perhaps it was erected as late as 1943 and wasn't there at the time of the great extermination? Unless it was the fifth building on Umschlagplatz? Many things still need to be explained. For example, the surface of the area commonly referred to as a courtyard. Did the deportees lie or sit on trampled grass? Bare soil? Cobblestones? Asphalt?

Apparently some Jewish historian or historians have formulated a methodological directive (I say apparently, because it was written in Hebrew and I know it only from hearsay) to the effect that the history of the Warsaw ghetto cannot be described using any of the conventional methods. What happened was so utterly without precedent and on such a scale that no known method of description can be applied. This particularly concerns the Uprising in April 1943, and appears to be substantiated by all I have read about Umschlagplatz.

A chronological narrative seems called for: how things looked and how they changed. But that is not feasible. A structural analysis would help to establish the inner links between individual facts, their inner necessity. But that is also unachievable. It would be of the utmost importance to decipher the historical significance of events; this would entail some sort of comparative study. But that is also out of the question: what happened there and then can be compared with nothing else. If I understand rightly, the Jewish historians are saying that as none of the traditional methods can be applied here, we should project for the benefit of posterity a vision that would, as I imagine, encapsulate some vague but acceptable interpretation of events. That strikes me as a judicious demand.

All that worries me is the word "vision"; it is so subjective. But let's stick to the word. This vision would have to be extremely sober, limited to what is strictly visible and to what a witness once saw. A broken window, a plate of cold soup in a deserted apartment, feathers. A lot of feathers above Leszno Street and Miła Street, because pillowcases were sold and people slept in feather beds. Jewish Girl Guides in the attic, a gangway at the level of the third or fifth floor, the wall up which they climbed. Enough for now.

HELP me, God of the Jews and God of the Poles, reflects the octogenarian Icyk Mandelbaum as he rides the elevator to the twenty-second story of the New York apartment building where he now lives, or sits at his desk. The building is at the corner of Central Park West and Seventy-first Street. On his desk he has a fountain pen, a Parker with a gold nib, and a photograph of Chaja Gelechter in a leather frame that my wife, Hania, brought him two years ago as a present from Warsaw. The photograph was taken on the Świder, there is no doubt about that, because Chaja stands ankle-deep in water clad in a bathing suit and cap, a sort of visor and kerchief affair tied behind her neck. In the background are clumps of willow brake, and there are children bathing in the far distance, at the bend in the river. It looks as though there are three, but no, there is a fourth crouching under the branches that overhang the water. So there are four children, and a second woman in a swimsuit. Chaja's is white, the other woman's is black, and her bathing cap also resembles a kerchief with a visor.

But here my memory fails me completely, for the woman's name is buried deep in my memory, beyond recall. It is unlikely I shall ever relocate the brain cell that was sealed off fifty years ago, unlikely that her name will ever rise again to the surface from that cell or bunker, the locked vault of my fickle memory. So I can say nothing about her, except that she died, for that is almost one hundred percent certain, in fact "almost" is almost certainly redundant here. As for the three children and the fourth child hiding in the branches at the bend in the river, it is a fifty-fifty chance either way, though the odds are they died. Unless they were Christian children, who on the day the photo was taken came running down to the Świder and hid in the branches overhanging the water: "Oh, Jewish women bathing," they said, laughing.

Now for the unidentified woman whose fate I am so sure about. What I find most distressing is not the fate of the 310,000 people who were deported between July and September at the time of the great extermination, because that is clearly unimaginable. No, that's not the way to put it; it is imaginable and obvious in the literal sense. One doesn't need much imagination to see a crowd crossing Żelazna Street or Lubecki Street and walking toward the siding a few hundred yards away from Gdańsk Station. So it is imaginable. But this visualization—I can think of no other word—impinged no further than my brain, which classifies it as distressing.

But when I look at the beautiful woman about whom my memory can tell me nothing, as she stands there ankle-deep in water, kerchief-cum-visor tied behind her neck, I am bewildered and confused, my brain ceases to function, I'm stuck again for words. I feel a kind of suction between my larynx and lungs, or a cramp in the lungs or windpipe, which impairs my breathing. My conceptualization of the beautiful woman as she stands ankle-deep in water and at the same time walks down Zamenhof Street toward the railroad siding appears to have filled me with panic. Or perhaps her fear, for I know she is utterly terrified as she walks down Zamenhof Street, unites with my fear or even becomes my fear.

In the grip of this terror, hers and mine, I have only one thought in mind, to drag her out from that crowd of 310,000. She will then let me embrace her, she will put her head on my shoulder, for just one moment she will stop trembling, for there is really nothing to fear. We'll both sit down on the edge of the pavement and wait for the crowd escorted by Lithuanian guards to walk by and turn from Zamenhof Street into Niska Street. Then I must somehow extricate her, and how can I fail, she doesn't look a bit like the others. She is dead scared, every inch of her skin, her every thought, is sick with fear. As I watch her paddling in the Świder I feel every inch of her skin, her every thought, somewhere inside me between my lungs and windpipe.

God of the Jews and God of the Poles, thinks Icyk, glancing at the photograph of Chaja and the woman in the black swimsuit, help me and guide my hand. If the prayer addressed to Thy Throne by someone who does not believe in Thy justice and mercy strikes Thee as a trifle impertinent, let me point out that it differs from the many other pleas dispatched each day, if I may so express myself, in that it is tailored to Thy skills. I am not asking for anything that might exceed Thy possibilities. I am not asking Thee to unlock the cell in my memory where the name of the woman standing next to Chaja in the photo was deposited, nor to describe her as she turns from Zamenhof Street into Niska Street in a crowd escorted by Lithuanians and Jewish policemen. My memory is something for me to handle; it is, after all, my memory, not Thine. As for the corner of Zamenhof Street and Niska Street, I know I cannot expect Thee to remember a woman who vanished from Thy sight in a crowd of 310,000 people, or the color of her dress and shoes, or the time when she was shoved into a freight car reeking of chlorine.

My prayer is thus tailored to Thy capabilities and should not prove unduly difficult to grant. Just guide my hand so that what I write is the exact transcription of my memories. That is all, I'm not really asking for much. Help me to describe the morning on the Świder when Chaja ran laughing and splashing into the river and the water was ankle-deep or at best knee-deep. As she stood by the woman whose name now eludes me, she said to someone who stood in the water holding a camera against his waist, "Come on, snap." To which the person peering into the camera said, "When your grandson sees that photo fifty years from now, he'll say, 'My grandmother was a giggler.' " Quite likely I was the person standing ankle-deep in the water and pressing the camera to his stomach.

Alternatively, God, for this might prove a better starting point, help me to describe the July afternoon in 1937, the climbing roses in bloom on either side of the veranda in Sara Fliegeltaub's garden. Also each of the steps—there were four—leading from the veranda down into the garden. Also the people sitting on the veranda that afternoon in wicker chairs—namely, Chaja, Jakub Wurzel, Sara Fliegeltaub, and Icyk Mandelbaum, then aged thirty. Help me, God, may my description be identical with what I describe. Let me omit nothing, for every word, every step, every smile, every leaf of the climbing rose, cries out for remembrance. Help me to give witness, God of the Jews that art also God of the Poles, and may my testimony be worthy and just. For it is just, righteous, and salutary that we should in all times and all places remember what once befell us here on earth. For what befell us here on earth also befell Thee, O Lord.

I'll start with the stairs, Icyk Mandelbaum muses. For a faithful rendering of the stairs, just four long planks, should be relatively easy. The steps were gray, grayish, indescribable shades of grayness, for Sara Fliegeltaub's boardinghouse was built at the beginning of the twentieth century and the timber, rain-washed and sun-dried over the years, had lost its natural color. In the middle of the first step a thin crack ran from the darker, almost black vein of the wood between the three rusted nailheads hammered in at the edge. The penultimate step was only a semi-step; someone had once planted his foot on it with excessive impact and broken it lengthwise, then thrown the broken segment under the veranda, where three empty rusted oil-paint cans, a white bottle with a curved neck inscribed "Odol," and a baby-carriage wheel without a tire were also to be found. As the supports had rotted and the nails had rusted, the step swayed perilously at the merest touch of a shoe tip, even if it was someone as light, ethereal, and evanescent as Chaja, who floated rather than walked, wafting and gliding above the graveled path, the gray-planked veranda floor, and the dining-room carpet, where an unsightly rip had been hastily patched up in the corner by the dresser. I do not remember the second and last steps. Unrecorded, unmemorized, undescribed, indescribable.

Grass now grows in the place where there were once four steps. Or else a bush, blackthorn let's say. Or there may be a driveway into the garage or a garage door, if a new house has been built on the foundations of Sara Fliegeltaub's residence, which is quite likely. Or if a new street was laid through the garden in the sixties, seventies, or eighties, which is also quite likely; there is a paving slab, closely cemented in with the adjoining slabs. Or else a hole, a pit, a tunnel. Just where the steps, veranda, and house used to be there is a hole leading to hell or Sheol or, worse still, a hole straight into nothingness, a hole into nonbeing. You return to your old haunts, place your foot where you placed it before, and suddenly you fall into a hole, into nothing.

"Confess, Szlojmele," says Sara Fliegeltaub, standing on the last step, the one I do not recall. "Now tell Mr. Wurzel how much I pay you."

Standing by the veranda against a backdrop of climbing roses, Szlojmele says nothing. For what can he say if both he and Sara Fliegeltaub know exactly how much she pays him and how much he earns and if they both know what Sara is driving at when she poses this rhetorical question. Sara wants Szlojmele to repair the step, which involves bringing a plank from the shed and nailing it in the place of what is now only a semi-step. Szlojmele feels no inclination whatsoever for this task, perhaps because he is currently engaged in deep subconscious debate with his Jewish God or with one of his God's demons and ripping up the old board and fitting and nailing a new one would inhibit him in his murky dialogue. But there again he may simply not be in the mood, and indeed why should he bother if the old plank still serves its shaky purpose. It is not surprising. Why should he buckle down to the job, who for, what for, if in three or four years there will be no more stairs and no more Szlojmele. The planks will be thrown into the stove; the first winter of the war was particularly harsh, freezing cold during the day, below zero at night. Both Szlojmele and the planks will go to the stove. Thus, for reasons best known to himself, Szlojmele makes no reply to Pani Sara and hobbles away, dragging his leg. I remember that he had a limp, but I cannot remember if it was his left or his right leg. The penultimate step will remain forever in my memory, and in the memory of my God, as a semi-step, wobbling underfoot.

So much for the steps. I should merely add that Icyk was standing on the steps one day, or rather rocking precariously on the semi-step. Chaja Gelechter was sitting on the veranda in a wicker armchair and smoking a cigarette? drinking coffee? reading a newspaper? a volume of poetry? Icyk's verse?—though it could just as well have been a volume of Rimbaud or Verlaine, in French, not that it matters. What matters is that Chaja was engrossed in Verlaine, in *Literarisze Blatter* or *Unser Wort*, smoking a cigarette, drinking coffee, though more likely she was reading the day's edition of *Our Opinion* or *Our Survey* and the review of Shloime Ansky's *The Dybbuk*, in which she played a secondary role. Playing the so-called utility parts was Chaja's natural destiny in life, for no one could claim she had any talent as an actress. "*Hélas*," she once said, "I am totally devoid of talent; there's not one spark of talent in me." In brief, Chaja was paying no attention to Icyk, who, as he swayed precipitously on the semi-step, said something he ought never to have said: "I love you, Miss Gelechter. I think you should bear that in mind."

When I recall that episode today, Icyk reflects at the corner of Central Park West and Seventy-first Street, I cannot explain how I brought myself to utter such a strange sentence and why, having finally plucked up my courage, I then called Chaja, whom I had been calling by her first name for well over a year, "Miss Gelechter." Why didn't I just say, "I love you, Chaja," or "I love you, I think you should bear that in mind"? I don't know. Perhaps by addressing her formally I wanted to make my declaration sound more like a solemn proposal? Unless, quite the reverse, I intended to strip my declaration of all solemnity and give it an ironic tone? I don't remember. On hearing me address her as "Miss Gelechter," Chaja ought to have burst out laughing, and that is probably what I thought would happen. But she did not laugh; she just gave me a strange sort of look, as though she felt saddened or alarmed by my formality or by the ironic tone of my confession.

Icyk was perplexed: should he assume that Chaja had not heard him and reiterate his declaration, or else that she had heard him and preferred not to react? So he continued swaying on the semi-step for a good two or three minutes longer. He then decided that the situation ought not to be prolonged, so he descended from the steps and vanished in the garden between the jasmine bushes. Where he still stands to this day, his hands in his pockets and his nose stuck between two branches, trying to resolve whether it had been a mistake to leave his declaration suspended in midair on the veranda and hovering above Miss Chaja Gelechter like a fluttery cabbage butterfly that never knows where to settle. Perhaps he should press his point, insist on an answer then and there.

Alternatively he could throw himself on Chaja and possess her on the spot, on the veranda, beneath the fluttering wings of the cabbage butterfly, in a wicker armchair or on the steps that once upon a time, thousands and thousands of years ago, led down from the veranda into the garden. But enough about the stairs; I have exhausted the topic. I shall now pass on to Sara Fliegeltaub's dressing gown. So help me God, who deserted the Jews and deserted the Poles, and even though it was almost half a century ago, no one knows to this day why Thou didst it.

Mrs. Fliegeltaub's dressing gown might conceivably be called a Turkish dressing gown, though I entertain grave doubts as to its authentic Turkishness. Even so, it passed as one; in fact, I hear a voice exclaiming, "Oh, there's Pani Sara in her Turkish dressing gown," though I recall neither the speaker nor the circumstances. All that remains is an utterance floating above the veranda and jasmine bushes, like a millennial cabbage butterfly, or more likely circling in my head, because I am quite sure that no one else remembers it. The dressing gown was black—I can't name the material—with large red and yellow flowers, and a great rip over the left side of the belly.

Now, Sara Fliegeltaub liked to be tidy, and loved to boast of this predilection of hers. Frankly, she ought to have mended her dressing gown, but for reasons best known to her, she never did. She sails out onto the balcony: "Just imagine, Mr. Jakub, sir, the little Yid who delivers the beef from Warsaw charges one zloty sixty the kilo. It's only one-forty at the market." If she noticed someone staring at her midriff, she would execute a royal gesture and position her palm over the relevant area to conceal the hiatus, and then continue, totally unperturbed: "Those Yids are only interested in pulling a fast one. But I'm not so easily fooled." As the proprietress of a boardinghouse, Sara Fliegeltaub felt that she ought to evince some mildly anti-Semitic views every now and again, because this was the proper thing to do. But in all other respects she was a perfectly respectable Jew. This did not prevent her from hurling such terms as "Jewy" and "Yid" and "kike" at the gaberdined tradesmen who delivered the groceries to her boardinghouse via the train that departed from the Kierbędź Bridge.

O God, what would I not give to sit with my gaberdined and capoted friends in one of the cars as the locomotive whistles and puffs and slowly proceeds from under the Kierbędź Bridge to Świder, to Otwock, and to Karczew. Not just because I am crazy about trains, be they the steam or the electric variety, commuter or suburban, overground or underground, and nothing gives me greater pleasure than to travel on all these lines and peruse their itineraries and timetables. But what I now want is to see my capoted and gaberdined friends, hear their hubbub and uproar, their fracas and din. O God, let me just once in my life travel by train to Świder amid that pandemonium and uproar issuing from Sheol, from history's abyss. But this clearly exceeds Thy scope, so I withdraw my request.

I am unable to explain why Sara Fliegeltaub walked around in her dressing gown. She was, after all, the proprietress of a respectable boardinghouse patronized by the intelligentsia of Warsaw and Łódź—or at any rate that was the reputation her boardinghouse genuinely or supposedly enjoyed. She was also, to put it mildly, a lady of utmost thrift (a fact that undoubtedly impinged on the amount of butter served at breakfast and the quality of the cutlets at lunch). Yet one time—at the beginning of the thirties, I think—she geared herself up to a major expense. In the hope of attracting new clients, maybe also to prove that her *ansztalt* was indeed of some standing, she had a brochure printed at Renom's of 17 Karmelicka Street to advertise her boardinghouse.

The leaflet, on gray-green paper, showed an advantageous view of the house and grounds with the following blurb: "Otwock. The Cozy Nook. Our boardinghouse is located in exceptionally lovely surroundings, in a large garden with flowers at the edge of a pine forest. Its appointments conform to all the requirements of hygiene, with full plumbing, electric lights, radio and gramophone.

Bathrooms, hot and cold running water, terraces for sunbathing and relaxing in deck chairs. Other features include exquisitely tasteful rooms, distinguished company, and good-humored patrons. Refined cuisine. First-rate meals served five times a day. From 5 zlotys daily for room and full board. Reduced rates in May and October."

Now, that is all a pack of lies—well, perhaps not all, but almost. Fair enough, there was a gramophone, for I can hear a tenor or baritone rendering "The Bargemen," Fejga's favorite record. But there was only one bathroom, and the water was usually cold. Apart from the veranda there was only one terrace, and even that was more like a balcony than a terrace. The state of the plumbing is best left unmentioned, for it is not a pleasant memory: the stench of latrine mingling with the fragrance of pine needles as I sit by the open window thumping on the keyboard of my dilapidated Remington.

The cuisine was nothing to write home about, the humor of the patrons ditto. My own mood was pretty awful most of the time, because Chaja refused to go to bed with me, the minced cutlets were distinctly suspect, and Hitler and Stalin were just around the corner. I am not a particularly cheery sort of guy at the best of times, and even if those gruesome trials had not been taking place in Moscow, even if Chaja had treated me more favorably, I'd still have been harboring a grudge against the world. You see—how shall I put it?—some of Thy concepts, O God, appeal to me in only a limited sort of way. That is how I was made, I'm always bearing some grudge, and that, incidentally, is also one of Thy concepts.

But let's drop the matter. In brief, the proprietress of such a refined boardinghouse ought never to have appeared before her guests in her dressing gown—no, not even a Turkish one. Mind you, I do not reject the theory that Sara Fliegeltaub wore her dressing gown only very occasionally, say just in the morning or just in the evening, and that most of the time she had a dress on. But I remember only the dressing gown with the red and yellow flowers and the split to the left of the paunch area. Dare I add that the dressing gown looked—in fact, it still does—somewhat past its prime, as its bell-shaped sleeves were worn and frayed at the seams. Unless that is just my imagination and the cuffs were not frayed at all.

The subsequent adventures of Sara Fliegeltaub's dressing gown are something I find particularly difficult to conceive. In a poetic vein one could visualize it as a kind of symbol adrift above the pines, the sanatorium rooftops, the raised platforms and the tower of Otwock Station: sleeves akimbo, it flounders above Otwock, a presage or a threat. But that is bad poetry.

Almost certainly the dressing gown was torn up for floor rags, though perhaps someone wore it first. Zosia told me that when the extermination or resettlement began in the place where she lived during the war near Ostrów Mazowiecka, Jewish women went around to the Poles with whom they had been friendly; they came to her parents too. "Do take our goat," they would say, or "Please have this chair." "All right," said the Poles, "we'll mind it for you." "No," said the Jews, "it's for you to keep."

Zosia, who was a small girl at the time, has another story. Some distance away was the wall of the Polish cemetery, and Zosia could see people standing against the wall with their hands crossed behind their heads. Then they vanished and more people came to stand against the wall, and then they vanished too, and others replaced them, and they vanished too. And so it went on and on. Zosia simply couldn't figure it out.

In discussing the last chapter in the life of Sara Fliegeltaub's dressing gown, we can imagine more than one scenario. Say it was worn for a couple of years, then torn up for floor rags by the proprietress of the house next door, who knows. "It's for you to keep." Alternatively, if Pani Sara had no time to change her clothes, her dressing gown will bob up against the cemetery wall. Then some Christian child, observing the scene from a distance, will fail to understand why in the place where red and yellow flowers have just blossomed there is now only a gray-plaster or red-brick wall.

Now, as he sits at his desk or rides the elevator to the twenty-second floor, Icyk reflects. With Thy help, O my God, that is all I have to say about the dressing gown, the steps, the brochure printed by Renom's, and other objects expedited by Thy decree to a place which in our ignorance we wrongfully call Sheol, nothingness, or words to that effect. And if, my God, Thou wouldst like to remain in this partnership and retrieve all we can from that pit, I shall continue to ask for Thy help. Only don't bank on my gratitude, for if we can expect no good of Thee, it's best not to expect any good from us either.

The Final Station: Umschlagplatz

SOME extracts from the diary of Adam Czerniakow, senator of the Republic and during the war years chairman of the Warsaw Judenrat. "January 4, 1940. Rinde came to the office with a black eye acquired in Nalewki Street. Wasserman had been punched in the nose by a street crowd on Theater Square as he tried to rescue a Jew who was being cruelly beaten up by the same crowd." "January 27, 1940. Many Jews were beaten up in Marszałkowska Street and Poznańska Street today. By daylight and after dark." "January 28, 1940. At ten o'clock at night a gang of street urchins that has been beating up Jews for the last few days marched past the Jewish Commune smashing the windowpanes across the street. A messenger of the Commune, Engineer Friede, was beaten till he bled." "March 24, 1940. After lunch Jews were beaten in the Jewish streets and windowpanes were smashed. A sort of pogrom." "March 25, 1940. Pogroms in the streets. Jews beaten and windows smashed on Żurawia Street." "August 19, 1940. Wasserman, an official of the Commune, was beaten up in Praga. Rabbis came by, terrified by the advance news of a pogrom. At three o'clock I went to the SS, where I was informed that a telephone call would be made to the Ordnungspolizei and a patrol sent to Praga." "October 26, 1940. Jews beaten up by rabble." "July 9, 1942. After lunch Polish street urchins threw stones over the wall on Chłodna Street. When we cleared the bricks and stones in the middle of Chłodna Street they almost ran out of ammunition."

Further information on this subject may be found in *Notes from the Ghetto* by Emanuel Ringelblum, *Chronicle of the War and Occupation Years* by Ludwik Landau, and "The Book of Life," the diary kept in the ghetto by Chaim Aron Kaplan. Kaplan writes as follows: "Never has Poland's capital seen such wild excesses as on March 24 and 25 this year [1940]. Someone behind the scenes organized gangs of youths, hooligans (there were even schoolboys among them), who attacked Jewish passersby. A gang comprising several dozen such individuals armed with sticks, stones, and so forth encircled small groups of up to a dozen Jews and beat them relentlessly. A Jew-baiting operation was being conducted in the streets of Warsaw." The editors of the *Bulletin of the Jewish Historical Institute*, where "The Book of Life" was published (No. 45–46/1963), omitted some fragments of Kaplan's entry for March, as they were presumably too distressing.

The incidents of March 1940 are also mentioned by Marek Edelman in his book *The Ghetto Fights*, published in 1945 by the Central Committee of the Bund. According to Edelman, a several-day pogrom was organized by the Germans, who enlisted "Polish scum, paying them four zlotys per working day." On the fourth day—this is also in Edelman's book—the Bund organized retaliatory action resulting in "large-scale street battles" in the region of Mirow Market, Grzybowski Square, Karmelicka Street, and Niska Street. Czerniakow says he often wondered whether Poland is represented by Mickiewicz and Słowacki or by the scoundrels from Chłodna Street and Żurawia Street. Next sentence: "The truth lies in between."

"Of course," I say, "there will always be people who use the favorite expression of the National Democrat journalists before the war and claim that this is typical Jewish bellyaching. The Germans were hatching their master plan for total annihilation, compared with which a stone thrown by a street urchin or a Jewish nose punched in Elektoralna Street is totally without significance. But when I read these impressions of Czerniakow, Kaplan, and Ringelblum, I literally shrivel up with shame and wail in a typically Polish fashion, "How could we ever have behaved like that?"

"It wasn't us," Hania protests, "it was those street urchins. You'll soon be saying I am responsible for what happened."

"You're a Jew," I say, "so it's not your responsibility. But it is mine. I'd gladly pass the buck and say, 'It's not me, it's those urchins, it's no business of mine.' But that would be indecent of me."

"I'm assimilated," says Hania, "so I'm not a Jew. Anyone who is assimilated is by definition a Pole. You might just as well call yourself a German, a Lithuanian, or a Tatar. As for window smashing, stone throwing, and Jew bashing in 1940 and later, I believe that only the culprits are responsible. And their instigators. Marek Edelman is a reliable witness, so those urchins were definitely recruited and paid by the Germans. Collective responsibility does not exist. You were only five or six at the time, so one could say you hardly existed at all. Why should you have to answer for such atrocities?"

"Collective responsibility does exist," I say, "though at the same time it doesn't. If the Nazis decide to arrest and deport everyone whose name begins with R and you hide me in the cellar, I see no reason why you should answer for that and be executed. That sort of responsibility doesn't exist, or at least it shouldn't. But to my mind there is such a thing as moral responsibility, in this case the moral responsibility of the Poles. In this sense I am responsible for the urchin who threw stones over the wall on Chłodna Street."

"You really do talk the most awful nonsense," says Hania. "It follows that you are responsible for everything the blackmailers, the dark-blue policemen, and the secret agents did at the time. And for the propaganda written by collaborators for the gutter press and blared over the loudspeakers. Pull yourself together. Moreover, may I remind you my name also begins with R, so when they arrest and deport all the R's we'll be arrested and deported together. So don't count on my hiding you in the cellar. Besides, in our cellar there's not even enough room for a decent bunker."

"The corner under the stairs could be walled up," I say, "next to the pile of boxes with the empty jars. But then there may be no more deportations in our lifetime. Coming back to the gangs who beat up the Jews in 1940 and smashed windows on Marszałkowska Street and Żurawia Street, I don't think you can just say it was the scum in the pay of the Germans. We good Christians were not involved and are therefore not guilty. The question is not who smashed the windows in the Jewish Commune, but what it was in the Polish moral climate that allowed windows to be smashed in 1940 and 1942, then of all times, just before the great extermination.

"I know you will say it wasn't only in Poland that such things occurred; the Germans found the same scum all over Europe. But that is a feeble argument, at least to my way of thinking, because I was born here. What went on elsewhere concerns me only on a purely theoretical level. A pretty or an ugly view, luckily it's not mine. It is precisely because I was born here, because I am a native, that I cannot pass the buck for what went on here whether then or now. If I shirked responsibility I'd cease to be a native. At least that's how I'd feel about it. To my mind everyone is responsible. Everyone born in this land. But anyone who says, 'It's not me, it's my compatriots, I'm not responsible for their villainy,' is behaving very meanly, as I'm sure you will agree. It's as though he wanted to be above or outside local concerns, and refused to be involved with his fellow countrymen. Those street urchins, as Czerniakow so mildly calls them, who threw stones over the wall on Chłodna Street spoke Polish. The home where one of those urchins grew up, the courtyard where he played, the church he attended on Sunday, they were all Polish. How can I pretend that it has nothing to do with me?"

"Think of the Jews," says Hania, "they too behaved quite abominably at the time. Well, at least a lot of them did. What you're saying about the Polish urchins from

Żurawia Street or Elektoralna Street applies just as much to the Jewish policemen and members of the Thirteen, to someone like Gancwajch or Szeryński, and even to Czerniakow and his colleagues from the Judenrat. The Czerniakow question is not so simple. For a long time he was thought of as a collaborator; now he is virtually a martyr. How did he put it? 'The truth lies in between.' So if you feel responsible for the urchins who beat up the Jews, then, logically speaking, Icchak Cukierman ought to feel responsible for Gancwajch, and Marek Edelman for Szeryński."

"I've never met Marek Edelman," I say. "I've seen him a couple of times in the distance, and each time I experienced a sense of almost religious awe. As though he were some great angel of terror sent by God to remind the Poles of what once happened in this land. An angel with a special mission. As I don't know him, I can't say what he feels responsible for. I don't even know if he feels like a Jew or a Pole; and even if I met him, I doubt if I'd dare ask him. But if he feels he is a Jew, I assume he sometimes worries about types like Gancwajch, Szmerling, or Szeryński, or may even engage them in conversation from time to time. Just as I occasionally chat with that urchin to try to discover what was going on inside his head. Of course, it may simply be morbid curiosity. But I am a writer and it is my job to find out what goes on in other people's minds."

"Fair enough," says Hania, "but your professional curiosity is neither here nor there. We're discussing responsibility, which is a completely different issue. Although they were of his race, I doubt if Marek Edelman feels responsible for the deeds of a Jewish policeman or a Jewish Gestapo officer. Did you know that Gancwajch managed to escape? Even though the Germans shot everyone from the Thirteen. I'm not absolutely sure, but no one knows what happened to him afterward."

"For that matter," I say, "no one knows what happened to Brandt. He apparently escaped from prison after the war. But you fail to grasp my point. I'm not saying that one man should answer for another man's deeds. We are talking about two different types of responsibility. Not all Germans are responsible for what Brandt or Mende did in the ghetto, I mean for their actual deeds. That's not what I am saying. But every one of them is responsible for the existence of such people as Brandt or Mende, for the moral sanction of their deeds, for the spiritual environment they operated in. To put it in a nutshell, I'd say they were responsible for the sanctioning of it."

"Every man is responsible for himself," says Hania, "and for himself alone. If you were right, one could argue that sanction was also given in the ghetto. That the Jews were collectively responsible for the shops selling oranges and chocolate in Leszno Street, for the restaurants in Sienna Street where rich Jews drank French brandies, and for the brothels in Nowolipie Street and Dzielna Street—while Jewish kids were dying of starvation on the pavement."

"It may be," I say, "that some people feel responsible only for themselves, while others feel responsible for everyone. And I may well belong to the latter category, which does not mean I lack respect for the former. If anyone feels that the anti-Semitic excesses of 1940 are not his business, I won't hold it against him. Everyone—I mean the Poles—must work it out for himself—that's what it's really all about—and not pretend it never happened.

"But I'd like to tell you something Krysia told me yesterday. It touches on the problem of collective responsibility. In 1942, Krystyna was imprisoned in Pawiak, naturally in the women's wing, so she was not in Pawiak but in Serbia. The windows of her cell overlooked Dzielna Street. She even drew me a small plan so that I could visualize the whole setup. This is Pawiak, here's the courtyard, here's Serbia, here's the window, and here—I'll draw it for you too—is the pavement outside the window.

"Her cell was on the ground floor, but she could see nothing of what was going on in Dzielna Street from the window, which, like most prison windows, was high up under the ceiling. But she could hear the sound of footsteps and voices from Dzielna Street quite distinctly. Maybe there was no pane in the window? I didn't ask. Not that she often heard voices from the street, because this incident occurred after the great extermination, in the late fall or early winter of 1942. By then the Jews were quartered in the workshops and were forbidden to walk about the streets. The nearest workshops were in Gęsia Street and Nowolipki Street, so Pawiak, which was once situated in the very heart of the ghetto, now stood, as it were, in a wilderness, still at the center, but the center of a hole, the center of nonbeing. A good symbol for a totalitarian state—that isn't part of Krysia's story, it just came into my head. Deserted houses, corpses, and silence all around. A wilderness. And in its midst a prison and guards yelling.

"Krysia could hear a convoy passing under her window in the morning and evening. Just the clatter of wooden clogs; they marched in silence. They went one way in the morning, and came back in the evening. Parties of Jews led by Ukrainians or Latvians were going to work. Do you know what that means?"

"They were working on the Aryan side," says Hania. "The walls around the ghetto's evacuated zone were being demolished. They were escorted back again in the evening."

"It usually took quite a long time for a column to march by," I say. "Their wooden clogs clattered past for ten minutes or more. So the women prisoners guessed it must be a pretty long convoy. As there was nothing much else going on in Dzielna Street, it provided—how shall I put it?—some sort of entertainment or distraction, and Krysia and her cellmates were almost tense with listening. 'What time is it? Why aren't they here yet?' I don't know—I didn't ask, but I shall—if they could be heard approaching from a distance or only as they passed beneath the windows. 'Now they're leaving Zamenhof Street. Now they're at Karmelicka Street.'

"Well, to make a long story short, as they came up to the prison window the Jews began to sing in very soft voices so as not to be heard by the Latvian or Ukrainian guards escorting the head and rear of the convoy, and Krysia's cellmates heard them singing 'Poland has not perished yet.' Very softly. I don't know if it was morning or evening. Let's assume it was morning. That evening they again heard the clatter of clogs leaving Zamenhof Street, passing Karmelicka Street, coming close. Then the prisoners began to sing in very soft voices, just loud enough to be heard in the street. 'Poland has not perished yet.' That is exactly what I mean by collective responsibility. By singing they assumed responsibility for Poland. It sounds awfully pathetic, but I can't tell it any differently. It was pathetic, so it's only right to tell it like that. But don't cry, Hania. It was almost half a century ago."

THE problem of the elevator in which Icyk Mandelbaum travels to the twenty-second floor of an apartment building at the corner of Central Park West and Seventy-first Street, reflecting on Sara Fliegeltaub's Turkish dressing gown and the four steps that led from the veranda to Sheol or from Sheol to the veranda. I'd like to describe that elevator, but I can't, as I don't know what New York elevators look like. I have never been to New York, even though I have been invited several times. I always managed to find an excuse not to go, as I never really wanted to go there anyway. This is something my would-be hosts could not figure out. They tried persuasion: "Someone like you can't afford not to see New York. You are a writer, aren't you? Without seeing New York you can't hope to understand what the twentieth century is all about. Without seeing New York you can't hope to understand what it means to live in the twentieth century."

"Actually you can. You only have to walk across Warsaw's Umschlagplatz."

Now, that's obviously not what I said to my persuaders. I merely explained that I wasn't interested in the trip because there was nothing in New York I particularly wanted to see. There are still a few streets I haven't seen in Warsaw, for instance Bolesław Bierut Street in Praga South, and that's where I ought to go first. But since I started writing this book I've changed my mind. I'd be only too glad to go to New York now. Why? Because I'd like to see the Northern District. Of course, I know there is no Northern District in New York, but there must be something comparable, as so many Warsaw-born Jews now live in New York. So if I went to New York, I'd want to see if they have taken their Northern District with them, and compare the Northern District in New York with our Northern District in Warsaw. To find out if they differ—it was, after all, almost fifty years ago—and how.

I have another reason for going, though the odds are I'll stay at home. I'd like to establish whether blockades would be feasible in New York—in other words, if the houses in Greenwich Village or the Bronx could be easily sealed off and evacuated. Whenever I visit one of the new Warsaw developments, as I alight from the B-2 bus at the corner of Bonifacy Street and Sobieski Street or from the 504 at the corner of Wałbrzyska Street and Puławska Street, I often wonder if what happened in the Northern District forty-five years ago could happen at some time now or in the future in Stęgny or Ursynów.

I have in mind only the practicalities of an evacuation: how the SS men (there are no SS men now, so it would be some other unit) would effectively blockade the eleven-story apartment buildings in Akermańska Street or Kaukaska Street. Or the huge house on Sonata Street—Służew nad Dolinką—where Jacek lives. Over a dozen stairways, over a dozen elevators. That would create totally new technical difficulties for the SS men or their successors. Difficulties which, God willing, they would be unable to surmount.

Also one other point: the absence of courtyards. The courtyards of Lubecki Street or Zamenhof Street played an important part in the great extermination. When there are no courtyards lots of men and equipment are needed to encircle and keep an eye on the evacuees. Compared with the Northern District in Warsaw, New York would present its own logistical problems. Which is not to say that a blockade in Queens, the Bronx, or Greenwich Village cannot be imagined. It can. Without even going there. All one needs is photographs and an average sort of imagination.

I look over the map of New York that Stás has lent me. He has been there, so I must ask him how he would visualize a great extermination in Manhattan. Where are the railroad lines? A siding could start at Pennsylvania Station and end somewhere on the edge of Central Park. Unless the siding started from Central Park? But then it would have to bypass the Pan Am Building—to get a full picture I may have to go there after all. The sentry would be at the intersection of Sixty-third Street and Central Park

West. The Befehlsstelle would be positioned in the vicinity of Columbus Circle, where Gulf & Western is. Central Park would be enclosed by a red-brick wall three meters high, topped by another meter of barbed wire. A vast Umschlagplatz in proportion to the city. At the point where West Drive cuts through Transverse Road (someone who visited New York told me one can drive right through the park from Central Park West to Fifth Avenue) there would be a wooden gate with a sign: "No entry under penalty of death." This is where the last selection would take place. I can't say what language the sign would be in. Time will tell.

Someone may protest that the idea of a siding at Pennsylvania Station, of an Umschlagplatz in Central Park, of blockades around the houses in Greenwich Village, is tasteless or frankly obscene. That someone is an idiot. For only an idiot could think that what began on July 22, 1942, in the area of Niska Street, Dzika Street, and Stawki Street is over. The extermination came to a halt. But we who live near Umschlagplatz know it is not the end. Our century can still go on for a long time. Living on the edge of Umschlagplatz we can be sure of only one thing. We wait on the corner of Dzika Street and Stawki Street for the next episode. For there will be a sequel, there is absolutely no doubt about that.

But enough of these gruesome ideas: if anything like that ever happens, I hope and pray I won't be around to see it. Now back to the problem of the elevator in which Icyk Mandelbaum passes the twentieth story, enjoying the view it offers him over Central Park and Seventy-first

Street. With his mind on Sara Fliegeltaub's Turkish dressing gown, Icyk glances down at the silver and yellow and red automobiles circling in the abyss as if God, with whom he is discussing the gown, were striding about among the blinking lights and neon signs of the abyss, between the cars, or enthroned in midair or levitating.

"Do me a favor," I say, "tell me what a New York elevator looks like. The type that goes to the twentieth or thirtieth floor. Icyk has to take the elevator to the twenty-second floor, so I have to describe it. But I don't know what it looks like, because I've never been to New York. The only ones I know are Warsaw elevators, and they're pretty dingy."

"There are several, maybe several dozen or several hundred different types of elevator," says Stefan. "I don't know which you want me to describe."

"I'm interested," I say, "in an elevator that's installed on the outside of a building in a sort of latticework shaft, or fixed to a rail, with a view of the street below, the pedestrians, cars, and the fountain in Central Park, if there is a fountain in Central Park. If you had an elevator like that at your house I'd spend the whole day riding up and down in it."

"Today," says Stefan, "I found graffiti in my elevator that might do for the book you're writing. An equals sign and 'Jews.' But I don't know who was being equated with the Jews, as it had been erased."

"Probably the Polish United Workers' Party or KOR. Our local anti-Semites claim all power derives from the Jewish God. Someone told me the other day that the Queen of England is also a Jew. Quite some family tree. But tell me about the elevator in New York. Remember, it must be on the outside."

"The winters are extremely harsh in New York," says Stefan. "That sort of elevator probably wouldn't operate in blizzards or in severe frosts. If you ask me, they don't have that kind in New York. Put your character in a warmer climate. Florida, for instance. They may have outside elevators there, though I can't vouch for it."

"The problem is that my hero really does live in New York," I say. "I can ignore reality up to a point, at least as far as the elevator is concerned, though I'm not happy about it, it's a bit like cheating. But I can't ignore it completely. I want him to look down and see the trees in Central Park receding at the speed of the elevator, and the red and silver cars, the neon signs flashing on and off. I also want him to see blacks sprawled on the park lawns receding from sight and toppling head over heels into the abyss, and Jews with sidelocks strolling by the fountain. If Jews in Hasidic hats go strolling by the fountain. And suddenly, as he comes up to the fifteenth story, the blacks, the neon signs, the fountain, the cars, all vanish in an instant. And what should then come to mind but a line from Mickiewicz: 'In the field of my vision a change then occurred.'

"The next snapshot is of the Polish-literature teacher testing him on Mickiewicz in the fourth grade of the Merchants Guild Grammar School, at the corner of Prosta Street and Walicców Street. Down below he sees the high windows of the Institute of Judaic Sciences receding at the speed of the elevator and next door to it the four columns of the entrance to the Great Synagogue, its two domes, one low and one high, and the crown on the top of the higher dome. A blue policeman is standing on the corner of Przejazd Street and Tłomackie Street, and Jews with sidelocks and without, with beards and without, in skull-caps or otherwise, walk along Przejazd in the direction of Rymarska Street and Żabia Street.

"Help me, God of the Jews and God of the Poles. And let me see them just as they were yesterday. Dr. Majer Bałaban steps out of the Institute building. A cartload of coal turns from Rymarska Street into Leszno Street. A youthful Isaac Singer stands with his brother Israel Joshua on the balcony at 13 Tłomackie Street, where the Union of Jewish Writers and Journalists is. In a pork butcher's shop on Przejazd a Jew in a yellow wig wraps up a kilo of sundry purchases. Niuta Tajtelbaum, with navy pleated skirt, sailor blouse, white knee socks, and two long braids, walks home from school swinging her satchel. She has a small elephant brooch pinned just above the knot of her navy tie in the cleft of her blouse. Emanuel Ringelblum bows to Dr. Bałaban outside the Institute door. He has come to exchange his books. The elevator rides on up, and everything, the crown on the dome and the cartload of coal, the Singer brothers and the blue policeman, the windows of the Institute and the five-pointed chandeliers on the wall in front of the Great Synagogue, Dr. Bałaban himself, race downward, subside, and are swallowed up there. And that is all one can say about it."

"It looks as though your elevator is climbing down the

gold skyscraper in Dzierżhyński Square," says Stefan. "Nowhere near Central Park."

"That's more or less where the Great Synagogue used to be," I say. "You know what people on the trolleys say when they pass the gold skyscraper? That it'll never be completed because the site is cursed by God."

"I don't know what you mean by cursed," says Stefan. "Do you mean God put a curse on the site because it had been desecrated by the Germans?"

"When anything horrendous takes place," I say, "the site where it happened is best avoided. When I go to the Jewish Institute to read *Our Survey* or *Our Opinion*, I do my best to avoid the skyscraper. I'm afraid it might collapse on me. Well, thanks. You really have helped me a lot," and I say goodbye to Stefan and put the receiver down. As Icyk ascends to the twenty-second floor of the apartment building on the corner of Central Park West and Seventy-first Street, he sees the last rays of the sun sinking beyond Muranow, beyond the Ring, beyond Bem's Fortifications, and gilding the crown on the green sheet-metal-covered dome of the Great Synagogue.

SOME facts about the ghetto in Otwock. In the conversation I had with my sister about the boy in white socks on the high platform and the girl being photographed by her father on the path between the pines, I stated that the Otwock ghetto was probably exterminated prior to the Warsaw ghetto, somewhere in the first half of July 1942. I subsequently chanced upon some references that suggested the extermination in Otwock actually took place shortly after the great extermination in Warsaw. I did not, however, succeed in pinpointing the exact date of the Otwock events. A passage in Leokadia Schmidt's book *We Escaped Extermination by a Miracle* suggests that they took place around the fourth week of the great extermination in Warsaw—namely, in the second half of August: "At that time a respite of several days was announced, as the Battalion was to be sent to Otwock. In the first days of the deportation many Jews had taken refuge there. It was mainly the wealthy who left, as it cost a lot. Besides, their respite was short-lived. It lasted just four weeks."

By "Battalion" Leokadia Schmidt means the Vernichtungskommando. The term Vernichtungskommando does not appear to have been used in the Warsaw ghetto. As I was informed by someone who escaped to the Aryan side at the beginning of 1943, in referring to this SS unit the Jews used the code name that the Germans applied to the entire operation: Einsatz Reinhard. Leokadia Schmidt writes as follows: "Finally the Extermination Battalion left Warsaw for a few days, heading for Otwock. As we later discovered, an out-and-out massacre took place there. The Jewish police did not follow the example of their Warsaw colleagues. When at the first briefing they were given orders for the deportation of the local inhabitants, they flung their police caps at the feet of the murderers and refused to obey. They were all executed. Most of the Jewish population was murdered on the spot. This is the only information we have on this subject." Władysław Bartoszewski, who wrote the introduction and footnotes to Leokadia Schmidt's book, casts further light on this passage: "The deportation from localities on the right bank of the Vistula near Warsaw was implemented over a period of several days, beginning on August 19, 1942."

Further information comes from a book on the history of Otwock. The Gestapo (probably the Sipo command and SD) was located at 60 Reymont Street. Kripo had a police station at 3 Sienkiewicz Street, where the headquarters of the blue police was also to be found. The head of the Otwock Gestapo was named Schlicht. Instructions for creating a Jewish residential quarter were issued by the Germans in November 1940. Two months later, on January 15, 1941, the ghetto was "closed" and anyone wishing to come out required a pass. I cannot establish what is meant by this "closing": was the ghetto fenced in (which in view of the straggly urban layout of Otwock seems unlikely) or just enclosed with barbed wire and patrolled by German, Ukrainian, and Latvian guards?

In 1942 the population of Otwock was estimated at 23,412 inhabitants: 11,355 Poles, 12,030 Jews. In 1943 the number dropped to 10,173. There was not a single Jew among them. The figures do not altogether tally, as the number of people disposed of in the extermination is slightly in excess of 8,000. It follows that around 4,000 Jews must have died in the Otwock ghetto in 1942 before the extermination began. If the ghetto was enclosed with barbed wire only, one can assume that many Jews succeeded in escaping and hiding—for how long?—in the nearby woods.

During the extermination, between August 19 and 30, though possibly at a somewhat earlier date, four mass executions took place in Otwock. The victims were the old, the sick, and the very young, those whom the Germans probably saw as unsuitable material for deportation. The remaining Jews, about 6,000 in all, were deported to Treblinka in forty freight cars. I do not know where those forty freight cars stood. Near the high platforms of Otwock Station? Most unlikely. Probably at one of the stations after Otwock on the line to Pilawa, where there is a railway junction: Pogorzel, Stara Wieś, Celestynów. One of the executions held between August 19 and 30 took place on the grounds of Zofiówka, on Wołczańska Street, now Kochanowski Street, where the Jewish psychiatric hospital was situated before the war.

During the war the Germans apparently set up, or perhaps they only had plans to set up, a maternity hospital in Zofiówka: *nur für Deutsche*. Pregnant German women stand at the windows and watch the performance being staged in the near distance, clearly visible through the gaps among the pine trees. They will give birth to fine Aryan children. Nowadays Zofiówka is a handsome two-story building with large windows and a second-floor terrace, set in a landscape of tall pines. It houses the Feliks Dzierżhyński sanatorium. What a nice name. Adam Czerniakow, who came to Otwock several times in 1940 and 1941 for a short rest and stayed in the Zofiówka or the Brijus sanatorium, recalls that in August 1941 he was accosted on the grounds of Zofiówka by a patient who thought he had black candles burning inside him.

"I don't remember," my mother says, "if the ghetto you mention was fenced in or simply wired. I'm not even sure I ever went to Otwock—I mean during the war. If I did, I guess I went no farther than the station. Unless I was passing through on my way to Celestynów. You know where that is?"

"Yes," I reply, "it's the third station after Otwock."

"Your grandmother," my mother says, "ran a boardinghouse there during the war. And the only Jews I remember are those your grandmother sheltered in her boardinghouse. Though I can't say for certain that they were local Jews; more likely they were intelligentsia, refugees from Warsaw. But at the time I didn't know who they were."

"When was that?"

"Probably 1943," says my mother. "Toward the end of 1942 or the beginning of 1943 your grandmother left her estate near Pułtusk and escaped to Warsaw. The estate was in the Reich by then and there was an obnoxious *Verwalter*, who had to be plied with vodka. What's more, they kept pestering her to sign the *Volksliste*. She was a Protestant, remember. That is why she escaped. Once she arrived in Warsaw she either bought or rented, I'm not sure, a house in Celestynów.

"At the time lots of people were fleeing from Warsaw

because of the Russian air raids, and your grandmother's tenants were supposed to be refugees from Żurawia Street or Wspólna Street. But in fact they were Jews. In 1943 when we were all together in Celestynów for Easter—Alinka and you were there too—two genuine Jews came to the house. By genuine I mean they didn't pretend they'd fled from the Warsaw air raids or ask if they could rent a room. It was obvious they were Jews, and they had two small girls with them. I had a terrible quarrel with my mother, who was your grandmother, because she didn't want to shelter them. She said they could sit for a while in the summerhouse—we had a summerhouse in the garden behind the house—but then they would have to move on. I remember bringing them food. Your grandmother had to choose between her lodgers and the two Jews with the little girls. The military police or the blue policemen could easily come looking for them. The Kripo police station was a stone's throw away. But I didn't understand; besides, I didn't know who her tenants were. The parents of the surgeon who took out your appendix after the war were living in the room upstairs. Later on the surgeon left for Sweden."

"What about the two Jews?" I ask. "And the two little girls? Do you have any idea what happened to them?"

"Don't ask me," says my mother. "They looked almost identical. The little girls also resembled each other, though less so than the two men."

"When they came out of the forest onto the road," I say, "and saw the military police marching toward them, it was too late to turn around and hide in the trees. Imagine what they felt about the Christian woman who fed them in the summerhouse and then told them to go away. They thought of her as the police ordered them to dig out the pit."

"I already told you," says my mother. "It was a question of choice. I am not sure if God exists."

"If He exists," I say, "they found out the truth later. What are you getting at?"

"Think as you like," says my mother. "If God exists. But that's not the end of the story; the end is really quite incredible. Before the two Jews departed, your grandmother agreed to keep the two little girls and deliver them to Warsaw. In Warsaw she was to call someone who'd come to get them. I don't remember the details, but that was the deal. The next day, though it may have been the same day, Uncle Antek took the girls to Warsaw. They rode in a wagon to Otwock, and in Otwock they caught the train. The elder of the girls was ten or twelve and understood everything; I mean she realized she had to keep her mouth shut. Her little sister was four or five, and simply couldn't understand she had to be quiet. The elder girl tried to explain, but it was no good. The moment the blue-and-yellow train set off, the younger girl, who was no doubt thrilled at the prospect of traveling on an electric railroad, began to jump up and down in the middle of the car, crying all the time, 'I am a little Jewish girl. I am a little Jewish girl.' Well, just imagine how Uncle Antek must have felt. It's almost an hour's journey from Otwock to Warsaw."

"But Uncle Antek is still alive," I say. "So a miracle

must have happened. A miracle that lasted almost an hour."

"Uncle Antek," says my mother, "is an incredibly lucky man. During the Uprising he was twice taken to be executed, and each time he got away. It cost him two wristwatches."

"Those Germans," I say. "Just imagine a band of pickpockets inventing some cretinous ideology to justify robbery. Thieves who disguise their theft through murder and ideological bunkum. They could have come in 1939 and said to the Poles and the Jews, 'Hand over all your watches and your rings, because we are stronger, from which it follows that your watches and rings ought to belong to us.' Instead they came and said, 'We will murder you because our ideology tells us to murder you. And as part of the package we'll take your watches and rings.' Have you ever seen the photos of the Germans in Grzybowska Street or Twarda Street cutting the beards off the Jews? The dignified biblical faces of the Jews and the asinine faces of the Germans tugging at their beards. Half-witted grins, gaping mouths. I am not a racist, but in this case one can only say that people, not superhumans, were being murdered by some wretched mutants or subhumans."

"Let me finish," says my mother. "The compartment in which Uncle Antek and the girls were sitting suddenly emptied, as though the other passengers sensed it was way too cramped. And that child kept on jumping up and down, crying, 'I am a little Jewish girl,' though she may have felt disappointed by her dwindling audience. And so

Uncle Antek traveled to Warsaw in style with the two little girls. But that is not the end of the story. Your grandmother lived on Koszykowa Street at the time, not on the same side of Marszałkowska Street as we did, but opposite, near Mokotowska Street. She rented an apartment there, though in fact it was only half an apartment. The corridor was partitioned by a cupboard, and some people we didn't know lived on the other side. For some reason the man who was supposed to pick up the girls turned up only a week or two later. For almost two weeks the people behind the cupboard could hear that four- or five-year-old boasting she was a little Jewish girl. What's more, that apartment was on the second floor; the SS or the SA lived next door and kept patrolling beneath the windows."

"The ones in light brown, light yellow uniforms," I say. "Round caps and a red armband with a swastika set in a white circle. I think it was an SA unit. They patrolled with dogs and I was absolutely terrified of those dogs. Do you remember once dragging me into the doorway on Koszykowa Street? There must have been a street roundup that day, but I'm not sure about the shape of their caps, so it could have been a different unit."

"I don't remember that," my mother says. "Now let's count. Your grandmother, Uncle Antek, the people behind the cupboard, the next-door neighbors, the house janitor—he must have heard. Plus the man who came to get the girls and the family to whom they were taken. I don't think we've anything to be ashamed of."

"I would also like to know about the financial side," I

say, "I mean how much the tenants in Celestynów paid. I read the story of Berman's wife, the other Berman, not Jakub. Apparently, Jews who were in hiding had to pay some deposit on top of their rent. As far as I can remember, anything from five to fifteen thousand zlotys. An astronomical sum. In 1942 a paper dollar cost forty zlotys."

"Gold dollars," my mother says, "cost even more."

"At the end of 1942," I say, "they jumped from one hundred and fifty to nearly two hundred zlotys. But what were the terms in Celestynów?"

"Your grandmother," says my mother, "was a very trying character. In fact, she was quite unbearable at times, she was always so sure she was right. But for all that she was a decent human being. Whatever her Jewish tenants paid her, I assume it was the going rate for a room in the Warsaw region. And even if it was not, allow me to think they paid the same as everyone else."

"The Jews are now planting trees and distributing diplomas and medals to those who hid Jews," I say. " 'Righteous among nations of the world.' That's all very nice and I'm sure it's a good thing to do, but I find it disturbing. There ought to be no reward for such deeds, at least not on earth, not here and now, but in the world to come, if at all. Something resembling absolute forgiveness. A voice addresses the sinner standing at the foot of the Throne: 'As you sheltered Jews, I grant you remission of all your sins.' And if I may ask Thee a favor, O Lord, then I pray that my grandmother be granted that reward."

"If God exists," says my mother, "I'm sure you don't need to ask Him. He will have thought about it Himself."

"LISTEN, Hania. If I were a Jew, I'd have left Poland at the latest in 1950. And if I'd never left, or else left at a later date, I'd feel I had basically made a mess of my life. By 'Jew' I don't mean an assimilated or Polonized or communist convert Jew, or one who is a mixture of everything. I mean a decent, pious Orthodox Jew, because if I were a Jew that is the kind of Jew I'd want to be, lighting the candles, reading the Books, speaking Yiddish and Hebrew, with only a smattering of Polish or even no Polish at all. At least that is how I would like to imagine myself. Now, if I were a Jew I could of course be an assimilated Jew, say if my grandparents and parents, in spite of being Jews, had attended a Polish grammar school or secondary school. In that case I'd probably have no option but to continue the assimilation process. I don't know what I'd do then. The problem of assimilated Jews is too intricate for me, unlike the problem of communist Jews, which is too simple to be worth discussing. But the problem of assimilated Jews is too complex for my stupid Polish brain, and if I were a religious Jew, I'd probably conclude it was no problem for my stupid Jewish head.

"Isaac Singer once said in an interview—it was a long time ago and I can't remember where I read it, so I may have garbled or distorted it—that an assimilated Jew ceases to be a Jew and should therefore stop plaguing and pestering the Jews until he rediscovers his Jewish roots and returns to his Jewish nature. I may be exaggerating. I love Singer and all he has written for us Poles and Jews, but here I think he's going slightly over the top. As though he'd solved this thorny issue just a bit too easily, dismissively.

"But as I said, this problem surpasses my skills, because a goy like me is quite incapable of understanding the agony and torment of assimilated Jews who continue to be Jews even though they don't want to be. So I don't know, I cannot say who I'd have been and what I'd have done with myself if I'd been an assimilated Jew. I guess I'd have tried to build my Jewish-Polish, Polish-Jewish nature, my duality and dilemma, into the shifting, mobile foundations of my existence, so as to derive some spiritual benefit or existential advantage, if one can put it that way, from my duality and ambiguity. I'd exploit my dual identity as a means of enjoying a double existence. I'd use the ambiguity of my existence as a means of discovering my ambiguous self. But what can I hope to know about these things? If I had the option, I'd still choose the life of a pious Jew: tallith, mezuzah, tefillin, Torah, Talmud.

"I grant you, I might well have ceased to be the pious religious Jew from Jadów or Radzymin after all that happened to me during the war. I'd quite probably conclude that the cruel jokes of my Jewish God make it impossible for me to continue believing in Him. I might even concede that my own pious person is one of His jokes. But despite all that I'd not stop being a Jew, a Jew who wants to be a Jew and nothing but a Jew.

"To return to my earlier point: that is why I'd have left Poland in 1950 at the latest. I might have left even earlier, right after the pogrom in Kielce, in the summer or fall of 1946. Why on earth should I live in a country where Jews are constantly beaten up, and not only beaten but murdered—forty killed in the Kielce pogrom? It can hardly be pleasant for a Jew to live in a country that is one great Jewish cemetery, an overhead cemetery where the smoke from three million bodies drifts between sky and earth. And why would I have left in 1950 at the latest? Because persecutions of Jews started up afresh in 1949.

"Compared with wartime events this was mere child's play, no bastinadoes, no murders, no torturing. At the time, the Poles were torturing and murdering fellow Poles with far greater gusto. But in this case communists were settling scores with Poles who didn't want them, and if I'd been a Jew I doubt if I'd have got very involved. Why should I feel pity for Poles who during the war had shown no mercy for Jews? At least that is how I would have argued as a Jew.

"How should I define this new wave of persecutions? Persecution may be too strong a word. No one was harmed. For the umpteenth time since the world began the Jews were simply denied the right to their Jewish separateness, Jewish autonomy, and Jewish dignity. In December 1949 the communists, who had already assumed control of existing Jewish organizations in Poland, delegalized all Jewish political parties. The Jews were given the option of continuing to live and function in communist Poland, to flourish and prosper even, on the condition that they obeyed the communists, collaborated with them, and helped them in the pleasurable pastime of tormenting the Poles.

"Many Jews accepted the proposal. If I'd been a Jew at the time I'd feel bitterly ashamed to reflect back on it now. But I am a goy—on that score my conscience is clear—so let the Jews feel guilty when they remember the Jews who behaved like non-Jews. If I'd been a Jew at that time I guess I'd have felt persecuted. For the communist proposal to collaborate contained a perverse and carefully veiled threat: either you renounce your Jewish separateness or you can pack up and go to your Palestine and Israel, we don't mind. So if I'd been a Jew at that time I'd have been forced to acknowledge that the only real option was to stop being a Jew or else get out. A sickening choice. What would I have decided if faced with this option? As I've already told you, I'd have chosen the second alternative as more palatable and dignified.

"Under the circumstances it is hardly surprising that a Jew who wanted to remain a Jew, and felt disinclined to build socialism in Poland for the Poles, packed his bags and left. One could obviously argue that the Jews were solicited, not by Poles, but by the very Jews who many Poles seem to think were governing Poland in those days, like Hilary Minc or Jakub Berman or Roman Zambrowski.

"One might also claim that the Jews were placed in this predicament, not by Poles or by Jews, but by communists—in other words, by people who were neither Poles nor Jews. A wise old Jew reckons that a Jew who converts to communism ceases to be a Jew, as he no longer deserves to be one. The fact that he has joined the party proves he is either terribly stupid or stark raving mad. That's supposed to be a joke. When telling this joke, wise old Jews with a communist past smile ambiguously to intimate that they were once rather foolish too, but that they have now outgrown their folly. So if it's a joke, it's meant provocatively, as it's not without relevance to some Poles.

"Yet even if we concede from the hindsight of forty years that it was not the Jews or the Poles but strange mutants who seized power in Poland and wanted to deprive the Jews of their Jewish separateness, it seems very unlikely that forty years ago Polish Jews should have seen it and understood it that way. They were living in Poland. The government that wanted to turn them by means of some new and unprecedented form of assimilation into the builders of Polish communism claimed to be the government of Poland. Whatever befell them was inspired and instigated by Poles. I imagine that's how they saw it. Even if they were acting on Stalin's orders, Stalin was a long way off, the Poles were around the corner. And whatever the Poles kept wanting of the Jews, it was never what the Jews wanted for themselves.

"If I were a Jew that is probably how I would have thought at the time. And I'd have been most unhappy in a situation in which the Poles ran my life according to Polish, Russian, communist, or whatever criteria. A pious Jewish adolescent, I have miraculously escaped from the ghetto, survived behind a cupboard, eluded capture in an attic, and I may be about to lose my faith. So why should I give a damn about their Polish or Russian communism? I think that is how I would have argued. What's more, I'd have insisted that my parents take me away to Israel. I'd have emigrated with my Jewish parents and my Jewish sister to Israel, Australia, or America, anything to get away from the country where someone constantly takes exception to my Jewish life and evolves theories that forbid me to live the way I like in accordance with the dictates of my religion, my separateness, and my Jewish nature, forcing me to adopt some newfangled Polish or Russian ideas. But, Hania, I would have left no later than 1949 or 1950. After that Jews had no choice at all in Poland. They were in Stalin's clutches and they had to renounce their Jewish identity. I don't know if they even ought to be called Jews."

"Wouldn't it be better," Hania asks, "to start teaching the Poles how to behave? Tell them when and where to leave or stay? If I were a Jew. If I weren't a goy. How can you ever hope to know what it means to be a Jew?"

"There's no need to get uptight," I say. "There's surely no harm in my trying to put myself in their shoes. Even if I never discover what it is to be a Jew, I might at least define what it is to be a Pole and thus pinpoint my thoughts about Jews. Especially as they aren't clear even to me."

"After all you've said," says Hania, "how am I supposed to feel about myself? I mean, it was my father the Central Committee sent around to dissolve the Bund in 1949. Also I am an assimilated Jew, so according to that foolish man

Singer I'm not even worthy of the name. And you want me to agree with you that my father was not a Jew because he renounced his Jewish identity, and that I'm not a Jew either because I renounced mine. But I'll never accept that. My father was a decent Jew and an honest man, even though he was a communist, and I'm a Jew too and always shall be. I'm the one who is going to spend the next hour weeping alone in the kitchen. But don't come to join me or try consoling me, because I don't want to be consoled by someone who's incapable of understanding who I am."

"I don't intend to try," I say. "Someone who's blubbering just because he doesn't know himself doesn't deserve to be consoled. In fact, he's inconsolable."

"You are callous," says Hania. "There's not an ounce of pity in you. And I don't know why I ever married you."

"Hania," I say, "I feel so much pity I don't know where it's all contained inside me."

"Oh, have mercy," says Hania, "and stop talking such nonsense."

THE wooden bench with iron legs had once been painted white, then green. But how that came to pass is a matter of speculation, as the white and green layers of paint both flaked and peeled off aeons ago. Years ago it used to stand in the park or perhaps in the hall of one of the Otwock sanatoria, though that too is a matter of guesswork. At any rate, the bench (who lugged it here and when?) now stands by the side wall of the shed in the southwestern corner of Sara Fliegeltaub's garden, the point farthest removed from the house, the veranda, and the white wicker armchairs.

Red-currant and white-currant bushes grow between the side wall of the shed, the wire fence behind the shed, and the iron-legged bench, then stretch farther along the fence. The shed contains coal and tools, a rake, spades, and hoes, which Szlojmele uses when the spirit moves him. Also a shovel he uses to heave coal into a bucket with a curved handle, muttering to himself all the while. But no one knows what foolish, lame Szlojmele mumbles to himself as he ambles with his bucket to the shed, for no one is listening. Yet it might be worth eavesdropping as he converses with the Powers in the shed. Not so much a conversation, I should add, as a stuttering, moaning, wailing, and chanting. Szlojmele's great solo arias as the shovel scrapes and the coal drops into the bucket with a thud. But no one listens. Only the shed has ears.

If anyone wanted to hide here, he could use Szlojmele's shovel to dig out a pit or tunnel between the coal and the rear wall of the shed, converting it into a perfectly acceptable refuge or bunker, especially as the rear wall adjacent to the netting has a loose plank and a hole in the netting facilitates a quick escape from the shed and the garden. You could survive several hours or even days or weeks in a hideout like that. However, if they came with the police dogs, they'd soon discover the tunnel and find grubby little Niuta or Gitla squatting behind the coal. So we can't say that the shed was a hundred percent safe as a shelter.

But now it is a sweltering, muggy late morning in July 1937. Lured no doubt by the white flowers and yellow stamens of the cucumber vine that climbs up the shed and along the fence, a bumblebee buzzes menacingly in Icyk's ear. At present there is no reason why anyone should wish to hide in the shed, which is kept shut by means of a large rusty padlock and therefore out of bounds. Anyone seated on the bench next to Icyk, be it morning, noon, or dinnertime, has his face in the sun, which diffuses only moderate warmth, because as it turns above Sara Fliegeltaub's garden it is screened by the treetops.

That tree on the left must be a maple, thinks Icyk, that other one could be a linden or a poplar. When will I ever learn to distinguish a maple from a chestnut, or a linden from a poplar? "There's nothing very odd about that," I say to Icyk. "If you spent your entire childhood on Stawki Street or on Zamenhof Street, and visited the Krasiński Garden for the first time at the age of thirteen or fourteen, you are going to have trouble distinguishing a linden from a poplar. As a city child myself, I had the same problem for years. Even though, when I was little, I used to play in Ujazdów Park near the green scales and the sculpture of the naked girl, which intrigued me greatly. In 1940 or 1941, children in Dzielna Street—or was it Niska Street? —saw an old Jew pulling a cow along on a rope. A Jew walking through the streets of the ghetto with a cow in tow, now that was an exotic sight. It may have been a goat, actually, but what's the difference. The children raced after the Jew and the cow-goat arguing about what it was. Do you know their conclusion?" "Yes, of course," says Icyk, though from a distance of fifty years he cannot hear me. "They concluded it was a horse."

The sun progressing behind the linden or the poplar warms Icyk's knees and hands pleasantly. A ruled notebook and a pen, a Parker with a gold nib bought at Siudecki's shop on Szpitalna Street for seventeen zlotys, lie by his side on the bench that was once white and then green. A substantial sum, and my Icyk is very proud of his Parker. He uses this pen and notebook to draft his daily column for *Der Moment*. The bench is a good place to work for someone who has deadlines to meet even on vacation, even on a fine, scorching July day. First, as we know, it is warm in a pleasant and temperate sort of way. Second, it cannot be seen from the veranda, and the voices of vacationers chatting on the steps or in the dining room are trapped and entangled in the leaves and branches of the jasmine, transformed into almost inaudible whispers and rustlings that do not disrupt the writer's concentration.

Icyk has to work, because his column in *Der Moment* is his main or rather his only source of income. He is paid thirty-four zlotys for each piece, from which we may infer that he is a highly rated columnist. For thirty-four zlotys you can buy two Parkers with two gold nibs. Or, for just one zloty more, spend seven days at Sara Fliegeltaub's boardinghouse. A pair of spats costs twenty-five zlotys, a meter of Bielsk worsted forty-one zlotys, a kilo of beef on the bone in Koszyki one zloty forty-seven groszy, a pickled cucumber nine groszy, and a trolley ticket twenty groszy. For a poem printed in *Literarisze Blatter*, Icyk gets nine zlotys if the editor can afford it, or nothing if he can't. The article he is writing or rather ought to be writing has to reach the editorial office of *Der Moment* in the morning mail the day after tomorrow at the very latest. But Icyk is idle. Not because the mellow heat of the sun is conducive to indolence. The ruled notebook lies unopened on the bench, with the pen on top, because Icyk's thoughts are not fit to be recorded, and even if they were, they would still not be fit for publication.

The die is cast, thinks Icyk, though I cannot say who cast it and why. But it may be the decision of the Jewish God, in whom sometimes I don't believe at all, though other times I partly believe and partly disbelieve. But the die is cast and it is patently clear to me that our chances here are nil. In view of what the future holds in store for us Jews, though probably even the God in whom I partly disbelieve cannot see that far ahead, the idea of shipping us all to Madagascar isn't so bad after all.

But Madagascar is not, alas, a Polish dominion. Even if it were, the shipment of three million Jews would not be feasible in logistic terms: just think how many times the *Batory* and the *Piłsudski* would have to sail around Africa. Mind you, I doubt if they'd put us on luxury liners; more likely we'd be packed under the deck of some dilapidated freighter, like the blacks used to be. That doesn't mean I relish the prospect of living in Madagascar—today of all days, when the sun behind the trees (linden or poplar?) warms my knees so delectably and the bumblebee heading for the cucumber vine buzzes so pleasantly in my ear. I feel good here and there's no other place I would feel better. But even if I were to be much worse off in Madagascar, I still think it's absolutely crazy to wait for future developments sitting on this bench here or in the white wicker armchair on the veranda.

You stupid Jews, Icyk shouts. Naturally he shouts softly to himself, and his shout is no louder than the buzzing of the bumblebee in his ear, because it's not really the right thing to do to shout something like that in Sara Fliegeltaub's garden or in the Great Synagogue on Tłomackie Street. You stupid Jews, can't you see that every single one of you should get the hell out of here now? Because otherwise they'll cook your goose for you. If not the Germans, the Poles. Failing the Poles, the Russians.

So raise your stupid heads from Gemara and look around you. Listen. Think about what is going on. Darwin and all the other evolutionists, Hegel and Marx and Nietzsche—their names are legion—were basically right. But they failed to foresee that evolution, a process that takes millions and millions of years, would suddenly gain momentum and start progressing at a horrific and unprecedented speed so as to embrace mankind. And that our own human race, evolving at a speed unprecedented in the history of nature, would give birth to new, hitherto unknown species: a super-race and a sub-race. Nor did they foresee that the unexpected new races of mutants would want to impose evolution on a race congenitally incapable of evolving at that rhythm, or indeed at any rhythm, because the very idea of evolution is contrary to their human nature.

Now pause to reflect, all you Jews: who are we talking about? You are the ones that refuse to evolve, you and your ancient, unchanging Jewish nature. There is no doubt whatsoever in my mind but that these mutants will get at you, maybe others too, but first and foremost you. They'll try to make you and the likes of you evolve at a faster pace. Your ancient customs, Old Testament beards, conservative gaberdines, antediluvian thoughts, and counter-evolutionary sidelocks will fill these mutants with fear and revulsion, because everything that is ancient and unswervingly human will fill them with fear and revulsion. If not Hitler, then Stalin. If not Stalin, then some Polish, Romanian, or Hungarian Mussolini. For these mutants, reflects Icyk as he fends off the buzzing bumblebee that has mistaken his ear for the cucumber flower, are already rife. Indeed they may already have landed in Madagascar, in which case there is no island on earth where the Jews can hide from them.

But are these thoughts of mine suitable for publication in *Der Moment*? In the first place, no one is going to print a piece like that. Second, they'd be quite right not to print it, as I may be wrong. Perhaps there has been and will be no mutation, so there is no reason to panic. A hundred thousand years ago, a million years ago, the bumblebee poised above the cucumber flowers hummed just the way it hums now, the same bumblebee above the same white flowers. If bumblebees could laugh and think, that bumblebee would laugh heartily at the very thought of an evolution of species for bumblebees, flowers, and humans—in which the human species actually believes!

Mind you, my way of thinking only goes to show that my Jewish mentality, being incapable of evolution and therefore undergoing no mutations, is categorically opposed to any form of this process. If I were to write and publish my thoughts, this would undoubtedly arouse the wrath and revulsion of the mutants. It would most likely provoke a similar reaction in my dear friend Moryc Kaplan. As a sympathizer of the Bund, Moryc must believe in evolution. Probably he'd like to make the Jews, including me, evolve at a slightly swifter pace. I wonder if he knows what the immediate future holds in store for us and what the mutants are planning. Moryc's good intentions are beyond doubt, but maybe I should advise him not to get too involved all the same.

So saying to himself, Icyk opens the ruled notebook on his lap and unscrews the Parker with the gold nib, having decided that his thoughts must be conveyed to paper. Otherwise, on this torrid, steamy day, when the weary bumblebees flounder through the air and not a single leaf stirs in the jasmine bushes, they will instantly evaporate from his head, and Icyk will never retrieve the notions he was hatching in Otwock on July 13, 1937, as he sat between the shed and the red-currant and white-currant bushes.

Now for a few headlines that appeared on July 13, 1937, in *Our Survey*, the largest Polish-language Jewish daily published in Warsaw. "War Rages in China." "Close to Madrid." "Frontiers of Jewish State Not Yet Defined." "The Truth about Leni Riefenstahl's Fall from Favor." "First Attempts to Introduce Aryan System to Craftsmen's Guild." "Ghetto for State Railroads?" "What German

Children Are Taught." "Apply for Foreign Passports as Soon as Possible." "Accused of Communist Activities." "Trial of Accused in Przytyk Scheduled for September 13." "Policeman Shoots Bicycle Thief." "Echoes of Bloody Incident in Otwock." "Problematic Friendship Between Austria and Germany." "Millions Pour into General Franco's Coffers." And so forth.

Reading these headlines fifty years later, in July 1987, one has to admit there was no lack of signs. But were there sufficient grounds? Leni Riefenstahl, "Hitler's friend and German film dictator" (her grandmother was a Polish Jew), was thrown out of the parlor by Dr. Goebbels. The Moscow newspaper *Trud* called for the total abolition of the Trotsky-Bukharin agency. Two thousand Moroccans landed in Algeciras, then took a train to the Madrid front. Were these sufficient grounds for prophesying, in July 1937, that it would all end in massacre? At the junction of Stawki Street and Dzika Street?

Admittedly, in February of the same year, the Warsaw weekly *Prosto z mostu (Plain Truths)* published a piece entitled "Poland Exploded in 1937," in which a certain young poet vowed that Poland would soon "smell of wheat, not of rabbinic intellect," and called upon the Angel of the Lord to send a night of the long knives on the readers of the Jewish writer Marcel Proust. But such threats were not taken very seriously. The mutants, as Icyk Mandelbaum called them, were not very much in evidence. Hence the question: Could Icyk foresee what the immediate future held in store as he sat on the bench that day with his notebook and the bumblebee buzzing in his ear? It seems improbable, for instance, that he could have anticipated the shout of the Jewish children when they saw a Jew pulling a cow on a rope on Niska Street in 1940 or 1941: "Oh, look at the horse, look at the horse."

"But I'm not claiming to have foreseen the future," says Icyk. "In those days no one could. I merely foresaw that something would happen; that's the difference. I wasn't alone in this. Others too sensed that our summer resort in Otwock was like a seismic shock zone. Deep underground something was cracking, ripping, shifting, splitting. Like a rumbling underfoot. And I heard it."

"My question may be inept," I say, "but I'd like to know why those who heard the rumbling and foresaw events didn't raise the alarm and tell everyone to get out immediately."

"Because everyone wanted to go," says Icyk. "Well, if not everyone, then almost."

"So why didn't they?"

"You reason like a child," says Icyk. "First of all, only a few heard the roar of subterranean forces churning scraps of bloody offal up to the surface. Second, not very many could afford to leave. It cost a lot."

"But was it really that expensive? Surely some of those who foresaw the horrendous future could have afforded the certificate."

"Of course."

"You mean they knew they should leave, they could afford to leave, but they stayed behind?"

"Precisely."

"Why?"

But Icyk does not answer my question, for Jureczek Wasiutyński has appeared among the jasmine bushes on the path leading from the house to the shed. White or rather cream trousers, not cloth but top-quality English wool, white shirt, and white V-neck with a navy-and-red band along the V. He holds a white-cased tennis racket in his hand. A short blond mustache, above his mustache the white visor of a white cap. Were it not for his nose, a trifle on the long side, one would say that Jureczek Wasiutyński was an exceptionally good-looking Aryan. One could also say, thinks Icyk, that Jureczek has an exceptional Aryan brain. I refer to his thoughts. He thinks like an Aryan. But if I expressed my view out loud Jureczek would be deeply offended, for to Jureczek's mind there is no better or more Jewish Jew than himself.

"But why didn't they leave?" I repeat my question from a distance of fifty years or seven thousand kilometers, depending on Icyk's whereabouts at the time of our conversation.

"You are tiresome," says Icyk. "Surely you know that idiotic questions like that have no answers. They didn't leave because they didn't leave. Incidentally, why don't you leave yourself? You're always expecting some calamity to strike you on the corner of Filtrowa Street and Sędziowska Street."

"But the zaddik from Calvary Mountain left."

"Now you just keep the zaddik out of it," says Icyk. "The likes of you will never understand the meaning of 'zaddik,' and I for my part have no intention of enlightening you on the subject of our zaddik from Calvary

Mountain. So kindly push off to a distance of fifty years, or seven thousand kilometers if you prefer. I wish to exchange a few words with Jureczek Wasiutyński. It drives me quite mad when that mutant produces his exceptionally Aryan thoughts from his exceptionally Jewish head."

"Allow me," says Jureczek, taking a seat beside Icyk and placing his racket over the blue notebook, "allow me to join you. I've won the match with Miss Chaja, just imagine, six–three. But although I have beaten her, I must admit she is magnificent. If all our young Jewish women were like her, we'd have been in Palestine a long time ago. Sometimes I even think our women understand the concept of Jewish statehood better than our men. Though perhaps I should phrase it differently. It's not that they understand better, they don't have to, they just embody it so magnificently. For me Miss Chaja is a symbol."

"Isn't that a bit exalted?" says Icyk. "Chaja symbolizing something in your head. I mean, really."

"Sometimes I wonder how best to encapsulate our notion of statehood," Jureczek says. "Let's say, to devise a poster that would induce our youngsters to leave. Then I always conjure up a picture of a young woman like Chaja in a short white skirt, hair blowing in the wind. A girl with a racket on a red tennis court. It would act as a summons or even a command."

"Summons to what?" asks Icyk, though he knows what Jureczek Wasiutyński is driving at. "Personally I'm not very enthusiastic about being summoned."

"You're not the problem," Jureczek says, "our youngsters are. They are certainly deficient in what one might call physical vigor. Racial vigor. Now take Soviet Russia, for instance, where they have various sports and military organizations for women, young people, and even children. That's what we need. We must become a healthy nation at last."

"Do you mean we are a sick nation?" Icyk asks. "The thought would never have entered my head."

"You surely aren't going to tell me," Jureczek says, "that a nation is healthy when it revels in its sores and wounds and keeps shoving them under everybody's nose, as it were? By forcing other nations to admire our infirmities we simply make ourselves ridiculous."

"What do you mean by our infirmities?" Icyk asks. "The fact that we have no state of our own? That might be seen as an infirmity of sorts, but you can hardly accuse us of wallowing in it."

"I didn't say that," says Jureczek. "What I mean is our sufferings through the whole course of history. We worship our own sufferings. I find this quite repulsive, because it is a kind of psychosis. A nation that enjoys suffering and persecution denies its own right to exist, because only strong and healthy nations have that right."

"If I understand you correctly," says Icyk, "a nation for you is a living organism, like a large animal, healthy or sick as the case may be. When it is sick, it lies low in its hole. When it is fit, it hunts other beasts. I have a somewhat different concept of nationhood."

"I've read your novel," says Jureczek, "and I'll tell you straight: I find your whole concept unacceptable. Sabbatai Zevi was a common impostor."

"But my novel doesn't pretend to resolve that problem," Icyk says. "It's about the Jews who believed in him. I wanted to explain to myself how they came to believe in him and embark on that journey."

"You've hit the nail on the head," says Jureczek. "Just a few more pogroms and another Sabbatai Zevi will appear in our midst. And the Jews will believe in him again. That is our tragedy, what I call a form of psychosis, though madness is probably a more apt word. As we wallow in our rare and glorious sufferings we subside into some sort of messianistic madness, as though that gave us the right and the duty to save all other nations. Please note that strong, healthy nations tend not to indulge in messianistic delusions."

"But don't you think a nation could be strong through its weakness?" asks Icyk. "Its weakness, be it genuine or apparent, might be its best defense. Our messianistic delusions, as you put it, are sometimes quite hilarious. And Sabbatai Zevi was an impostor. Yet we've still managed to survive a few thousand years. We may even owe our survival to our messianistic delusions. We believed God had some special mission for us. That may have enabled us to survive. We shouldn't really be here at all, Jureczek."

"It's absurd," says Jureczek, "to believe that we should make Judaism the spiritual center of all mankind. Messianistic delusions are absurd too. We have to conquer a real territory, not some spiritual realm. And we won't succeed unless we become a healthy nation. That's why I consider racial fitness to be the order of the day. The injunction of nation and state."

"Chaja with a tennis racket?" says Icyk. "Or Chaja with a machine gun? That might be a better idea for your patriotic poster."

"Throughout history," says Jureczek, "colonization has always had to reckon with the resistance of the natives. Palestine will be no exception. Right now the Jews are outnumbered by the Arabs there six to one. So?"

"Six to one?" says Icyk. "And so what?"

"If we want the Arab majority and the mandate government to take us seriously," says Jureczek, "we ought to have at least two thousand soldiers there right now. Without an army we don't have a hope in heaven of creating our own state. But I assume the matter leaves you cold."

"Far from it," says Icyk. "But I don't consider it to be our top-priority problem just now." Yet, he thinks, I am a funny guy. I know exactly what Jureczek is driving at and I know exactly how our conversation will end. So why do I provoke him? Chaja must be on the veranda by now, and if I went up I could see how she looks in her white pleated skirt. White ankle socks. A short-sleeved white blouse above her elbows. A glimpse of her elbows would certainly be more enjoyable than conversing with old Jureczek.

"That is what I used to think," says Jureczek. "Don't take offense, but you always look to me like someone who has lost his homeland. Palestine will never be a homeland for you."

"You fail to perceive the subtle difference between homeland and state," says Icyk. "I've nothing against the idea of *Judenstaat.* I'm well aware of the obligations that will devolve on me when it comes into being. But my homeland is everywhere."

"I see," says Jureczek. "You're like our Orthodox Jews, the Talmud is your homeland, or to quote Dr. Bałaban, a sort of mobile homeland. That is simply preposterous. We live in a specific situation. Specific states conduct a specific international policy. And we'll gain nothing by invoking the Talmud, or shoving it under the noses of English or French politicians. We must convince these politicians that we have an instinct for statehood. That we are a force to be reckoned with."

"It's not only a question of the Talmud," says Icyk. "I should have phrased it differently. It would have been more appropriate to say that everything is my homeland."

"What do you mean by everything?" asks Jureczek. He is no longer sitting on the bench, but pacing up and down in the confined space between the shed, the currant bushes, and the jasmine, pausing every now and then in front of Icyk and gazing at him intently. Perhaps he wanted to put my Jewishness to the test, thinks Icyk, as if it were impossible for someone like me to be a Jew. Or maybe he is simply flabbergasted that a Jewish intellectual living in the first half of the twentieth century should store such Talmudic nonsense and Orthodox delusions in his head. But in that case Jureczek acknowledges my right to be a Jew, he acknowledges my Jewishness. So I'm not doing too badly. "What do you mean by everything?"

"I mean the luggage we Jews carry with us," says Icyk. "All we've achieved in history. All that has befallen us.

That is what homeland means for me, in the etymological sense: the heritage of which I am the heir. So please"—and here for no particular reason Icyk flies into a fearful rage and starts shouting at Jureczek, who seems somewhat unnerved by his outburst—"so please don't try to tell me about a state. There is not a state in the world that could shoulder such a burden. A state is a fine thing in itself. But it is not its vocation or its raison d'être to shoulder the burden of the heritage we carry with us and without which we are nothing. I don't want to be hampered by a state. Our heritage is our concern, not that of a state. Because only the nation, the entire nation, can shoulder it."

"I fail to see the basic difference between nation and state," says Jureczek, mildly disconcerted.

"You fail to see the difference because you are a mutant," Icyk has it on the tip of his tongue. But as he's not in the mood for explaining to Jureczek what he means by mutant, he says something else instead. "It is the job of the state to print trolley tickets and ensure that they cost no more than twenty groszy. If that is the historical task you assign to the nation, congratulations."

"You simply don't want to understand the essence of statehood," says Jureczek in a more conciliatory tone, or at any rate more sotto voce, though perhaps he ought to start shouting too, "which I wouldn't hesitate to describe as sacred. The sacred essence of the state. To my mind this is identical with the essence of the nation. This worries me. At present we need every manifestation of Jewish energy. But to derive some benefit from it, different strands must combine to create a single form transcending all others. If every Jew is going to think just what he pleases, and we Jews are inclined that way, we are individualists, anarchists even, so if every Jew, including you, is going to think just what he pleases, our state will never be built. For instance, you may have an idea that strikes you as beautiful and noble, but if it is in conflict with our ideal and hinders its realization, it must be ruthlessly axed. We can have many ideas, but only one ideal for the present. Two or three ideals is pure nonsense. One can only serve one ideal."

"But I don't intend to sacrifice a single one of my noble and beautiful ideas for your ideal," says Icyk.

"There you have it," says Jureczek, "the root of all our Jewish bad luck. We Jews are incapable of uniting into a single iron fist to strike when necessary."

"Fist?" Icyk shouts. "Who are you going to fight?"

"Words don't matter," says Jureczek. "If that one doesn't suit you, another will do instead, say 'machine' or 'orchestra.' You'll tell me, I know, that it's not very pleasant to be part of a machine, or one of the instruments in an orchestra. That it's even unworthy of a free man, as it restricts his sense of freedom. So I'll anticipate your objections. Only people who are and feel themselves to be genuinely free will be able to work together with the splendid precision of a machine. The absolute and infinite freedom of every man here finds its supreme expression. Proud to be free, the individual subordinates his will to the collective needs of state and nation. I must confess, this innate desire and ability to harness the individual and the communal is what I see as the finest feature of the human race."

"When your orchestra," says Icyk, "is perfectly attuned and starts playing just what you want to hear, who is going to conduct? You, I expect?"

"You must be joking," says Jureczek. "I don't feel worthy. I'm not the only one who thinks along these lines. There are many more worthy candidates, better trained than I am to 'conduct' the orchestra. I shall subordinate my will, of course, as I am convinced that success depends first and foremost on this principle of subordination. Now, that doesn't mean I want to submit to someone else's will, or indeed intend to. Far from it. The man above me will be the depository, so to speak, of my freedom or my free will, disposing of my will but acting by my will and according to my will. One ideal, one aim, one will—I see no other possibility for rebuilding our state. Otherwise we shall languish in the diaspora for the next thousand years."

"So that someone," says Icyk, "will be a sort of leader?"

"The whole point of discipline," says Jureczek, "is that one man subordinates himself to another, who is in turn subordinated to a third. Without discipline we shall never realize our ideal."

"When you get the opportunity," says Icyk, and as he rises from the bench he tucks the gold-nibbed Parker behind the blue cover of the ruled notebook, "tell the someone to whom you will all be subordinated that he can kiss my ass." Then, as he walks along the path, he turns around again from between the jasmine bushes and adds, "When you get the opportunity, you can say the same to Mr. Hitler and Mr. Stalin."

"Which obviously I ought never to have said," says Icyk,

as we brake at the corner of Mordechaj Anielewicz Street and Karmelicka Street fifty years later. "I felt pangs of guilt for years afterward. But, dear boy, how could I have known in the summer of 1937 about the opportunities that lay in store for Jureczek Wasiutyński?"

"I DON'T like what you're writing," says Hania at the wheel of her red Renault, a present from her aunt who lives in Israel. It has ugly reddish stains on the roof and right fender which I made with special paint when the chassis began to rust and the first hole appeared. "I don't like what you're writing," says Hania as our, or rather her, Renault turns downhill from Płowiecka Street and courses along the crosstown track of the blue-and-yellow railroad. Our conversation takes place along the Warsaw Anin, Warsaw Międzylesie, Warsaw Radość, Warsaw Miedzeszyn stretch.

We are on our way to Otwock, because I have decided to examine the posts that once supported the fencing around Mrs. Sara Fliegeltaub's property. Such posts are notoriously resistant to fires, bulldozers, evacuations, death sentences, dictators' speeches, and sundry cataclysms of history, and I am quite convinced we'll find them still in situ on this torrid morning in July 1987, albeit with a new fence.

"And the reason I don't like it—only don't fly off the handle—is that you're fabricating. I'm not saying I don't like fiction, but in this case I feel it is unacceptable, a bit indecent even. Not one of them survived. Then a mere spectator of their death starts inventing a novel. I don't know how to put it. It's not that you're belittling them, it's as if you didn't believe what they lived through and what they suffered, and found your own imaginings more reliable than the facts. That's what I find so distasteful. I don't want you to fabricate."

"If you don't like what I'm writing," I say, "I won't read you another page. You'll have to read it for yourself in that fuzzy samizdat print and you'll ruin your eyes; you've damaged them enough already reading all those clandestine publications. Besides, you are barking up the wrong tree. In my story I invent nothing. I quite agree it would be indecent to fictionalize."

"Invent nothing, my foot!" Hania explodes. "You mean you didn't invent those tennis courts in Otwock? How can you know if there were tennis courts in Otwock at the time? Not to mention the fact that your Jews certainly never learned to play tennis. The Jews who came here on vacation were the urban poor from Nalewki Street and Krochmalna Street. Don't you know what their summer exodus looked like? They would load all their Jewish bedding on carts or furniture trucks and roll up in Józefów or Otwock with their wives and kids perched on top of the bedding. A gaberdined Jew waving a tennis racket. Just try to visualize a cart stacked high with bundles trundling along this stretch of road with two splendid tennis rackets sticking out of the pile. The whole thing's ludicrous."

"You don't know much about the Jews who came to

spend the summer here," I say. "Those Jews who brought cartloads of bedding went to Falenica or Józefów or other resorts along the line, as it was then called. A totally different class of Jew came to Otwock, a much wealthier, tennis-playing type, no two ways about it. As for the courts, you're wrong again. I can't say for sure if there were tennis courts in Otwock, but there were definitely some in Śródborów, and that is where Chaja Gelechter and Jureczek Wasiutyński used to play, at the Śródborowianka boardinghouse. They used to walk to Śródborów through the rachitic pine trees of the forest holding hands. When my friend Icyk found out about these walks—I think I can call him my friend in spite of the difference in age—he said to Jakub Wurzel, 'Jakub, I've discovered that they walk through the forest holding hands.' To which Jakub Wurzel replied, 'I always told you you should marry some respectable Jewish woman, not just any old trollop.' There would have been nothing very strange in his remark, were it not for the fact that Chaja Gelechter was Jakub Wurzel's mistress at the time, though that is something Icyk found out about long after the event."

"Kindly refrain from telling me what happens next in your novel," says Hania. "I've already told you there's something I find personally offensive in your lucubrations."

"I'm only trying to explain," I say, "that what you call fabrication is not fabricated at all. The tennis courts in Śródborów are a good case in point. I know for a fact that there were tennis courts there. But Andrzej, who told me about them, couldn't remember if they were grass courts or hard courts with some reddish surface, whatever it's made of. So I pass over that point in silence and forbear to describe the tennis courts. Only established facts deserve to be retold. The same goes for the garden shed and the iron-legged bench.

"I can't say for sure if Pani Eliza hid a Jewish child in the shed in 1942 or 1943 when she was living in Sara Fliegeltaub's house, but the chances are she did. Before the war she had Jewish friends and she conversed quite freely in Yiddish, which she had picked up as a child on Krochmalna Street, where she lived with her parents. 'If you'd like, Mr. Rymkiewicz, I'll teach you their tongue, I can speak it even faster than they can.' But I don't know if Pani Eliza used Szlojmele's old shovel to dig out a cavity between the coal and the rear wall of the shed, so I have merely said that the shed would have made a good hiding place. To have the right to tell stories, there's no use doubting the veracity or accuracy of certain things; you must know what really happened and have the guts to say exactly how things were."

"That's the whole problem," says Hania. "How can you possibly know the facts? And I wouldn't put it past you to invent the shed and Pani Eliza. I also have my doubts as to whether Szlojmele's shovel ever existed."

"Now you listen," I say. "Maybe I invented it all, Pani Eliza, the shed, the iron-legged bench, the white armchairs on the veranda, the pansies in the flower bed, and Szlojmele's shovel, likewise Chaja Gelechter and Icyk. But you have met Pani Eliza and Icyk. And your aunt was friends with Chaja. Besides, even if I've invented it all, including you and the red Renault and the blue-and-yellow railroad too, it is no less true for all that.

"Back in 1937 I was a kid. Of course, you can say I'm an unreliable witness, because I remember nothing; all I recall is broken scraps and disjointed fragments flying at a phenomenal speed through my memory into some cosmic void or intergalactic darkness. A bench. A white armchair. Two veranda steps. Someone sitting in the armchair and reading a newspaper. A pince-nez. Wrist cuffs above the long fingers holding the newspaper covered with weird scrawls, the likes of which I'm unacquainted with. My paltry testimony, my deficient memory.

"But I reject your claim that as a second-rate witness I have no right to testify, and you have no right to deprive me of that right. Why should I be so deprived? They are all inside me, in my memory. Chaja, Jakub Wurzel, lame Szlojmele, Jureczek Wasiutyński, Sara Fliegeltaub, with all their strange adventures and tragic martyrdom. It was all half a century ago. But whether I like it or not, those scraps and fragments that made up their lives, all that remains of their lives, will continue to spin around in my memory until it is plucked away one day and engulfed in cosmic darkness.

"So I think I am a suitable witness, and I feel that I not only can but should testify. Even if I cannot testify to their lives, it will be my own personal act of remembrance. Not much, perhaps, but it will do. So you're wrong to accuse me of wholesale fiction-mongering. You surely can't mean that my great dirge for the Polish Jews is imagined; I'd be very upset if you thought that. And surely my testimony is not imagined either. My dirge is a lament for myself. When I mourn for the Polish Jews it is an act of self-mourning, the lament of a Pole forever forsaken by Polish Jews. You'd have to be really mean to call that fiction."

"Then I beg your forgiveness," says Hania, planting a kiss on my cheek and simultaneously losing control of the steering wheel, as the red Renault with the russety spots swerves violently toward the railroad track and the high platforms of Miedzeszyn Station.

"That's no reason to kill me," I say. "I'm getting on in years, and if you kill me I'm not sure that anyone else will be able or willing to testify. My juniors by only a couple of years remember even less than I do, and sometimes I feel that those biographical fragments of theirs exist only in my mind. Besides, it's unlikely that my juniors can even begin to gauge the extent of the loss."

"I promise not to kill you," says Hania, "if you promise not to fictionalize. As for those posts, I bet you anything they're no longer there."

"Then we can go to Anielin to see the Jewish cemetery, or what remains of it," I say. "If you weren't an assimilated Jew, you could make yourself useful deciphering the inscriptions on the broken tombstones."

"If you're unhappy about my not reading Hebrew, you'd better divorce me and marry a pious Jew."

"As far as I know," I say, "pious Jewish women knew no Hebrew; knowledge of Hebrew was a male prerogative. That's my first point. The second is that no pious Jew would marry a goy like me. The third is that there are no pious Jews left in Poland now." Whereupon the red Renault climbs down from the sandy road into a rest area and grinds to a halt alongside some rusty posts supporting a brand-new wire fence, which has been given a protective coat of silver paint.

WHAT a lot of sand. If we accept that our world was created by God, which is fairly probable, or by some other Power, which amounts to the same, it is evident that the object of creation was conceptualized prior to or in the moment of creation. It was thus created for a purpose. To infer that things exist for no purpose would be to cast doubt on the wisdom of God or of the Power. But why did God create the sand? What use could He have of it? What is His reason for my shoes, my hair, my nose, and my ears all being so full of sand? Rabbi Symcha Bunam of Przysucha: "He who disbelieves that God wants this grain of sand to lie just here has no faith in Him." Rabbi Symcha Bunam may have been right. But a God who ponders where to place the sand grain that has adhered to my moist fingertip is a God I do not comprehend. So I've decided not to air my views on the subject, or even give the matter another thought, because whatever ideas my brain churns up, God remains unfathomable and enigmatic. Hidden behind ten *sephiroth*—I think that's the number—in the unfathomable depths of proto-air or proto-light. Or in the unfathomable depths of proto-sand.

Beyond the pines there is sand, beyond the sand there

are more pines, beyond the pines still more sand. Beyond the sand flows the Świder, and we sit on its sandy beach; the bank opposite is overgrown with willow brake. I sit on the latest issue of *Our Opinion*, spread out on the sand to protect my gray trousers. Sitting by my side, Szymon Warszawski ignores such trivial matters, but Szymon's father is a banker (the bank on St. Andrew's Street in Łódź), so Szymon does not have to worry about keeping his trousers clean. Chaja perches on a sloping tree stump, probably a willow, that protrudes from the water, its crown broken and sawn off, its grain clearly visible. A pale blue dragonfly, a small glider, circles just above Chaja's white sailor cap. Miss Lilka, wearing an identical white cap and a white-and-navy-striped garment that might be described as a pajama or a suit, paddles with her wide pajama legs hitched up above her knees.

The Świder is shallow at this point and one can cross over to the opposite bank without getting one's knees wet. Chaja's white shoes and silk stockings lie by my side on the sand. Miss Lilka's white shoes and socks are next to Szymon. What a lot of sand. If God in creating the sand dwelt upon the destiny and location of every grain, He must have worked overtime. Though, ever unfathomable, He may have solved the problem in half a second, or even outside of time, in proto-time or timelessness. The grains of sand exist in time, and like all of existence, they may even be identical with time. But they were conceivably created outside of time and then hurled into time. Unless their creation in time resulted from a decision taken out of time.

It is so pleasant to sit on the banks of the Świder on today's issue of *Our Opinion* and reflect upon the position and destiny of each and every grain of sand. If I select one grain from among its fellows and place it here on the picture in *Our Opinion* of a palm leaf swaying above the flat rooftops of Jerusalem, who is responsible for this move? Who made the decision and when? But Szymon clearly won't allow me to ruminate on the inscrutable destiny of this grain of sand, because he wants to know why I don't write in Polish.

"I simply cannot understand," says Szymon, "why you don't write in Polish. It beats me why a writer of your talent should use a language that in fifty or a hundred years from now will be totally forgotten—that must be painfully obvious to both of us. It is a doomed language. I assure you, fifty years from now you'll not have a single reader."

"It may be that I write in Yiddish for the very reason that its days are numbered," I say. "But my answer is much simpler. I don't write in Polish because I don't want to write in Polish."

My reply will never satisfy Szymon Warszawski, who is bound to treat my admission as a joke not to be taken very seriously. How could anyone capable of writing in Polish (and Szymon knows I could) simply not want to? In Szymon's opinion, someone who writes in Polish ipso facto achieves a far higher standing than a writer in Yiddish.

I wonder how he'd put it. He'd probably say that Polish is better adapted to the requirements of twentieth-century civilization, better able to convey the progressive ideas of the century than the Jewish lingo or patois, as he has occasionally been heard to call it. Szymon reads the patois, because he learned the alphabet as a child, but I'm not sure that he speaks it. Probably he is too ashamed to speak it. If he were to converse in patois he would put himself on a much lower rung than when he speaks Polish. He would prove he is a Jewish obscurant, befuddled by the effluvia of the Jewish Dark Ages, and that he's not yet become a European. And Szymon is every bit a European.

So I wonder why he spends his vacation in a Jewish boardinghouse, in the company of such Jewish obscurants as me and Jakub Wurzel. I guess that's because Miss Lilka, a great philo-Semite, felt that a vacation in a Jewish boardinghouse would be a fitting sort of testimony. Anti-Semites say, "Don't consort with Jews," so she spends her vacation with us here to prove her love for Szymon and all other Jews. Slightly grotesque, but also quite appealing, especially as Miss Lilka is a stunning beauty. It is a sheer delight to watch her paddling in the Świder in that pajama suit with the navy and white stripes.

"You'd have far more readers if you wrote for *Wiadomości Literackie*," says Szymon. "What's more, they'd be members of the intelligentsia, who would understand you so much better than your Jewish audience. Not to mention the fact that you'd earn more that way. How much do you get paid for your column?"

"Dear Szymon, sir," I say, "can't you see I'm on the breadline?"

"Mr. Słonimski is paid fifty zlotys a piece," says Szymon. "And a hundred if it's reprinted elsewhere."

"Quite convincing," I say. "But you know, what I write probably wouldn't interest the readers of *Wiadomości Literackie.*"

"If you wrote in Polish," says Szymon, "you'd obviously write about different topics."

"That's the whole point," I say. "I don't want to write about other topics."

"I see," says Szymon. "The perennial problems that vex the residents of some Polish or Romanian ghetto. The secrets of the Jewish soul. Riddles for yeshiva pupils to puzzle out. You refuse to come to terms with the fact that we live in the twentieth century. But the twentieth century is with us to stay, so perhaps we should be faithful to it and admit that its problems are also our problems."

"The ghetto," I say. "Now, that is a problem for the twentieth century."

"As I foresee it," says Szymon, "in fifty years there'll not be a single ghetto left in Europe. A few days ago I was on Zamenhof Street. Those ghettos are the disgrace of Europe. When all Europe is living in the twentieth century, you can't have small enclaves only two streets away lingering on in the Dark Ages. I find that totally unacceptable."

"Any idea how to change it?"

"Well, how?"

"That's what I'm asking you. What should be done to ensure that no ghettos survive in Europe fifty years from now? You say the ghettos will vanish, because something so infamous has no right to exist. Good. But the Jews who live in the ghettos won't vanish. So what do you intend to do with them? Do you think they'll be assimilated? All of them?"

"I don't know," says Szymon. "The intelligentsia will all have to assimilate sooner or later, I'm sure of that. I can't speak for the others. I mean, can you imagine our Orthodox Jews ever assimilating? Clearly you're right in saying that something ought to be done with them, but I don't know what."

"I didn't say something ought to be done with them," I say. "To my mind it's best to do nothing at all. God places each grain of sand exactly where He wants it to lie."

"Fair enough," says Szymon. "You don't want to write in Polish because your God has placed you among Jews. But as a man of the twentieth century, I refuse to see myself as a grain of sand."

"If you roll in the sand," says Chaja, leaping down from her willow stump and towering above me. Just above me, against a background of sky and willow brake on the opposite bank, I can see her knees, her white dress fastened from bottom to top with large, shiny mother-of-pearl buttons, her double chin and her cloud of black hair outlined against the blue sky. "If you roll in the sand and knock your head about in it, your hair will be full of the stuff. And washing one's hair in Mrs. Fliegeltaub's bathroom can hardly be described as one of life's pleasures."

"I've got sand in my head," I say. But Chaja can't have heard me, as she has just retreated behind the willow brake to pull on her silk stockings. I consider it a mean and dastardly trick that she should go behind a bush to put her stockings on, for there is no sweeter sight in the whole world than Chaja pulling on her stockings and tying her garters. In my lying position I am denied that prospect, and that I consider to be a mean and dastardly trick. To tie her garters Chaja should stand where she was only a moment ago, towering above me, outlined against the blue sky. There could be no more suitable background for her silk stockings and silk-stockinged legs than this almost translucent July azure. "I've got sand in my head. Listen to me, Chaja, my head is full of sand. Sand instead of brain. Whatever will become of me. Oh, woe."

"Mr. Icyk is putting us on as usual," says Miss Lilka, sitting down on *Our Opinion*, the issue I put aside before I started rolling in the sand, and pulling on her white socks. A pleasant enough sight, no doubt, but surely less charming than that of Chaja slipping on her silk stockings. Though perhaps I should not call it a sight, as it is hidden from sight behind the willow brake and no one can behold it. Yet invisible though it be, a sight it remains, especially if it is visible to God, for whom no willow brake can be an impediment to contemplating Chaja. "Away with that willow brake," says God, "because I want to watch Chaja tying her garters." The bush promptly slips away before God's eyes and God gazes at Chaja's knee sheathed in shiny silk, her fingers pulling the pink elastic of a garter. That I also consider to be a mean and dastardly trick.

Not that I deny God the right to contemplate Chaja's lovely knees. It is a truism that God, having created Chaja in all her beauty, has the right to contemplate her whenever and wherever He chooses, on the beach and the veranda, in her bed and in her bath, naked or dressed, putting on or removing her stockings, fastening or unfastening her garters. I don't object to the fact that God contemplates His beautiful creature, but that He views her egoistically—don't blaspheme, Icyk—and in so doing He screens her from my eyes behind that willow brake.

That is what I find so mean and dastardly and incomprehensible. For if God created that beautiful woman, those fingers poised on her garter, that knee sheathed in a silk stocking, and if His own creation gives Him so much pleasure that He cannot refrain from contemplating it even when it is hidden behind the willow brake, why does He screen her from my eyes, thereby intimating that He does not wish me to enjoy her beauty on the beach or the veranda, in her bed or in her bath? This is what I consider to be so very egoistic—calm down, Icyk, don't blaspheme—and a serious restriction of my free will. "Mr. Icyk is putting us on as usual. It strikes me that a tendency to exaggerate is a major feature of your psychological makeup."

"What are you going on about?" Szymon asks. "What's going to happen? And to whom?"

"To my head," I say, "and to the rest. I have a sandy desert in my head. Infinite stretches of sand. Dunes, nothing but dunes."

"I told you so." And Chaja in her silk stockings emerges from behind the willow brake, a sight as pleasurable as ever to behold, though less enchanting than what God contemplated only a moment ago in His solitude, marveling the while at His own creation of an object so exquisite as Chaja's knee. "I told you not to roll in the sand. Now you'll have to wash your hair."

"Before lunch there's usually warm water in the bathroom," says Miss Lilka.

"Let's go," says Chaja. "If we hurry you'll have time to wash your hair before lunch."

"Spread out the newspaper for me," says Hania. "And you'd better sit on it too; it's unhealthy to sit on damp sand."

I sit down on today's issue of *Warsaw Life*, on the headlines "Sunny High-Pressure Zone over Poland" and "Did Hitler Die in Argentina?" "If they came to the beach and bathed in the Świder, this is roughly where they would have come. It's barely a twenty-minute walk from here to the boardinghouse, twenty-five at most. But I have a feeling that I bathed in this spot in 1942. It's vaguely familiar. That bend, that backwater. The willow brake."

"The Świder is full of meanders here," says Hania, "and sand is the same everywhere. How long are you planning to stay?"

"Please, Hania," I say, "just don't speak to me right now. Let's sit here for a while, but don't speak to me."

"How long do you want me to keep quiet for?"

"Just a few minutes."

"If you insist." And Hania lies down on the sand and crosses her hands under her head, gazing into the almost transparent July azure. Her red hair cascades over the headline "Sunny High-Pressure Zone over Poland." A red whirlwind. A red cloud traversing a sunny high-pressure zone.

"Come out," I say. But Hania cannot hear me, for there is no reason for her to hear what I am saying. "Please come out. I know you are there, standing behind that willow brake. Don't be scared, come out. No one will harm you. Come out, I want to see you. In your white dress with the mother-of-pearl buttons. In those luxurious silk stockings. Please, please come out. For just one second. For a fraction of a second. Do it for me. Chaja."

BACK to the description of Umschlagplatz. What did the two, three, or four buildings standing in or near the Square look like inside? The best-documented is the ground-floor room in the Old Archives building, where deportees were detained prior to being loaded into the freight cars. Sometimes they were allowed to walk around; other times they had to sit still and the Ukrainians killed anyone who stood up. In *We Escaped Extermination by a Miracle*, Leokadia Schmidt writes that the floor was covered "with secretions and mud." There were, however, several crates one could sit on. The room had a barred window, or perhaps several, for Leokadia Schmidt's husband spent the night by a barred window. The panes had probably been smashed. In *The Ghetto Fights*, Marek Edelman writes: "The nights are cold, there is no glass in the windows." But we do not know which rooms and building he is referring to.

According to Leokadia Schmidt, there was a water tap on the ground floor of the Old Archives building, though I'm not sure that this is the large room in question, and this is not confirmed by other sources, most of which state that there was no water at all in Umschlagplatz, and even if there was the detainees had no access to it. Marek Edelman writes: "There is no water in the taps, the lavatories are blocked." Henryk Nowogródzki in *Three Days on Umschlagplatz*: "There is no water." But when Nowogródzki was in the ground-floor room of the Old Archives building it was forbidden to get up from the floor or walk around, so he was unable to go upstairs, where Leokadia Schmidt states that water was also to be found. I do not know on which floor this was; and the water had to be paid for. In a letter written in 1943 to her family in Palestine and entrusted to the Poles who were hiding her (it was published by Józef Kermisz in the second volume of *Documents and Materials Concerning the History of the German Occupation in Poland*), Franciszka Rubinlicht writes that on Umschlagplatz her father "tramped about for several days without a drop of water." Władysław Szpilman, in *Death of a City*, mentions a woman begging for water, of which "Transfer Square was deliberately deprived by the Germans." The problem of water in Umschlagplatz seems to me insoluble. Maybe there was water at some times but not at others, or maybe it was available for the wealthy—Leokadia Schmidt and her husband were rich entrepreneurs—while those less fortunate could not afford it.

A word about the ground-floor room in the Old Archives building. It follows from Henryk Nowogródzki's account that it was dark there at night: "The rooms in Umschlagplatz are not lit. We sit in the dark." Elsewhere he writes of "large rooms." Also: "There is no furniture." So perhaps there was not one, but several rooms on the ground floor? The sentence about the furniture refutes Leokadia Schmidt's reference to several crates. But not necessarily. One more detail from Nowogródzki: "gray walls." These were probably in the ground-floor room.

We know far less about the rooms on the upper floors of the Old Archives building. Leokadia Schmidt entered a large room—I do not know on which floor—with several large tables on which the detainees slept pending deportation. "There were several gas outlets on the wall." The gas supply was not cut off and could be used. Perhaps the large room was the gymnastics room which Marek Edelman mentioned to Hanna Krall in *To Outwit God*: "On the third floor there was a large room for gymnastics. Several hundred people lay on the floor." But the gas outlets were located in the big room—they were less likely to be in a gymnasium—so there were probably two different rooms.

We know even less, in fact next to nothing, about the rooms of the building in which the children's hospital was located. When I first broached this topic I made a mistake. I wrote that the children's hospital named after the Bersons and Baumans was transferred from Śliska Street to Stawki Street. In actual fact, the hospital which was situated between Śliska Street and Sienna Street was first transferred to the building on the corner of Żelazna Street and Leszno Street, from where the sick children were subsequently transferred to Stawki Street. From Adina Blady Szwajger's *Short History of the Berson and Bauman Hospital (1939–1943)* it appears that this happened halfway through August 1942. Later, at the beginning of September, to quote from the same source, "all the sick from all the hospitals" were taken to the building where the children were kept on the third floor.

A question here arises that I am unable to answer. If, as we must infer from Adina Szwajger's account, the children's hospital was set up on the third floor of the building only halfway through August, then what was to be found there in the early days of Umschlagplatz, from July 22 to the middle of August? Adina Szwajger worked in the hospital on Umschlagplatz for three weeks. Although stories of the Warsaw ghetto ought not to be graded on the basis of their documentary value, Adina Szwajger's account belongs in a category of its own. Its eschatological significance—I don't think that's too strong a term—makes it one of the most important documents of our century. Anyone curious to know about the times he has to live in should read that text. It is not easily obtainable, so here are the bibliographical details: Alina Blady Szwajger, *A Short History of the Berson and Bauman Hospital (1939–1943)*, in *Zeszyty niezależnej myśli lekarskiej* [Independent Medical Thought] (No. 10, December 1986), a periodical printed by the Independent Publishers Press. Perhaps I should say more about this document, which is a charter of the Covenant sealed on Umschlagplatz, but I feel that no one but the author has the right to relate the most salient facts.

Back to the rooms in the building that I shall continue to call the children's hospital. On the ground floor there was a sort of vestibule and duty room. As Adina Szwajger writes: "the women were not lying in the room for the sick, but down below in a small room next to the duty room." Some stairs led to the rooms on the upper floors: "I reached our third floor at last and there was only a room for babies. There were no rooms for children, since the sick, the wounded, and the dying were lying everywhere." Marek Edelman describes a door in some detail: "He stood behind the door of the hospital building. Once it had been glazed, but the panes had been smashed and the holes boarded up with planks. Through the chink in the boards I could see his face." The reference is to someone Edelman ultimately failed to rescue.

Finally there were some rooms on the ground floor. They were unfurnished, and Leokadia Schmidt lay next to a radiator. Higher up were windows with bars. If anyone wanted to escape he had to crawl on all fours to avoid being seen from the street. That street baffles me. I cannot figure out how the Old Archives building and the children's hospital interconnected. They were definitely adjacent to each other. But how were they situated in relation to Stawki Street and Niska Street? If there was a street outside, both buildings overlooked it; at least the children's hospital did. Was that street, be it Stawki Street or Niska Street, part of Umschlagplatz? And if so, was it fenced off or divided in half along the roadway or the sidewalk? Marek Edelman says nothing on this score; as a messenger at the children's hospital, he presumably had a pass and had no problems circulating between the buildings in and around Umschlagplatz. But then none of the other sources mention it either. Something may be gleaned from Leokadia Schmidt, but just this once her account is rather nebulous. Apparently the children's hospital could be entered from a back entrance, from Umschlagplatz and from the Old Archives building.

There was a courtyard that both belonged and did not belong to Umschlagplatz. It seems to have been divided from Umschlagplatz "where the rear part of the hospital was situated." How was that courtyard connected with the area referred to as a backyard, large backyard, or a small square of "oval shape"? I do not know. But there was definitely a passageway from the oval backyard to the courtyard. And from the courtyard one could enter the hospital by the back door. This is the door Leokadia Schmidt entered when she decided to hand her child over to one of the nurses. In *The Ghetto Fights*, Marek Edelman also refers to the door of the children's hospital. "People knock at the hospital door, which is guarded by a Jewish policeman." But Edelman's door may well be the main one.

From the ground-floor room in the Old Archives building one could reach the front door of the hospital by going out into the street. But it was not easy and anyone who decided on this venture did so at the risk of his life. According to Leokadia Schmidt, one had to go out of the

Old Archives building through an iron gate into the street, probably Stawki Street, and then "step across the sidewalk." "My husband collected our son from Frager on the sidewalk outside the building." Frager is the Jewish policeman who carried Mr. and Mrs. Schmidt's child out of the hospital. The iron gate was a few dozen yards from the front entrance to the hospital.

Apart from the policeman there was also the lawyer Szmerling, whom Leokadia Schmidt calls "the senior district officer" of the Jewish police, and who figures in other accounts as the Jewish commander of Umschlagplatz. Szmerling sat in the middle of the roadway outside the hospital or outside the Old Archives building. Leokadia Schmidt could see him from the Old Archives building through a crack, or perhaps a small window, in the iron gate. One had to walk the distance between the iron gate and the front entrance in such a way as to avoid being seen by Szmerling.

Szmerling in the middle of the roadway, the Jewish policeman or policemen outside the entrance of the children's hospital, are all important elements of Umschlagplatz topography. Their positions suggest that the pavement and roadway outside the two buildings (which probably overlooked Stawki Street) both belonged and did not belong to Umschlagplatz. They belonged in that one could step out onto the sidewalk, and in Szmerling's absence presumably into the roadway. But this was not synonymous with getting out of Umschlagplatz. There must have been further obstacles such as a fence, a wall, or barbed wire to bar their way. Yet at the same time they did not belong because they were guarded, and those who stepped out onto the sidewalk or roadway were treading on forbidden territory.

Other parts of Umschlagplatz were also out of bounds, yet within certain limits one could stay there. Cellars, attics, probably all of the children's hospital, which we can define as being part of Umschlagplatz or separate from it, depending on whether we apply the term to the entire area or only to the oval backyard and the rooms in the Old Archives building. Umschlagplatz may thus serve as a perfect sample of totalitarianism. Virtually everything is prohibited, and anyone who breaks the ban risks being shot. But only he who steels himself to take the risk stands a chance of escaping. He will hide in the hospital building. Bribe the military police on sentry duty. Disguise himself in a doctor's coat. Purchase a cap and armband from a Jewish policeman.

Let's return to the roadway outside the hospital. When Szmerling went off duty, what prevented the people behind the iron gate from escaping? A wall, barbed wire? Maybe the gate was locked? In *The Extermination of the Ghetto in Warsaw*, Adolf Berman, Jakub's noble brother, a mythical figure straight out of a bloodcurdling fairy tale about the two brothers, one good and one bad, writes as follows: "We were all escorted behind wires onto the Square." Wires—this time barbed wire is clearly implied—also appear twice in Emanuel Ringelblum's *Notes from the Ghetto*. I do not know if it's possible to determine the position of the barbed wire on Umschlagplatz. Berman, I think, mentions barbed wire near the wooden gate where

Edelman stood. He then refers to the exit from Umschlagplatz. "After which, following just a couple of steps behind him [i.e., the Jewish police officer who led the Bermans from Umschlagplatz] we passed by the sentry." The wire was near here, so it must have been part of a main or subsidiary barrier.

From Ringelblum's comment about Szmerling—"He threatened to throw me behind barbed wire"—one might infer that the barbed wire was situated outside the children's hospital. But Ringelblum could have met Szmerling elsewhere. The barbed wire is also mentioned in the notes Ringelblum made at a later date, in September and October 1943, and which were transferred from the shelter on Grójecka Street to the archive of the Jewish National Committee. There we read: "I walked onto Umschlagplatz. In a large square surrounded by barbed wire I saw a vast crowd pressing for all it was worth toward the exit." This would seem to suggest that the oval backyard—for that is surely what is being described—was entirely surrounded by barbed wire.

Another place that was both part and not part of Umschlagplatz was the end of the siding connected to the railroad line by Gdańsk Station—in other words, the loading ramp and tracks where the freight cars were waiting. According to eyewitnesses, though some repeat this from hearsay, the siding was outside Umschlagplatz. To quote from Emanuel Ringelblum's *Notes from the Ghetto*: "they led us straight to the freight cars—not to Umschlag, but straight to the freight cars." Leokadia Schmidt likewise notes that there was a gate between Umschlagplatz and the siding, a detail not found elsewhere: "At the end, beyond these buildings, one could see a great gate with the words: 'No entry under penalty of death,' and beyond it the railroad tracks." The inscription must have been in German.

On the basis of the account by M. Passenstein (I know only his initial) entitled "Contraband in the Warsaw Ghetto," written in 1943 but referring to events before the great extermination, one might even infer that the 'No entry' gate was erected later, perhaps as late as July 1942, by which time it was serving a different purpose. Passenstein mentions a railroad barrier that previously stood in the place where the gate was, or may have been, erected, for we may be referring to different sites: "At the junction of Dzika Street and Niska Street were the Transferstelle bureau and warehouses, to which the railroad sidings led. The square was partitioned into two sectors, one of which belonged to the Jewish district, the other to the Aryan side. At the narrowest point of this demarcation, a railroad barrier enabled automobiles and carts to cross over between the districts upon showing a pass issued by the Transferstelle bureau." It was surely not far from Umschlagplatz to the loading ramp and the tracks, at most several dozen meters, possibly less. The poplars were in the same place as the ramp and tracks. As Hanna Krall's text tells us: "the engine stood waiting near where the poplars were."

Otherwise little is known about the road linking the ramp to Umschlagplatz. I found a further reference in Henryk Rudnicki's *Martyrology and Extermination of the Warsaw Jews*, the book with the plan of Umschlagplatz, but I cannot vouch for his reliability. As I believe I have already mentioned, he visited Umschlagplatz three times; and he hands us one absolutely capital fact. The Square, in his estimation, measured "around 80 meters in length and 30 meters in width." To my knowledge, this is the only source to give the dimensions of the Square—namely, the courtyard that was entered from the Old Archives building.

Rudnicki's book is, however, full of glaring mistakes, and contains a number of eccentric or even farfetched ideas. He claims, for instance, that the Polish officers murdered in the Katyn Forest massacre were Warsaw Jews rigged out in Polish uniforms, whom the Germans shot in order to accuse NKVD officers of Jewish extraction of the crime and thus trigger a pogrom in Warsaw.

According to Rudnicki, a path led from Umschlagplatz to the ramp. "A pathway was contiguous to Umschlag; along it the Jews were escorted toward the freight cars." Rudnicki's book contains several other references to this path: "they began to drive the Jews who were gathered there together along the path to the freight cars." Elsewhere the way to the siding is described as "sandy ground." As Rudnicki says that blood and tears soaked into the ground, this sandiness is probably a poetic license. But perhaps the ground really was sandy there. So I don't know what to make of the path. Rudnicki went along it, so one wants to believe him. One has to believe him. But Katyn? I am nonplussed.

What else do we know about the ramp? Next to nothing. For entering the freight cars, there were two wooden contraptions resembling steps. Were they put into position only when the train drew in, or were they a permanent fixture? The ramp was quite long: a deportation train comprised up to a maximum of fifty-seven freight cars. I read this in a story entitled "I Built a Railway Bridge near Treblinka" by Engineer Jerzy Królikowski, to whom Polish railroad workers from Malkin had explained all about train lengths. The track behind the wires at Treblinka was long enough to accommodate nineteen cars, so the number of cars in any transport must be a multiple of nineteen. I have seen no photograph representing Umschlagplatz in 1942 or 1943, and I assume no such photograph exists. The Germans, as we know, loved to be photographed with their victims. We have countless snapshots showing a row of men against a wall or above a ditch, but in this case no picture was taken. So why didn't Brandt or Hoefle pose for a photographer on Umschlagplatz? It's worth giving the matter a moment's thought.

I have admittedly seen a photo taken on the ramp, when the freight cars were being loaded. But it doesn't tell us much. Several cars, one with a sentry box. Several Germans in helmets, one in a cap. Two or three Jewish policemen. Some distance away, almost in the background, a crowd is huddled around the freight cars, small figures with indistinguishable faces. Bundles and packages are scattered on the ramp, which appears to be overgrown with grass, but the photo is blurred, so I cannot say for sure. Behind the freight cars, in the far distance, one can see the roofs of two houses, the windows of the top story, and chimney stacks. We do not know how the German photographer positioned himself, whether he faced Umschlagplatz or the locomotive or had his back turned, so we cannot say if the houses are in the ghetto or on the Aryan side.

There may well be other photos of the ramp or of Umschlagplatz. Personally, I hope that there are not. Visualizing by verbal means is to see through a semi-transparent veil. Words reveal, but they can simultaneously conceal what they reveal. A photograph is different. In a photograph we would glimpse something I strongly feel to be taboo.

THERE was a time in my very early manhood when people used to think I was a Jew, and the label accordingly stuck. What is more, in the process of being generally thought a Jew and commonly passing as one, I was already partly Jewish and by autosuggestion was fast becoming a Jew. So in my very early manhood I was frequently given to understand that I was a Jew and that I ought to come clean with it. The best proof of being a Jew is not to admit to it. I refused to let on, and that created a bad impression.

In later years, much to my chagrin, my pedigree ceased to arouse such interest until not very long ago an elderly gentleman with a trim gray mustache asked me which of the Rymkiewiczes I stemmed from. "Oh, the wellborn Rymkiewiczes," I replied. The elderly gentleman said nothing in reply, but offered a weird sort of smile, as though hinting at forgiveness, whereat his gray mustache twitched upward and his smile made it patently clear that I was neither a wellborn Rymkiewicz nor any kind of Rymkiewicz, but a Rozenkranz, Rozenfeld, or Rozenduft. The sickly smell of roses, the sickly smell of anti-Semitism. The elderly gentleman would certainly have taken offense if I had called him an anti-Semite to his face. For all I know, he may not have been an anti-Semite at all, heaven preserve him. In my very early manhood, it must have been around 1955, my would-be mother-in-law used to proffer the same sort of smile as the mustachioed gentleman. But as my would-be mother-in-law had the chance of actually becoming my mother-in-law, she felt that a smile of forgiveness was inadequate and resolved to tell me frankly what she had on her mind.

"You know how I like you, Jareczek," she said. "Personally I see no difference between a Pole and a Jew. So if you are a Jew you should make a clean breast of it."

This conversation took place in the house where my would-be fiancée used to live in Marysin. My would-be mother-in-law received telephone calls from her women friends.

"You really do amaze me. I mean, everyone knows he is a Jew."

"Do you want her to marry a Jew?"

"His father was a policeman in the Warsaw ghetto. That much I know for sure."

"I've nothing against Jews. But I'd never let my child marry one."

I don't wish to wrong anyone, I want to be fair, so I

should stress that Marysia, my fiancée, had no such silly notions in her head and couldn't have cared less whether I was a Jew or not. I guess my mother-in-law *in spe*, who in the event became my mother-in-law manqué, did not really mind either. Perhaps she ought not to have had such moronic friends, but that is her business. The marriage never came off for other reasons which I shall not go into. Neither then nor now have I really understood how I managed to pass as a Jew in Łódź. I had fair hair, gray eyes, and a snub nose, somewhat rounded at the end. So why? A snub nose proves nothing, as I said to myself when Marysia told me what her mother's friends had been gossiping. There must be Jews with snub noses, so why shouldn't I be a snub-nosed Jew. But my father was definitely not a policeman in the ghetto. For the whole of the war up to the outbreak of the Uprising we lived on the corner of Koszykowa Street and Marszałkowska Street, and as far as I know my father never even visited the ghetto. I could still be a Jew, though. These things aren't always clear-cut, and my parents could have concealed the fact from me. That is how I argued at the time as I scrutinized my snub nose in the mirror, from which it would appear that I was not totally indifferent to my Polish or Jewish pedigree.

Why did people keep thinking I was a Jew? Two reasons spring to mind. In the first place I was making my debut as a writer. As a cocky nineteen-year-old, I saw prodigious talent in myself, and made no secret of that. I can imagine one of my fiancée's mother's friends contorting a smile into the telephone receiver and saying, "He writes and what's more he is awfully bumptious. So he must be a Jew." Ally Polish envy to the Polish inferiority complex, then add a small pinch of anti-Semitism to prove that someone who writes and thinks he's a cut above others must be a Jew, for what else could he be? He's smarter than we are, so he's a Jew. He's no smarter than we are, but he makes himself out to be, so he's a Jew. They print him, so he has connections, ergo he's a Jew. He has connections, the Jews fixed it for him: QED.

Second, my parents were members of the Communist Party. In those postwar years many Poles could see at best only a marginal difference between communists and Jews. By and large, though, anyone who was a communist had to be a Jew, and the reverse also held true. Incidentally, some people may still think that way, so it might be worth conducting a sociological survey. The Poles had some grounds for arguing along these lines. They remembered the prewar activists of the Polish Communist Party, who dreamed of transforming Poland into the seventeenth republic. They couldn't fail to notice the large number of Jews among the ranks of the communists who had just seized power, and were wielding it in a manner scarcely calculated to beguile them.

Their argument, I should add, does not hold water, and to identify communists with Jews is merely one of the symptoms of the anti-Semitic distemper. This equation, you see, was not a postwar idea; it was concocted before the war, and the intentions of its authors were painfully obvious. Father Trzeciak, who turned out anti-Semitic brochures, wrote in 1936: "Bolshevism is not a disease of the soul, but a great Jewish hoax. To discuss communism without mention of the Jews is to have no understanding of communism, for at present communism and Judaism are virtually synonymous concepts. . . . Bolshevism is the most terrible and treacherous weapon the Jews have ever used against Christianity. Bolshevism constitutes a new, satanical form of Judaism's eternal struggle with Christianity."

This text was written in 1936, but the quotation is taken from a German propaganda leaflet printed in Warsaw in 1943. Father Trzeciak was grist for the Germans' mill; he suited them to a tee. His knowledge of communism, by the way, is amazingly and terrifyingly simplistic. At the time, in 1936, a large number of Poles probably saw communism in similar terms, not as a sickness of the spirit, but as a Jewish conspiracy. To the list of casualties caused by anti-Semitism one must add all the Poles who, having once succumbed, became bereft of their wits and failed to foresee the sweet surprise history held in store for them.

Another brief digression. The German leaflet of 1943 provides an interesting specimen of spurious sensibility, if that is not a misnomer, in that the mental vision of the Germans is dually or doubly distorted. The Germans revile Bolshevism without seeming to realize that the comparison with Judaism assigns it an exceptionally high spiritual grade, which Bolshevism obviously never enjoyed. The upshot is that they extol and advertise Bolshevism. My second point is that when they revile Bolshevism the Germans quite unconsciously denigrate themselves, vilifying the very subsoil that gave birth to the totalitarian, alias the gangster, ideologies of the twentieth century.

To return to the equation of communist and Jew that was common currency among Poles in the forties and fifties. Instead of following the example of the anti-Semitic Trzeciak, the Poles ought to have analyzed the tenets of communism, one of whose principal aims is to transform Jews, Poles, Russians, Germans, and all others into weird creatures stripped of nationality, and thus bring about mutation and eliminate the differences between mutants of Jewish and Polish extraction, culminating in the total assimilation of noses and mentalities. But maybe I expect too much. In those days the Poles were subject to persecution themselves, and a man undergoing torture can hardly be expected to fathom the essence of oppression. The man on the rack cannot collect his thoughts, so he screams out, "They're torturing me!" "Who is?" "Him, that commie Jew." So up to a point I can justify my fiancée's mother's friend when she said, "For heaven's sake, don't let Marysia marry him. He's a Jew, because he comes from a communist family."

I wish, though, to make it perfectly clear that I never had any objections to being labeled a Jew. It's no problem. If you, fellow countrymen of mine, tell me I am a Jew, a Jew I shall be. In so doing you honor me greatly. I like being a Pole and, certain difficulties notwithstanding, I can just about cope. But if you think I'm a Jew, I can cope with that too. The Jews are a splendid nation and there are times when I regret I was not born a Jew. If I were a Jew there would be times when I'd probably regret I was not born a Pole, because the Poles are a splendid nation too. If I'm allowed to voice my preferences, I'd rather be a Jew of my own nomination and choose my Jewishness for myself than have it thrust upon me by the ladies who assured my fiancée's mother that someone like me cannot possibly be a Pole.

As for our Polish equation of communist and Jew, it no doubt stems from the Poles' virtual ignorance about Jewish life in the interwar period. I'm not sure whose fault it was, and probably both sides should share the blame. Few people knew about Poalej Sion, Aguda, Mizrachi, and the Bund, or were interested in Jewish customs, Jewish politics, or the spiritual life of the Jews. A Jew was a rabbi or a Hasid, in which case he lived in the Northern District. Alternatively he wore a goatee and pince-nez, in which case he was a Polish poet or lawyer, though in the eyes of the Poles he did not cease to be a Jew.

So the Poles could easily be brainwashed into thinking there was no difference between Jews and communists. Stalin, when the time was ripe, exploited this to his advantage: I'll fix the Poles and let them think the Jews have done it, then they can vent their fury on the Jews. But never mind about Stalin. The problem is my nose. Could a snub nose such as mine be Jewish? Several years later, when I had lost my Jewish label, people somewhat unexpectedly began to dub me an anti-Semite. Again my ostentatiously anti-Semitic nose was the problem, not for the anti-Semites this time, but for the Jews, the communistic ones of course, who raised a great hue and cry: "He's an anti-Semite!" I really had a problem. But I'll tell you about that some other time, Hania. I'm curious about what you're going to say about all that.

"As usual, you're exaggerating slightly," says Hania. "It's typical of you to pile it on. There's nothing wrong with your nose; it's my nose that's the problem. And there's nothing very unusual in the fact that you were called a Jew. You know the saying—I can't remember who coined it—that it's only being called a Jew that actually makes you a Jew. But I'm intrigued by that Zosia or Marysia of yours. Whoever was she. You never told me about her before."

"She had a ponytail," I say, "spike heels, a skirt with a stiffened petticoat, and a bodice à la Brigitte Bardot. In those days all the girls dressed like that. Oh, and she was exceptionally beautiful, which shouldn't come as a surprise, because all my girlfriends have been exceptionally beautiful. But do you know who lived in those houses in Marysin during the war? Rumkowski's men, he was the king of the Łódź ghetto. The commander of the Jewish police and suchlike, all the Jewish elite of the time. They spent their holidays there and enjoyed the good life until they were exterminated. I didn't know that at the time, more's the pity, because when my mother-in-law manqué was pressuring me to confess my true identity, I could have pointed out that she was living in a country house and wearing a fur coat that had formerly belonged to Jews. I wonder how she'd have reacted to that."

"She'd have kicked you out of the house," says Hania.

"And with good reason. I don't think you ought to print that."

"What don't you want me to print, the remark about the ex-Jewish country house and fur coat?"

"I don't want you to print any of it. If you do, there are bound to be people who will say you wrote about being mistakenly labeled a Jew simply to conceal your true origins. So that no one would ever suspect you again. Just you wait and see. They'll say that only a Jew could have written a thing like that, and that your book only goes to prove you are a Jew. A Jewish sympathizer ends up becoming one himself, remember. And to top it all off, you've got a Jewish wife—namely, me. That will also be held against you."

"They can say what they like," I say. "I'll be just delighted. You remember what the papers were writing in March 1968? I recently looked through that year's issues of *Warsaw Life*. And most instructive it was too. Paweł Jasienica was an assassin, Antoni Słonimski was conspiring with Zambrowski, Andrzej Kijowski was active as an anti-Polish brawler. I've copied down a quote: 'Some of them have sullied their good name by collaborating with international Zionism.' Anyone who fell afoul of those magnificent Aryans with their potato noses and potato brains was automatically classified as a Jew. I often consult with Andrzej and Antoni now that they are no more, and seek their advice. To be an anti-Polish brawler with Słonimski, an assassin with Paweł Jasienica, an international Zionist with Andrzej Kijowski, and to be a Jew with all of them together is really a tremendous honor, and I am not even sure that I deserve it."

ICYK Mandelbaum's car, a silver-gray Toyota, proceeds down Andriolli Street on its way from Otwock to Anielin. Before reaching Anielin, however, near the edge of the pine forest, it turns left, then right, then left again. Not far from here, Icyk thinks, should be the Jewish cemetery where Jews who died of tuberculosis in the Otwock sanatoria were buried, and where Sara Fliegeltaub may have been buried too if she managed to die at the right time, when Jews were still being buried in their own cemeteries.

This somehow strikes me as improbable, and I doubt if I'll find a stone with her name engraved in Hebrew and Polish, or just Hebrew letters. Yet perhaps she lies there, her bones and wig buried in the Otwock sand, and the roots of dwarfish pines thrust through the white shroud and rip apart the last veil that separates us from the inconceivable concept of nonexistence (in the earthly sense of being and nonbeing) and from the view that is not a view, though who knows if in some otherworldly sense of the word it remains a view notwithstanding. But even if Sara died when it was best to die, in 1939 or in 1940 at the latest, the vertical stone slab with Hebrew lettering was probably removed from the Anielin cemetery by truck and used by the Germans for laying the surface of a highway or sidewalk, long before it became coated with a greenish patina and a greenish moss filled the cavities of the letters. Instead the slab was placed smooth side up, the Hebrew letters filled with yellow or gray sand, and Sara's name with her dates of birth and death, 5647–5699, could be deciphered only by someone reading from underneath, from the bowels of the earth, through a layer of sand and clay and lava.

"Here we are," Icyk says in English to the young man at the steering wheel, and the silver-gray Toyota stops outside Sara Fliegeltaub's boardinghouse. The young man in a long black gaberdine overcoat, a shiny black felt hat, and long blond sidelocks whom Icyk calls Ben—"Ben" (again in English), "are you sure we are still Jews?"—is Icyk's cousin's grandson. He translates Icyk's novels from Yiddish into English.

Ben first opens the car door, then the trunk of the Toyota, and takes out Icyk's two large black leather suitcases. Icyk opens the wooden gate and is pleased to note that nothing, but nothing, has changed here. The rusty hinges of the gate creak as of yore. The bell tucked away in the foliage and flowers of the convolvulus can be heard ringing as before, and the spring that closes the garden gate behind the visitor snaps as it always did. The gate too is the very same gate that Sara Fliegeltaub wanted lame Szlojmele to paint. But Szlojmele never got around to doing the job because he was never in the mood for it, and later, when he might have felt the urge, he could do nothing about it, because he was no longer of this world. Beyond the same gate there is the same path, and the same nettles grow to the left.

Followed by Ben, who is lugging the suitcases, as drops of sweat run down the lovely sidelocks he has pushed behind his ears, Icyk walks around the house and pauses on the same steps of the same veranda, of which the penultimate, as we know, is a semi-step. There is no one on the veranda or in the dining room. But there must have been someone in the dining room only a moment ago. On the table, covered by a green crocheted tablecloth, there are three glasses of undrunk tea and a newspaper, *Folkscajtung* or *Hajnt*, dated July 13, 1937.

That's the glass I think I was drinking from, Icyk muses, the one on the left, above which a fly is now circling. Unaware of its impending fate, that foolish buzzing fly will shortly descend into the depths of the glass and will drown without cognizance of its doom. It is the same fly as fifty years ago, a quinquagenarian fly, so to speak. The wooden stairs creak. The stairs lead from the dining room to the second-floor landing, to the right of which, if my memory serves me well, was the attic door, secured with a wooden hook. That was where Sara Fliegeltaub hung out all the bed linen after a great laundry session, the faintly yellowed sheets and duvet covers and pillowcases. To the left was a corridor and the doors to three or four bedrooms. Behind that last door the clatter of a dilapidated black Remington could be heard first thing in the morning.

The wooden stairs creak and someone enters the dining room. It is Chaja Gelechter. She is wearing a gray suit and a closely fitting gray hat, a toque with a veil of a slightly lighter shade. Chaja Gelechter loved veils and wore them even when they were out of fashion. She presumably thought that a veiled woman assumes a greater air of mystery, and she was no doubt anxious to be thought of as mysterious. But I may be mistaken. She may have worn a veil because she was timid and wanted to conceal her nervous twitches and smirks, a sudden twist of the mouth prior to tears, the uncontrollable quivering of an eyelid.

On closer inspection the toque proves to be made of something resembling shiny gray hexagonal scales. Toques with veils were highly fashionable in the spring of 1936, but in 1937 the fashion changed and ladies started wearing small curved- or straight-brimmed hats. Chaja felt, however, that the new style did not suit her, and she remained faithful to her toque. The lower edge of the veil is not straight but scalloped, and there are darker gray spots or dots on the veil and each of the scallops. From a distance of five or ten paces, it is impossible to tell if the spots are on the veil or on the face of the person wearing it, gray freckles and patches that for some unknown reason appear on her cheeks, nose, and eyelids. Address of the milliner: 57 Krochmalna Street, second courtyard, second door on the left. On the door a sign in Polish said: "Watch out for the step!"

"Are you looking for Mrs. Fliegeltaub?" Chaja asks.

"No," says Icyk. "Or rather yes, I am looking for Mrs. Fliegeltaub."

"Mrs. Fliegeltaub has gone to Józefów," says Chaja. Icyk then recalls that Sara Fliegeltaub had a younger sister living in Józefów, whom the whole family thought was mad and with whom she, Sara, was forever quarreling, though Icyk cannot remember the cause of their feud. It may have been because Irena, the sister's daughter, went to the Institute for the Propagation of Art and drank coffee there with the goyim. Sara Fliegeltaub might well bear her sister a grudge for allowing the daughter to behave in that way. "She is mad," she used to say to her brother-in-law, the sister's husband, "and she'll drive you to your grave. Artur, you ought to lock her up in Zofiówka." Chaja lifts her veil; the gray patches vanish from her nose and eyelids. She peers intently at Icyk.

"You've come from Warsaw? Do take a seat on the veranda. Mrs. Fliegeltaub should be back shortly."

"Then I'll wait," says Icyk. Chaja walks through the dining room, past the table with the three glasses of un-drunk tea, in one of which the quinquagenarian fly beats its wings to intimate its intentions of fighting for its life until it is ultimately engulfed in the chasm of tea. Now she is on the veranda, about to descend the steps and vanish behind the house. Icyk wants to detain her. He has come back to Otwock and to this villa especially to see her, to be told by her all he needs to know, to find out at last the truth about those gray patches—are they skin markings or darker spots on the veil? Wanting to detain her, Icyk repeats very softly this time, "Chaja."

"You must be mistaken," says Chaja. "We have never met."

"Take a look," says Icyk. "Can't you see it's me? Icyk. Icyk Mandelbaum. Do you recognize me now?"

"Yes, of course. But you've changed so much."

"That's only to be expected," says Icyk. "It was fifty

years ago, after all. I am now a very old man. I am eighty years old, Chaja. Eighty-one."

"It's a fine age, Icyk," says Chaja. "Where have you been all this time? Whatever happened to you?"

"Better to ask me where I haven't been, Chaja," says Icyk. "I have been everywhere. I've been in Kazakhstan and in Persia and in Palestine. And now I live in New York. On the twenty-second floor."

"Then why have you come back?" asks Chaja. She lowers her veil, and the gray patches reappear on her eyelids, nose, and right ear, the one that Icyk can see. "I'd never have returned. Aren't you happy in New York?"

"Oh, I'm happy enough," says Icyk. "But please, Chaja, remove your hat, the veil is hiding you. I want to look at you, and I can hardly see a thing through the veil."

"All right," says Chaja. She removes her gray toque and veil and shakes her hair, her shiny, ink-black hair, fragrant with Guerlain's Mitsouko, so that it tumbles loose over her brow, her tiny ears, and her neck. My lips close by her hair, just above her tiny pink ear, fifty years ago. "But promise not to look at me like that, it makes me nervous."

"I promise," says Icyk, with no intention of keeping his word. "And now I shall tell you why I've come back. I wanted to see you, Chaja. You and everything else. This veranda, the steps, the nettles, and Pani Sara's dressing gown—you remember, the one with yellow and red flowers. The gray patches on your right ear. I wanted to see it all again, I wanted to find out for myself."

"You'll discover nothing," says Chaja, and Icyk sees her

trying to control the tic of her right eyelid. "What can you hope to find out from the Poles? They don't want to remember and there's nothing very surprising about that. In their place I wouldn't want to remember either."

"But I want to find out how you all survived," says Icyk. "How you fared."

"I did not survive," says Chaja, and Icyk notices how in speaking she closes her eyes, almost clenches her eyelids, perhaps to control her quivering, her nervous tic. But perhaps she does not want to look at Icyk or at anything any longer—the three glasses of undrunk tea on the table, the piece of cheesecake on which a quinquagenarian fly is strutting, its predecessor having been engulfed in the abyss, the crystal and the porcelain ballerinas in the glazed cabinet, the Virginia creeper climbing up the veranda columns, the pale blue sky, pale blue and white, pale-bluely translucent, hanging above Sara Fliegeltaub's house, above Otwock, and above Poland. "No one survived."

"But I survived," says Icyk. "That is why I want to know. What would have happened to me if I hadn't left. I don't mean what would have happened to me; I know all about that or at least can make a pretty shrewd guess. But I want to know how and what I would have felt. If the Russians hadn't deported me from Lwów in a cattle truck in '41."

"That is something you will never know," says Chaja, "for you have no right to know. That is something only we know," and Chaja falls silent. They look at each other, look into each other's eyes, Chaja Gelechter aged twenty-four years forever and eighty-year-old Icyk Mandelbaum.

But it lasts only ten seconds at most, because Icyk then lowers his eyes: what Chaja knows is unendurable for us survivors.

"According to some sources," says Icyk, "the Jews on Umschlagplatz, not all of them but those who had a long wait because there was no room in the freight cars, so they waited for the next train, these Jews, when the hour of prayer came around, took out their tallith and prayed, praising the God who—there's really no other way of putting it—had arranged all this for them. When I was fourteen or fifteen, certainly not later, but when I was still living with my parents, I was a very pious Jew, so I ought to understand them. But I just don't understand. To whom were they praying then? Does it make sense to you?"

"There is nothing to understand," says Chaja. "They were praying because they were praying. That's the way it was. But I'd rather you didn't ask me what things were like. Tell me about yourself and what it is like to live on the twenty-second floor. Do you write books?"

"Yes."

"Doing well with them?"

"I can't complain. With a bit of luck I should get the Nobel Prize in a year or two if I'm still alive."

"That's what I wish for you, Icyk. I wish you to win that prize and any other prizes that may come your way." Chaja puts on her gray toque with the veil, then walks up to Icyk and strokes his cheek with her hand, which is sheathed in a gray suede glove. "I am sure you will win all the prizes. I'm delighted you are so successful. Remember? I always said you'd be famous one day."

"I'm famous, all right," says Icyk. But perhaps he only thinks it, and if he says it, it is more to himself than to Chaja. "I am as famous as one can hope to be. But what do I, an old Jew, get out of it? Who will tell me that?"

"I really must go now," says Chaja, "or I'll miss the train to Warsaw. I have a date with Jakub at the Ziemiańska Café. But you can stay here if you like. Take a seat on the veranda and wait for Mrs. Fliegeltaub. She'll be back shortly."

"Don't leave yet," Icyk begs, "because I'd like to look at you just a little longer. This is my grandson. Well, not mine, but my cousin's. He translates me into English."

"Your grandson," Chaja says, and walks up to the young man with the sidelocks pushed behind his ears, who is standing on the veranda with Icyk's suitcases in his hands. "So there are still Jews in the world. How very odd. I thought there would be no more Jews, we are the last Jews on earth." And Chaja touches Ben's sidelocks with her suede-gloved hand, takes one of the locks between her fingers and twines it, untwines it, and twines it again.

"He was born after the war," says Icyk, "and does not understand Polish. But you can speak to him in English or Yiddish."

"If he was born after the war," says Chaja, "what are we going to talk about?"

"But he is a Jew," says Icyk. "Can't you see?"

"You mean the same?" asks Chaja.

"The same as who?"

"The same as us."

"Identical," Icyk replies. Yet he is not at all sure whether his grandson in the Hasidic hat is the same as the Jews in Hasidic hats who used to come for their summer vacation to Świder, Józefów, and Falenica. "Or almost. Well, a bit different maybe; he was born in the Bronx, not on Krochmalna Street or Lubecki Street. But does it matter? A Jew is a Jew everywhere."

"Then I'm glad he is almost the same," says Chaja. "A good-looking boy. You're almost the same too." Then from the veranda steps she adds for some unknown reason, "My poor, poor, poor Icyk. But I must run, I'll miss my train. Bye!" and Chaja runs down the steps. In actual fact, she does not run, but rises gently in the air, just a few inches above ground level, and sails or floats down the stairs, then drifts, glides, and hovers just above the nettles and thistles and path, again not too high, almost but not quite touching the dandelions, almost brushing the tips of her gray suede shoes against the yellow and mauve pansies at the edge of the flower bed and the broken pieces of red roof tiles stuck aslant into the yellow sand along the edge. The gray veil flutters above the dandelions and nettles. The white heads of puffballs lightly caress her fine gray silk-stockinged ankles. A gray cloud above the path and the flower bed. A gray cloud, gray ashes, gray dust. Above this flower bed, this path, this abyss.

They translate me, thinks Icyk, replacing the cap on his fountain pen. His Parker has a gold nib and piston, and as our century reaches its end, it is fast becoming a museum piece. He then gets up from his desk and walks over to the window. They've translated me into seventeen languages, maybe even nineteen by now. It would follow that

I am not just anybody. And even if I exaggerate in thinking I am not a nobody, I can at least say I am a pretty competent professional writer.

So why is it that whenever I try to visualize my return visit and my conversation with Chaja, my imagination runs dry and all I can conjure up is Chaja rising, drifting, hovering above the yellow and mauve pansies? The time is either simultaneously 1937 and 1987, or else somewhere between 1937 and 1987. I have no difficulty in imagining her gray toque and veil and stockings and gloves, the quivering of her left or right eyelid, her black hair tumbling loose over her tiny ears. Restored to life by me or by my imagination, in some mysterious way she exists both in 1937 and in 1987, though at the same time she does not exist.

Yet what she says or could say or might have to say to me is unimaginable, and the conversation of octogenarian Icyk Mandelbaum and twenty-four-year-old Chaja Gelechter is tentative and faltering and then it breaks off, even though nothing of essence has as yet been said. Why? Does that mean that after all that has happened we have nothing, absolutely nothing, to say to each other? But if our conversation is to take place, if I am to imagine it, perhaps I should go to Otwock—I wonder what the Polish Otwock looks like now and what the Poles have done to the Jewish Otwock—and stand in the place where there was once a flower bed with an edge of broken roof tiles, a gate with a spring and creaking hinges, and a veranda with three wicker armchairs.

There is obviously no flower bed, gate, veranda, or armchairs there now. But the place still exists where they once used to be. And who knows, if I stood on that spot I might hear or at least imagine what Chaja could have to tell me. If the dead appear among us from time to time, which I doubt, for frankly why should they bother if they have no business with us, and of course they have no business with us, we're no longer of any use to them, for what use could we be? If the dead sometimes appear among us, albeit against their own better judgment, they are bound to appear in the places they loved and which they remember, where they enjoyed being when they were alive. Chaja was fond of Otwock, so if she felt a strong enough urge she ought by rights to appear in Otwock—by the gate, on the path or on the steps, in a wicker armchair.

But I shall not go to Otwock. Not because I don't want to open the gate that is no longer there, or stand on the steps that have been chopped up for firewood, but because I fear that after all we've been through we would have nothing to say to each other; we speak different languages and can no longer communicate. The language of the dead. They still use Yiddish or Polish, but it is as though they uttered or we heard only disjointed words that fail to constitute a logical sequence of intelligible sentences, unless, of course, they form the sentences of a secret language whose rules we are unable to decipher. The same words, but without knowing the syntax no one will grasp the sense. Perhaps it would be more apt to say that the words and the syntax of this secret language are the same but the words have a slightly different meaning that eludes us. Icyk leans his palm—the skin encasing his octogenarian bones is dry and wrinkled and covered with brown markings—on the metal window frame and looks down from the twenty-second floor into the deep pit of the unfathomable, the pit of Sheol. Chaja stands behind him and places her gray-gloved hand—the skin inside her glove is white, fine, taut, almost translucent—on his palm.

"Poor Icyk Mandelbaum," she says. "But just think how rich and famous you are."

But we do not know what "rich" and "famous" mean in the unintelligible language spoken by Chaja. We do not even know what the names Icyk and Mandelbaum mean in Chaja's language. Language as a gray cloud, or dust. The disintegrating language of the dead.

MORE about the ghetto in Otwock. I have located a number of sources giving the date of the final extermination of the Otwock ghetto. In fact, there are two dates, a discrepancy that I fear cannot be resolved. Franciszka Rubinlicht, who, according to the notes furnished by Józef Kermisz in his collection of documents, was a Warsaw theater scene painter, wrote in 1943 with reference to 1942: "On August 20, the Jews were driven out of Otwock and on the same day Anka was shot on the highway together with her family." According to sources describing events along the crosstown railroad line between Anin and Otwock in August 1942, victims begged to be executed on the highway—a boon that was but seldom granted.

The date given by Franciszka Rubinlicht is corroborated in accounts collected by Wiktor Kulerski. In an article entitled "The March" (*Krytyka*, No. 15/1983), he quotes an extract from the diary of Celek Perechodnik, which has been deposited in the archives of the Jewish Historical Institute. "On August 20, on Thursday, operations began in Falenica. For a change, the Germans started not at 7 a.m. but at 3 a.m., when it was still dark." The date is further borne out by the statements of witnesses taken down by Kulerski. Jadwiga M. from Miedzeszyn: "It happened on August 20, 1942. I shall not forget that day, because they dug a pit for children in my square." Kulerski's article in *Krytyka* is illustrated with several photographs of Falenica and the reproduction of a plaque which, according to the caption, was published "privately" in 1977 and commemorates the march of the Jews "from Rembertów to Falenica and the extermination of both ghettos on August 20." The plaque is inscribed: "August 20, 1942." The extermination in Falenica definitely took place on the same day as the extermination in Otwock. I am full of admiration for Kulerski's meticulous care. He has described the march from Rembertów to Falenica exactly the way one should, accurately and soberly, though I have some misgivings about the date he gives.

During the night of August 20–21, Warsaw was bombed by Russian planes, and one of the bombs fell on a building close to Umschlagplatz. The next day a rumor spread through the Warsaw ghetto that the Russian air raid was intended as a warning to the Germans, to make them understand that their criminal activity was being monitored and would be tolerated no longer. The rumor was justified to the extent that after the air raid on August 21 the Germans suspended activities, though admittedly not for long and certainly not because the Russians had deterred them. At the time, the Russians had no intention of cautioning or intimidating the Germans. If Stalin had any inkling of what was going on in the Warsaw ghetto, being the specialist in deportation and annihilation that he was, he would doubtless have observed the scene with a twisted sort of smile. But the great extermination was suspended: on August 21 there were no blockades and no freight cars waited on the tracks behind Umschlagplatz. The last day of the blockades before the lull seems to have been August 21.

That evening or the next morning the Vernichtungskommando set off for Otwock, Falenica, and Miedzeszyn. This version of events is corroborated by Adolf and Barbara Berman, who appear to have been fairly well informed. They wrote their story, entitled "The Extermination of the Ghetto in Warsaw," in October 1942, as soon as they had escaped to the Aryan side shortly after these events. According to the Bermans, the extermination in Otwock, hence also in Falenica, began "on Friday morning," after the night of August 20–21. The Bermans do not give the date. But Friday was August 21. One might conceivably suppose that the operation in Otwock and Falenica was started by some local SS or military police units and that the Vernichtungskommando joined forces with them a couple of days later. That does not, however, seem very likely. The extermination of the ghetto was carried out by professionals, and nonspecialist units were not permitted to take part in the action. Adolf Berman makes it clear that the entire staff of the Warsaw team came down to Otwock. He mentions Brandt, and Hoefle was almost certainly there too, maybe also an ethnic German named Brzezinski, who, as I have just read in Henryk Makower's *Recollections of the Warsaw Ghetto*, recently published by Ossolineum, "loaded the majority of the Warsaw Jews."

After arriving in Otwock, Brandt drove around the town ghetto and the so-called sanitary ghetto—so there were two ghettos in Otwock—in a small black Opel and gave orders for sentries to be posted. If Celek Perechodnik and the inhabitants of Falenica and Miedzeszyn quoted by Wiktor Kulerski are correct in stating that the action commenced at 3 a.m., before dawn, Brandt must have arrived in Otwock during the evening of the previous day—in other words, on August 20. It is clear from the Bermans' account that if the action on the blue-and-yellow railroad began on August 21, it lasted four days at the most. On August 25, blockades started up afresh in the Warsaw ghetto, which means that the Vernichtungskommando had returned to base. During the operations the patients of Zofiówka and the Brijus sanatorium were executed. The children in two Centos orphanages were also shot—the Bermans quote a figure of about 250 children. Apparently several of the older children managed to escape. In Śródborów eight Polish families who had sheltered Jews were shot.

Many Jews living in Otwock had moved there from Warsaw since it seemed a much safer place in the first half of 1942. One month before the extermination of the Otwock ghetto, on July 19 to be exact, two well-known Jewish Gestapo officers, Kohn and Heller, collaborators of the Thirteen and owners of the horse trolleys, dispatched their families to Otwock. According to Emanuel Ringelblum's *Notes from the Ghetto*, some of these Warsaw Jews managed to escape from Otwock by ambulance. I don't know if this includes the families of Kohn and Heller, who were both killed in Warsaw, their bodies being removed to the cemetery near Okopowa Street at Brandt's special request on a rubbish cart or carts. In connection with the Warsaw Jews who took refuge in Otwock, the Bermans and Ringelblum mention a journalist named Ajnhorn, one of the editors of the daily *Hajnt*. He was given the opportunity to escape from Otwock in the aforementioned ambulance. He refused and remained in his room, where he was shot, probably in the Brijus sanatorium. I don't know why, but I am curious to know what happened to the prewar owner of the Miramare cinema at 29 Warszawska Street. He was named Mojżesz Łopata.

Earlier on in writing about the extermination of the Otwock ghetto, I hazarded the guess that forty freight cars pulled in at one of the stations between Otwock and Pilawa: Pogorzel, Stara Wieś, or Celestynów. But Wiktor Kulerski's article would seem to indicate that this was not the case. A fragment of Celek Perechodnik's diary quoted by Kulerski reads as follows: "Several hundred people were dispatched on foot from Otwock under police escort and were then crammed into the freight cars at Falenica. Mothers departed by the Otwock transport, their children the next day with the Falenica contingent, their fathers the day after that on the Mińsk convoy." So loading took place in Falenica and Mińsk Mazowiecki. Likewise on the high platforms of Otwock. Most probably on August 21, 22, and 23.

As Kulerski writes, the ramp in Falenica was situated "to the south of the station and the crossing, between the tracks and the highway." The Jews of Falenica were herded into the square between the station and the synagogue, and several hours later they were shunted toward the siding. Here too there is a discrepancy between Kulerski and the Bermans, who state that "apparently" the Jews of Falenica refused to come out of their houses and even put up armed resistance to the Vernichtungskommando. As a result, all the local Jews were murdered on the spot by Brandt's henchmen. As far as the Jews of Falenica are concerned, the testimonies adduced by Kulerski are beyond question. The Bermans could thus have been ill informed as to the date.

"Just imagine him," I say to Hania. I am sitting on the headlines "Sunny High-Pressure Zone over Poland" and "Did Hitler Die in Argentina?" in today's issue of *Warsaw Life*. "He is sitting right here in the sand. He has four days of vacation. Or almost, because he has one small assignment. A weekend break for Karl Brandt. In the morning he will start murdering, which is very pleasant, and in the afternoon he will paddle in the Świder, which is also very pleasant. On this beach, beneath this willow brake. He unbuckles his belt, pulls off his uniform and his boots, then enters the water. Brzezinski, the hardworking military policeman, folds his boss's uniform in a neat square. A beautiful August day, warm sun, cool water. In those days there was no polluted stench emanating from the Świder. Hoefle also steps into the water and cries: *Karl, diese Juden hatten es hier gut.* Whatever could have been going on in the mind of that goggle-eyed brute named Brandt when he paddled here in the Świder?"

"Oh, for heaven's sake, stop," says Hania. "I honestly don't care."

"But what was going on inside his mind?" I say. "Brandt and Hoefle splash about in the water, roaring with laughter, then roll in the sand. How very sweet and pleasant to be alive. He sensed and apprehended the pleasantness of being alive. I mean, he was a man."

"No," says Hania.

"No what?" I ask. "What do you mean by no?"

"That I don't want to think about it," says Hania. "Not now."

"Then let's think about something more pleasant," I say. "About Hitler dying in Argentina." And I pull the issue of *Warsaw Life* from under me and shake it clean of gray sand.

"What Hitler?" Hania asks. "What are you talking about?"

"In the paper it says he died several months ago in Argentina," I say, "at the age of ninety-seven. Some Argentinian has documents to prove it and wants to sell them to the Jews for five hundred million dollars. He even knows where Hitler's grave is, and knows Eva Braun's address. Because she lives there too and has four children. Adopted ones."

"That's nonsense," says Hania. "The Jews would be mad to pay five hundred million dollars for something like that."

"I bet you they'll pay," I say. "Hitler's grave is worth even more than five hundred million. Its price for mankind is simply inestimable."

"Let's get going," says Hania. "I really don't care much for that either."

"As for Hitler being in Argentina," I say as Hania drives the red Renault toward the Miedzeszyn Rampart, "I bet you anything that Comrade Stalin is still alive too. Hiding in the taiga or tundra, a holy hermit aged one hundred and ten. He ambles around the taiga puffing on his pipe and gazes at the lights of a hard-labor camp twinkling in the distance. He is alive. They are all alive."

"In your head," says Hania. "And stop throwing yourself around, you'll cause a horrible accident. I don't want to end up in the hospital because of you."

A BRIEF guide to the Warsaw ghetto. Our tour is best begun at Żelazna Street, as it is the most "ghettoish," by which I mean it has the most buildings that once belonged to the ghetto and for some reason were not burned down when the Germans razed the Northern District. As you proceed up Żelazna Street in the direction of Nowolipie Street and Nowolipki Street, you have the Aryan district to your left and the ghetto to your right. Forty-five years ago the Poles walked on the western side of Żelazna Street, the Jews on the eastern side. The junction of Żelazna Street and Krochmalna Street is particularly noteworthy. Krochmalna Street was once a very long street, starting at Iron Gate Square and ending at Karolkowa Street. Today it is substantially shorter, beginning at Ciepła Street and ending at Żelazna Street.

Now you should turn right, preferably into Grzybowska Street, then walk down Krochmalna Street from Waliców Street as far as Żelazna Street. The view ahead is uninteresting: a new, postwar building stands on the opposite, Aryan side of Żelazna Street. There are old houses, though, one on the left-hand corner, two on the right, all badly damaged. The five-story corner house on the left has retained its balconies with their beautiful balustrades, but for the safety of pedestrians they will soon have to be demolished before they collapse of their own accord. The plaster is falling off in places; otherwise the house is in reasonable condition. But the house on the right has been stripped of its plaster for many years, and rusty iron girders now protrude from the dirty-red brickwork where the balconies used to be. A curved metal contraption secured to the front of the house looks like the upper part of a crozier. A street-lamp once hung from it.

It seems that few people stroll along this stretch of

Krochmalna Street. At about noon I was alone among the old houses. The atmosphere here is hard to describe, probably because one is simultaneously walking through prewar Warsaw, the ghetto, and the Warsaw of today. In the house on the right-hand corner, a carpenter's shop displays bottles of lacquer, tins of glue, baseboards, strips of timber, and shelving in its window. Forty-five years ago someone could have stood looking at this window. He may now be standing by my side and we both glance at each other, the difference being that only he can see me. We earth dwellers are thick-witted and sluggardly, and when we are given a rare chance to sense the dual or treble density of time, to capture the sense of being in several temporal strata at once, we are too slow and dense to seek deeper insight.

Double or treble time. The tourist on Krochmalna Street heading for Żelazna Street can choose to walk down Krochmalna Street in 1987 and imagine he is walking there in 1942. Alternatively, he walks down Krochmalna Street in 1942 and imagines how it will look in 1987. As a last option, he walks down Krochmalna Street in 1939 and has a premonition of how History will deal with these houses and with him. A several-minute walk is therefore recommended along this stretch. It is useful to exist in three different epochs at once, as it helps one visualize the extraordinary scenarios of History. In Żpelazna Street our stroller should peer into the doorway of the dirty-brick corner house with the rusted balcony girders. Inlaid with blue, navy, and dark yellow tiles, just about half of which are now broken, this gate must once have afforded a good view of the wall dividing the Aryan district from the ghetto.

Proceeding up Żelazna Street you come to Chłodna Street: the crossroads marks the end of the little ghetto and the commencement of the big ghetto. Chłodna Street was guarded by a sentinel and barriers that were later replaced by a bridge linking the two parts of the ghetto. I have seen several photos of the bridge, but the new blocks on either side of Chłodna Street make it difficult to locate it. According to my calculations, access to the bridge in the little ghetto, on the south side of Chłodna Street, was, roughly speaking, from the present-day site of the one-story pavilion and "Oral Surgery No. 12: Prosthetics, X Rays, Extraction under Anesthetic," and that sign hangs in the very place where the steps once led up to the bridge.

The steps up to the bridge in the big ghetto—on the north side of Chłodna Street—were on the site of the entrance to the candy store, the one in the large gray building at the corner of Chłodna Street and Żelazna Street. Before taking the high road or the low road from the little ghetto to the big ghetto, it is worth spending a few more minutes in the little ghetto. Turn right along Chłodna Street. Halfway down Chłodna Street or, if you prefer, between Chłodna Street and Elektoralna Street, obviously on the Aryan side, you will find the church of St. Charles Borromeo. From the church steps there is a good view of the bridge and the trolleys passing underneath. Numbers 5, 11, and 21 travel westward along Chłodna Street. The tracks end just before the corner of Żelazna Street, no doubt where the bridge used to be. If you keep to the southern sidewalk of Chłodna Street, note the peculiar shape of the curb at the level of the small square outside number 11, proof that there once used to be a large porte cochère here. The old trolley lines run alongside. There is obviously no house and no gate there now. All that survives is that historic curb, the only evidence that this was once a way in and a way out.

Beyond Chłodna Street the big ghetto begins. Turn now into Ogrodowa Street and go out to the rear of the Law Courts, or else continue up Żelazna Street, passing the sentinel posted at the beginning of Leszno Street. The corridors of the Law Courts were the meeting ground of Jews and Poles. Jews entered the building from Leszno Street; Poles, as far as I can make out, from Ogrodowa Street. So it is an important landmark and undoubtedly well worth a visit. At the junction of Żelazna Street and Nowolipie Street there is the old building—90 Żelazna—of the present maternity hospital. The building has been renovated. I don't know if there was a maternity hospital there during the war. There must surely have been one maternity hospital in the ghetto. Numerous sources mention that Jews were getting pregnant at the time and that children were born in the Warsaw ghetto. This is not easy to understand and it calls for a moment's thought. Did those Jewish women believe that their offspring would live, or that the Jewish God could or would save them?

In a conversation with Benjamin Fondane in July 1938, Lev Shestov, arguably the only philosopher of this accursed century who deserves to be read, and undoubtedly one of the few who have something relevant to say about our epoch, quoted the following verse from the Prophecy of Jeremiah: "Cursed be the day on which I was born!" (20:14). For Shestov these words were proof that the prophet Jeremiah, even as he prayed for God's help, was of the opinion that God does not help men. Shestov appears to have shared this view: God may be asked to help, indeed He must be asked, but help is not forthcoming. Fondane then took down the following words: "St. Augustine refused to admit that our God does not help us. Nietzsche knew it. Not content with ascertaining the cruelty of nature, he began to glorify it. What on earth for? Jeremiah knew full well that God does not help us, and the Jews knew it too."

To my mind, this is the weakest point in Shestov's argument. Shestov's God is the God of the Old Testament, a God not yet limited in His actions by the crazy notions of philosophers such as Plato, Spinoza, and Hegel. Accordingly, He did not submit to necessity or to what our reason considers to be necessary. He is a God more powerful than sunrises, sunsets, and the ocean's tides, more mighty than two plus two equaling four. Shestov kept harking back to Pascal's evocation of the God of Abraham, Isaac, and Jacob, who is not the God of the philosophers. And, of course, he endorsed this opinion: his God was not the God of the philosophers either. But can it be that the God of Abraham, Isaac, and Jacob is a God who does not help men?

Shestov interprets the Old Testament in a manner I find incomprehensible. The God of the Old Testament was and still is an omnipotent God. Nothing can limit Him, because

He is above all things and is mightier than all things. If He so wishes, the sun will rise tomorrow in the evening and set in the morning, and whenever He wants, two plus two will equal five. But we cannot foresee, only He can foresee, if this will happen tomorrow or ever. Can we claim that such a God does not help men? "Jeremiah also knew that God does not help us." But how could Jeremiah know, if his God was above all things and acted according to His own will? The God who does what He wants may or may not help men, as the case may be. It depends only on Him and on His will, which is unknown to us and unknowable.

Incidentally, the notion of a God who has withdrawn and handed History over to men, the notion of History as the result of human activity and of man endowed with free will doing with History whatsoever he chooses, is incompatible with Revelation. The God of the Old Testament keeps intervening in History. He is constantly present and constantly participating. This is not to say that He is acting under constraint. He reveals Himself when He wills, when it pleases Him, and there is nothing more to be said on the subject. Except that it has nothing to do with our prayers. For God, who can do all things, cannot allow our prayers to constrict Him. Though He may if He so wishes. He reveals Himself when He wants, invited or uninvited. The Scripture, that is to say Revelation, provides ample evidence. A few examples will suffice.

Who in Genesis 9:5 concluded the covenant with Noah and closed the door of the Ark? Who in Genesis 11:6–7 confounded the tongues of those who were building the

Tower of Babel? Who in Exodus 12:12–13 ordered that the doors of the Jewish houses be marked with blood: "I shall pass through the land of Egypt this night, and will smite all the firstborn in the land of Egypt, both man and beast; and against all the gods of Egypt I will execute judgment: I am the Lord. . . . And when I see the blood, I will pass over you, and the plague shall not be upon you to destroy you, when I smite the land of Egypt." In his conversation with Fondane in July 1938, Shestov also invoked the Books of Maccabees as proof that God does not help. "The Jews knew it perfectly: the stories of the Maccabees, etc." But the Second Book of Maccabees (11:10–11) says something else: "They advanced fully armed, having their ally from Heaven, because the Lord had taken pity on them. They assailed their enemies like lions and slayed eleven thousand, also sixteen hundred horsemen, and they forced all the others to flee." There are other passages in this Book where Yahweh intervenes in History to help the Jewish people (viz., 3:24–29; 9:4–5; 10:29–31).

In 1933, in his essay on Martin Buber, "Martin Buber, Jewish Mystic of the German Language," Shestov wrote that God does not change: "One must adhere closely to Buber's principle: theophanies may be subject to change, but that does not mean that God changes." I do not think I am misrepresenting Shestov's thought if I infer from this sentence that the God of Abraham, Isaac, and Jacob who closes the door of the Ark is the same God who appears above the Jewish horsemen in the Second Book of Maccabees. The God who appears as the ally of the Jewish horsemen is the same God who appears above the Warsaw ghetto if we want to see Him there.

When we deprive God of the right to intervene in History, we are doubtless more concerned with His interests than with our own. We accept that our History proceeds outside Him and that it is our doing only, because we do not want God to be responsible for all the atrocities we have witnessed. But in depriving God of the right to intervene, we strip Him of His omnipotence: He can no longer act as He wishes, so He ceases to be almighty. A God who has pulled out, whom we have pulled out from History, ceases to be God.

I may be going too far, as Shestov did not say that God does not appear; he merely said that God does not help. But if He does not help He cannot be the God of Abraham, Isaac, and Jacob. And if He is not the God of Abraham, Isaac, and Jacob, then He does not exist. By eliminating God from History we reiterate Nietzsche's act of a hundred years ago: we kill Him. Nietzsche wrote: "He choked one day from a surfeit of mercy." To phrase it slightly differently, we have stifled Him by our excessive pity for Him. But there is no reason why we should feel sorry for our God. Pity for the Almighty is an incongruous feeling. And there is no reason why we should kill Him. God is alive, the proof of which is or should be our faith, which states that God does with us what He pleases.

Standing as we are at the junction of Żelazna Street, Nowolipie Street, Żytnia Street, and Wolność Street, a stone's throw from the maternity hospital, we should now turn right and go along Nowolipie Street, Smocza Street, and Nowolipki Street until we come to St. Augustine's Church. This church is a must for the tourist for two good reasons. In the war years it stood in the very heart of the ghetto, and in the middle or late fifties—I've forgotten the year—a miracle took place, and the Virgin Mary appeared above its steeple to the people of Warsaw. An acquaintance told me he used to live in this neighborhood and was only a child at the time: "I saw her. I was standing on the embankment there, and I saw a transparent figure above the steeple. They daubed it all over with pitch, but that didn't help."

Back at the junction of Żelazna Street, Nowolipie Street, and Żytnia Street we can turn left and go along Wolność Street, known during the war as Uhrmacherstrasse, in the direction of the cemetery, or cross over Nowolipie Street and walk as far as Nowolipki Street, which is where Żelazna Street ends. One of the ghetto gates was on Nowolipie Street close to Żelazna Street. If the maps are to be believed, there were twenty-one gates, a number that for some reason strikes me as symbolic. The visitor to the ghetto should not overlook the final stretch of Żelazna Street. First, though, he should turn left. Walking along Wolność Street—house number 2A, still standing, was annexed to the ghetto in July 1942—one comes to the small square outside the Jan Śniadecki High School. The ghetto boundary used to run through this square or in the immediate vicinity. Beyond it we have Kacza Street, Okopowa Street, and the cemetery.

In the middle of the square stands an advertising pillar,

a cylinder painted green surmounted by a sort of metallic cornice bristling with spikes. Before and during the war advertisements were affixed to cylindrical posts, but they could also house electric substations or newspaper kiosks. The pillar in the square near Wolność Street, which is really more like a small meadow, must have been used as a kiosk, to judge by the metal flaps on which the newsdealer no doubt displayed his newspapers. Did it stand in the ghetto, at the ghetto boundary, on the Aryan side? I do not know. If it was at the boundary, it may well have been used as a hiding place: smugglers, seven- or eight-year-old kids, could have hidden in it; likewise their German pursuers. If it was on the Aryan side, the odds are it accommodated a kiosk where the inhabitants of Żytnia Street and Kacza Street came to buy cigarettes and newspapers. Leaning against the counter, they would chat with the kiosk owner and discuss recent events on the other side. The cylinder is a sturdy prewar construction, and although the metal has rusted in places, it will no doubt stand there for quite some time to come.

It is worth viewing the advertising pillar from somewhere in the middle of the square. Without excessive spiritual exertions the stroller may well be rewarded by the same emotion he already experienced at the corner of Żelazna Street and Krochmalna Street. He crosses the square, and within spitting distance of the metal cylinder of 1987, he suddenly steps back into 1942. Not that the present dissolves or evaporates: the time is still 1987. The process could be termed a change in the consistency of time, or a change of time's constituents. The present becomes rarefied and absorbs components of the past. Or the reverse: some elements of the present pervade and permeate the past. The red-and-yellow Fiat 125s and the Polonez cars are still parked at the rear of 29A Nowolipki Street. But who knows, any minute now a patrol of three military policemen armed with metal shields will emerge from among the Fiats and Polonezes. As they race off in pursuit of an escapee, their metal shields clank against their uniform buttons—a sound familiar to every inhabitant of Warsaw over fifty years of age.

From the square outside the high school we return via the backyards or else through Nowolipki Street to Żelazna Street. The last house in Żelazna Street is number 103. Step through the entrance of prewar terra-cotta into the corridor of the stairwell, where there is a door leading out into a courtyard. It is best not to enter the apartments or ask the residents if they know what took place between their sofa and their gas range. Adjacent to the house on the Nowolipki side is a vegetable stand with radishes, small onion bulbs, chicory, and lettuce visible through the glass.

Between the ground-floor windows of 103 Żelazna Street a plaque carries the words: "In this house in 1943 in the dungeons of the Gestapo, thousands of Jews from the Warsaw ghetto were tortured to death." There are three mistakes in this caption. There were no Gestapo dungeons at 103 Żelazna Street, for the Gestapo was elsewhere. Thousands of Jews were not murdered here, because not even the most proficient murderers could have pulled that one off. And what occurred here "in 1943" had already reached its peak in July and August 1942. Number 103

Żelazna Street is where the SS men from the unit known as Vernichtungskommando had their offices. It was the headquarters of the SS.

A few words about the often glaring mistakes made by historians specializing in the Warsaw ghetto. In one book, whose author I shall forbear to mention, I read that the house at 103 Żelazna Street was situated at the corner of Żelazna Street and Leszno Street. Karl Brandt frequently appears in footnotes as an SS Sturmführer, SS Untersturmführer, and SS Obersturmführer. On the plan of the Warsaw ghetto printed in the Polish edition of Adam Czerniakow's diary, a small square on the corner of Żelazna Street and Leszno Street is meant to designate the Law Courts, while on the opposite corner a second square indicates the "Hospital of the Orthodox Jews on Czyste Street."

The inhabitants of Warsaw do not need to be told where the Law Courts are. In fact, the Arbeitsamt and quarantine buildings were located at the corner of Żelazna Street and Leszno Street, on the west side. On the east side, where the plan locates the hospital, there is a building that had been a school before the war. During the war, in the autumn of 1941, an annex of the Berson and Bauman Children's Hospital was to be found here, the one which up until the extermination of the little ghetto was situated between Sienna Street and Śliska Street. It was only in August 1942, and only for a brief period, that a few departments of the old hospital on Czyste Street—internal medicine, I think—were transferred from Stawki Street to the building on the corner of Żelazna Street and Leszno

Street. The building of the Arbeitsamt was on the Aryan side. To reach it from the ghetto one had to cross the bridge over Żelazna Street. In writing this book I may well have committed some embarrassing blunders. But I am not a specialist: I adduce only what I have read or seen with my own eyes. It is important that certain facts should be established once and for all before it is too late. Time is of the essence.

It seems, though again I am not sure, that the house at 103 Żelazna Street also accommodated the SS mess hall with a Jewish band and Jewish waiters. There are two more houses on this stretch of Żelazna Street, numbers 99 and 101. So the mess hall could have been situated in either of these, or even somewhere quite different. Number 103 is one of the most significant houses in our ghetto. During consultations or briefings held here every morning in the summer of 1942, Hoefle or perhaps Globocnik himself indicated on a German map of Warsaw the areas where blockades were to be set up for that day. His finger hovers above the streets and chances on a house in the block between Eisenstrasse and Gerichtstrasse: *Die fahren heute.*

I imagine that they operated according to a logical plan, sealing off and deporting street by street, block by block, house by house. They were, after all, Germans, and first-rate professionals. Work must be carried out with accuracy and rigor—that was important to them. But if they operated according to a system, the neighbors of an area under blockade would catch on pretty quickly that their turn was next and would have time to hide or escape. From the German point of view an element of surprise was essential.

The system or sequence of annihilation should not be obvious to the victims. A haphazard system was thus called for, if that is not a contradiction in terms. The finger hovering above the plan chances on a house or a backyard. That's the house to strike, those are the people to get today. *Die fahre heute.* Pure chance? Maybe. There must have been a master plan or underlying system, intelligible only to the occupants of the house at 103 Żelazna Street. It would not have made sense to the inmates of the yard over which the finger was poised. At the level of the backyard it must all have been fever, chaos, and gibberish. But nonetheless it was a system: unintelligible, inscrutable, undecipherable. Unknown and unknowable.

Anyone who lives some distance away and dislikes long walks, or else feels disinclined to tramp the full length of Żelazna Street, can catch a bus in the city center and ride all the way to the Befehlsstelle SS. Get off at the bus terminus in Nowolipki Street. After inspecting the house at 103 Żelazna Street, go along Nowolipki Street, then turn left down Smocza Street in a northerly direction. We pass Dzielna Street, Pawia Street, Gęsia Street, which in those days probably followed a slightly different course and were definitely much narrower.

Nowadays there are broad squares, almost like small parks, between Dzielna Street and Pawia Street and also on Gęsia Street. We reach Miła Street. Compared with Żelazna Street, this part of the Northern District contains far less ghetto or even, to be quite honest, no ghetto at all. I am not saying the neighborhood is not worth visiting. In walking down Smocza Street and Miła Street one cannot, however, reconstruct the scenery and events of forty-five years ago, or even imagine them. We need data to build images, but here no data are supplied, and the imagination flounders. What books and photographs tell us about this neighborhood fails to connect with the present panorama. Houses, passages between houses, pavements, squares, everything is new and divorced from what was once here. If total annihilation ever took place, it was here. Every manifestation, concept, and embryonic image of life was exterminated here in 1943. Perhaps this is the true aim of totalitarianism. The crossing of Esperanto Street and Miła Street is arguably the one place on earth where totalitarianism has ultimately triumphed: it has annihilated the past. Nothing remains. History can start again from scratch, and if History fails again, annihilation will recur at some future date.

Turning from Smocza Street into Miła Street in the direction of Marchlewski Street, we should remember that the numbering on Miła Street has been changed. Number 18, the old number, is now at the beginning of Miła Street near the little square at the junction of Zamenhof Street and Stanisław Dubois Street. We pass the garages on Miła Street, the sand pit in the square by Karmelicka Street and the house at 2 Miła Street, where the Urban Building Works have their offices. Number 2 on Miła Street strikes me as being the only historical monument in this neighborhood. It has been restored to an acceptable standard, yet something about the shape of the windows hints at a more ancient provenance, so it must have been built before the war. We are close to the square, still on the northern side of Miła Street, near the low mound covering the bunker where Mordechaj Anielewicz committed suicide. "He was a communist," someone who knew Anielewicz once told me. "He belonged to Haszomer Hacair, but in fact he was a communist. A crazy guy. They were all waiting for the Reds to come." But now it is irrelevant whether Anielewicz belonged to Haszomer Hacair or to Dror, Poale Syjonu of the Left, the Polish Workers' Party, the Bund, Mizrachia, or Auguda. Now Anielewicz and his girlfriend, whose name was Luba, belong to God.

At the end of his essay on Kierkegaard (1935), Lev Shestov says that God is not only above reason but also above ethics. "He takes our sins upon Himself and confounds the monstrosities of life." Perhaps this ought to be translated as the horrors of life. Was it Nietzsche who initiated the trend of placing things above ethics? I have no proper philosophical training, so I cannot answer that question. God is above ethics—that is to say, He is above good and evil. He is not compelled unto anything, because He cannot be bound by our humans ethics. Shestov naturally means the God of Abraham, Isaac, and Jacob, not the God of the philosophers.

Yet he does not seem altogether sure if we can set God above ethics. He may have changed his mind on this point, I do not know. In his last text, the essay on Husserl he wrote in 1938, he says with reference to the Prophets of the Old Testament and the Apostles: "They say that God cares for every man and that God will ultimately triumph over an unjust and merciless reality, God, who 'counts the hairs on a man's head,' God who is love and who promises that each tear will be wiped away." Shestov—there can be no doubt about it—was of the same opinion. Can God who is love and wipes away our tears, can God who judges an unjust and merciless world, justly and mercifully be a God above ethics, unconstrained by our wretched earthly concept of good and evil?

What did the Old Testament really say? It repeats time and again that God is good, merciful, and just. The Book of Deuteronomy (7:12–13) states that God obliges man to be good and merciful, but simultaneously requires the same of Himself: "If ye hearken to these judgments, and keep, and do them, that the Lord thy God shall keep unto thee the covenant and the mercy which He sware unto thy fathers; and He will love thee, and bless thee, and multiply thee." The covenant of mercy, often mentioned in the Scripture, is eternal. The First Book of Chronicles (16:41): "because His mercy endureth forever."

From the Prophecy of Jeremiah (33:11): "for the Lord is good; for his mercy endureth forever." But from Jeremiah (16:5) it would appear that the eternal covenant is not eternal, for mercy may be withdrawn: "for I have taken away my peace from this people, saith the Lord, even loving kindness and mercies." In Jeremiah the expression "saith the Lord" refers to words uttered by the Lord Himself through the mouth of the prophet. It is possible for mercy and kindness to be taken away because there is nothing that God cannot do. This first crops up in the Book of Genesis (18:14): "Is anything too hard for the Lord?" and is reiterated in Jeremiah (32:27): "Behold, I am the Lord, the God of all flesh: is there anything too hard for me?"

Revelation tells us simply this: God can do and does everything He wants—viz., Jeremiah (27:5): "I have made the earth, the man and the beast that are upon the ground, by my great power and by my outstretched arm, and have given it unto whom it seemed meet unto me." For that reason, God, by His great power, is simultaneously above ethics—in other words, above good and evil—and not above ethics. When He wants, He takes on obligations. When He wants, He breaks his allegiances. When He wants, He sees every hair upon our heads. When He wants, He sees not a single hair. All that counts is His will, His act of willing. But with our own notions of good and evil and our concept of an eternal covenant, all this is beyond us.

The inherent obscurity to be found in Shestov's thought—or is it his vacillation?—can probably be explained as follows: Shestov was supposedly an assiduous reader of the Old Testament. If he changed his mind about God's ethical stance or the relation of God to ethics, it was probably because his favorite prophet, Jeremiah, was not sure of God's own attitude toward the words on the tablets given to Moses. This is not a reason to think—indeed, such an interpretation is to my mind inadmissible—that by placing God above ethics Shestov distances Him from man and frees Him of responsibility for creation, for all the monstrosities and horrors of our life on earth. Or that divorcing God from our ethics was simply one of the many strategies to which a cognitive mind resorts in submitting to necessity, alias pragmatic reality.

It is worth dwelling on yet another obscurity in Shestov's system, or rather his thought, for clearly he created no system. Philosophical systems were something he despised. In 1934, Shestov met Buber in Paris. The conversation, transcribed by Benjamin Fondane, touched on the situation in Europe. They discussed communism, fascism, Hitler. Buber said that humanity in its despair was beginning to commit acts of incredible stupidity and probably intended to kill the biblical serpent. To which Shestov replied that the serpent ought by rights to be killed. "I have been struggling with the serpent day and night for many years. What is Hitler compared with the serpent!"

I cannot comment here, as I find Shestov's thought, or Fondane's account of Shestov's thought, quite incomprehensible. The biblical serpent is a symbol of cognitive reason, knowledge, necessity, of everything that separates us from God, and everything Shestov abhorred. So I understand that he desired the death of the serpent. But Hitler is what bothers me. Did Shestov think that totalitarianism is one of the deeds of the biblical serpent, and that the serpent which gave us knowledge, the fruit of the tree of knowledge and freedom, is therefore responsible? I do not know. "What is Hitler compared with the serpent!"

This was in 1934, and Shestov could not know what the immediate future held in store. Today the prophetic nature of his remark is only too apparent, and it informs our future, not that of the participants in the Paris encounter of 1934. Basically it says: Hitler is nothing as yet, but you'll soon see what the biblical serpent, or rather the diabolical reason bestowed on you by the serpent, is capable of, you will see what it can do. A discomfiting omen. You can argue that it was only an off-the-cuff remark: Lev Isaakovitch had to say something to Buber and that is what came to mind, and it is quite without significance. God. Great is Thy might. Spare us.

Steps lead up to the top of the mound erected above Mordechaj Anielewicz's bunker. There is a commemorative stone with inscriptions in Polish and in Hebrew, or perhaps Yiddish, I don't know. The letters are Hebrew, so I cannot decipher them. But every visitor will ask where Anielewicz's bunker is. When we stand on top of the hill, are we just above it? Or was it somewhere in the vicinity, by the wider modern roadway of Miła Street, or perhaps where the square is now? It must have been much lower than the present level of the square, roadway, and pavement. What about the mound? I wonder if anyone remembers what is underneath the stone and the mound; the men who built it can't all have died. Was it built of rubble and then covered over with a layer of soil? Or was it ready-made, so to speak, the ruined house above the bunker being simply buried in a layer of earth?

I also do not know—but then I don't think I want to know, so the question is a rhetorical one—if Anielewicz and those who died with him are all lying there beneath the mound. I have not found their graves in the cemetery by Okopowa Street, so their bodies were presumably not exhumed. The stone on the top of the hillock is weather-beaten, and the Polish and Hebrew lettering will soon be illegible. Anyone wishing to visit this site would do well to choose the time I came, between noon and one o'clock on a weekday. As at the junction of Żelazna Street and Krochmalna Street, there are few pedestrians there at this hour. The surrounding streets are virtually empty. With a bit of luck there will not be a single soul in the small square where Miła Street, Zamenhof Street, and Dubois Street all meet—at least that's how it was the day I went there.

Standing upon the eminence the tourist will have the impression of being in a town whose inhabitants left their chattels behind and went off for an unknown destination without closing the doors: during the blockades all apartment doors had to be left open. This impression will last no more than a couple of seconds, for soon a pedestrian is bound to appear on Zamenhof Street or Dubois Street. But it is a valuable experience. Brief though it be, it is spiritually enriching and instructive. The bunker buried under the mound, surrounded by the deserted streets of the Northern District. On top of the hillock—*cwiszn lebn un tojt*—the real meaning of the terms "evacuation," "deportation," "extermination," will be revealed. I do not think their meaning can be conveyed in words.

After descending from the mound we turn from Miła Street to the right and via Zamenhof Street and Anielewicz Street we come to Świętojerska Street. We are now walking in the direction of Bonifraterska Street and Koźla Street. To the right we have Krasiński Garden, to the left a wall abutting on the territory of the brush makers. It was, I think, somewhere in this vicinity, at the level of that embassy, that the Germans who were about to enter the workshop precincts in April 1943 were blown up by a mine. I wonder what being blown up by a mine actually looks like. Hunks of flesh, scraps of uniforms spiral up in the air, somersaulting and dripping with blood? At what altitude? If one has never seen anything like it, it is difficult to imagine. Even though I was born before the war, I find it impossible to visualize the speed of the ascent and somersaulting, the pious levitation of hunks of flesh, scraps of body and blood.

"IF you don't mind," says Icyk, hunkering down by the deck chair where Jakub Wurzel dozes beneath the black-and-yellow sunflower shields, "I could read it to you now."

"Read what?" asks Jakub Wurzel. He seems unable to figure out why someone whom he fails to recognize should offer to read to him when he is in the middle of a deliciously drowsy nightmare and has no wish to be roused from it until it ends in accordance with its own nightmarish logic. "Oh, it's you. What do you want to read?"

"The column I've just written," says Icyk. "We were discussing it at breakfast. I've called it 'A Reply to Mr. Słonimski.' "

"I doubt if I can be of much use to you," says Jakub

Wurzel. "I admit, I observe literary polemics from a distance, because it's so funny to see writers jumping at each other's throats. But the opinion of a businessman, a second-rate speculator at that—I mean, my trade in starch and yeast is hardly what you would call big-time business—is neither here nor there. However, do go ahead."

" 'A Reply to Mr. Słonimski,' " Icyk repeats. He perches on the edge of the pea patch, where the tall beanpoles tower above him, and opens his blue ruled notebook, the cover of which carries the appeal "Give a grosz to build state schools." This is how I begin: Mr. Słonimski may not love the Jewish God, and that is his right. Mr. Słonimski may consider the Jews—or as he often calls them, the Yids—to be Talmudic twisters. That is also his right. Mr. Słonimski may refer to the Old Testament commentaries as trash that costs a pretty penny in Świętokrzyska Street. Here too, albeit with sadness, we recognize his right to do so. It might be preferable for Mr. Słonimski not to refer to the exodus of the Jews from Egypt as a swindle, for what is the point of offending the tribe to which one belongs or once belonged? It might also be preferable for Mr. Słonimski to dip every now and again into the Old Testament; then he would know there were not seven, but ten plagues of Egypt, a fact that any Jewish child could tell him.

"Yet we Jews must recognize Mr. Słonimski's right to that too. Mr. Słonimski is free not to read the Old Testament. He is free to think of the Old Testament as a 'picturesquely gloomy work,' and free to offend the tribe to which his wise and learned grandfather Chaim Zelig Słonimski belonged. It might, however, be advisable for Mr. Słonimski to make up his mind. If he thinks the Jews are Talmudic twisters, why does he defend them against the attacks of the hooligans from *ABC Magazine* and of Mrs. Wielopolska, a pure-blooded Aryan who relishes the pure Aryan atmosphere of Nazi films.

"I understand that Mr. Słonimski wishes to defend the lofty ideals of humanity and mankind. May I therefore point out that mankind and humanity are abstract concepts, whereas nations such as Poles, Jews, and Germans exist in a tangible way. The murky intentions of the two colossi threatening Poland from east and west give me reason to believe that we should relinquish our lofty ideals and our abstract vision of mankind, at a time when living nations and their vital space, to use Hitler's expression, are under threat."

"I'll tell you something," says Jakub Wurzel. And he half shuts his eyes as though to sink back into the sweet drowsy nightmare that I disrupted with my blue notebook and the slogan "Give a grosz to build state schools." "And do take the advice of an old man, a small-time speculator who knows a thing or two about life."

"But that's not all," says Icyk. "There's more to come."

"You can read me Part Two some other time," says Jakub Wurzel. "Now for my advice. You're a young writer with hardly any following. One day you'll definitely be a great writer, but I'm talking about now. Mr. Słonimski is an established writer who enjoys considerable authority among the Jewish educated classes as well. So what's the point? If you go ahead and publish, he'll make minced cutlets of you, or beefsteak in the English manner, oozy with blood. Your readers will enjoy it all enormously. Also, if you don't mind my saying so, you've got the wrong end of the stick. The ideals which you so scathingly refer to as lofty must be defended under all circumstances."

"I'm not so much concerned with Mr. Słonimski's ideals," says Icyk. "After all, I respect him for his courage. What bothers me is his apparent inability to decide whether he is with the Jews or against them. That's my next point, the age-old problem of assimilated Jews: they don't know who they are or who they want to be. Being assimilated, they are Poles. But they are still Jews. They're obviously driven into this dichotomy by the local anti-Semites who keep reminding them that even though they are assimilated they are still condemned to continue being Jews. But assimilated Jews seem to accept these anti-Semitic assumptions. As though they agreed to this enforced duality."

"I see no harm in being dual," says Jakub Wurzel, "in feeling both Polish and Jewish at once. Someone who is dual is bound to be richer than someone who is not. It creates a far more complex spiritual life. A valuable asset, don't you think? Though, of course, only for someone who can exploit this duality and does not hide it under a bushel."

"I don't agree at all," says Icyk. "Such a dichotomy is a disaster for a writer. Someone who is both Jew and Pole is neither a Jew nor a Pole. It's a question of roots. One cannot take root in two places. A Jewish writer ought to be anchored in the Jewish language, Jewish customs, the Jewish religion. Otherwise he is not a Jewish writer, so you can tell him to stop being obstreperous. But I'm not sure that I'm making myself clear. What I'm trying to say is that someone who is not a Jewish writer, because he is not rooted in Jewishness, shouldn't try to convince me that he is one. So tell him to stop pestering people with his Jewish problems, because they are not Jewish problems. But you may be right when you say that I am too young to air such bold views in public. Fifty years from now, when I get the Nobel Prize, I shall say it in an interview. And Jewish journalists will kiss my feet."

"The Nobel won't help," says Jakub Wurzel. "If you say that fifty years from now, someone else will make English roast beef of you. Do you think that in fifty years the problem of assimilation and dual nationality will have ceased to exist?"

"Search me," says Icyk. "Fifty years from now nothing will look quite the same. Meanwhile there is probably not an educated Jew in this country who doesn't feel the dichotomy at least some of the time. Even Mr. Jakub Zineman, though he worships Jabotinsky and sees himself as a loyal citizen of the *Judenstaat*, writes more often in Polish than in Yiddish. May I also point out that the two of us are conversing in Polish?"

"Really?" says Jakub Wurzel. "I hadn't noticed. I was dreaming of Miss Chaja only a moment ago, and I am quite sure I spoke to her in Yiddish in my dream. But I didn't even notice. How odd. I switch from one language to the other quite unconsciously."

"Are you going to tell me your dream?" asks Icyk, anticipating a slightly doctored version of how and where Jakub Wurzel meets Chaja Gelechter in his dreams, and what they talk about in Yiddish on these occasions.

"Fejga appears to be standing on the veranda," says Jakub Wurzel, and closing his eyes, he stretches out in his deck chair. "She'll soon be ringing for lunch, so you'd better go. I'll carry on snoozing for a little while. And do listen to the advice of an old speculator. Your article's not fit for publication."

"I'll think about it," says Icyk. Sticking his blue notebook inside his white shirt, he saunters off in the direction of the veranda, where Fejga stands waving a brass bell with a wooden handle. He is halfway between the sunflowers and the veranda, near the jasmine bush and the molehill that was not there yesterday, when he hears Jakub Wurzel calling: "But don't take it to heart. You'll publish it in fifty years' time."

Fifty years, Icyk broods, trampling on the molehill and thereby saving the foolish underground mole from ineluctable doom. On Mrs. Sara Fliegeltaub's orders, lame Szlojmele pours a foul, stinking black fluid into any molehill left untrampled by Icyk, resulting in the ignominious death of the mole that lives down below. Fifty years from now my present thoughts will be quite incomprehensible, and no one reading my column will have a clue what it was all about. Who was Mrs. Wielopolska? What was *ABC*

Magazine? No one will remember what Mr. Słonimski wrote about the plagues of Egypt. We can't be sure that there will even be Jewish writers in the world fifty years from now, or that the problem of roots will still exist, or that there will be Jewish journalists to kiss my feet. Chaim Bialik said at the Philharmonic Society that a language cannot exist without its own territory and that the days of Yiddish are numbered. Who knows, he may be right. If so, in fifty or a hundred years there will be no one to speak and read my language, apart from a few humdrum scholars at the Institute of Judaic Sciences on Tłomackie Street.

So why then do I cling to it, why do I write in it? Because I have nothing else to cling to. My language is my last anchorage, a scrap of rope to save me from drowning. Or a rope up which I climb between heaven and earth. Not that I expect to reach heaven, but then that is not the purpose of the exercise. I'll be content enough to reach those low-lying clouds, or even the dome of the Great Synagogue or the skyscraper in Napoleon Square. As I clutch at the rope in midair, I'll have a pretty good view of everything that's going on down below on Bielańska Street, Mylna Street, and Ptasia Street, also on Moniuszko Street, Jasna Street, and Marszałkowska Street. If the rope snaps I'll come crashing down and break both my arms and legs, for I am not one of your levitating Jews. Do not forsake me, O my language. Abide with me just a little longer. Remember there is no other rope for me to grasp should I begin to fall. Bialik didn't mind either way. He wrote in Hebrew, so he was never at risk. He will be read in fifty years and in five hundred years. But when the rope snaps—oh, horrors—only the eggheads will read me. In the whole world there will be just four scholars specializing in the specific variant of Yiddish spoken in Warsaw in 1937, which in a hundred or two hundred years will regrettably be all but forgotten.

But let's say there are as many as seven specialists to debate the hypothetical or probable meaning of the word used by an all but forgotten writer, Icyk Mandelbaum, on page 237 of an all but forgotten book, which according to the title page was published in Warsaw in 1937. It is the fourth day of a conference being held in London a hundred or two hundred years from now, attended by six eggheads, because one egghead stayed at home with the flu. "Colleagues," one of the seven eminences will say, speaking in Hebrew, German, or French. I really don't care what language they use to discuss me. "Colleagues," the most highly specialized of the seven specialists will say, "as we are unable to define the meaning of this word, I propose we omit it from our dictionary. The aim of any dictionary is to give the meanings of words. A dictionary that failed to define the words it contains would be nothing short of ludicrous. We shall file an index card for this obsolete word. Who knows, if any further material comes to light in the future, we may one day be able to discover the meaning it had in 1937." The scholars will then indulge in a long, tedious discussion about the correct methodology for editing dictionaries of the twentieth-century dialects of the so-called Yiddish language, now defunct, also known as Jidysz or Jiddisch. A quarrel may flare up, perhaps even a real brawl, escalating into an exchange of blows, when one of the eggheads inadvertently uses the term "dialects."

"Do you know, Fejga," says Icyk as he climbs the stairs up to the veranda, "in a hundred or two hundred years' time no one will know that Gęsia Street ever existed in Warsaw? Well, I suppose someone might know it existed and what it meant. Four eggheads, maybe seven. But no one will ever know for sure how it was pronounced by the residents of Gęsia or what it signified."

"Oh, Mr. Icyk, sir, you do carry on," Fejga says. "I was on Gęsia Street only last Tuesday." And she pronounces "Gęsia" exactly the way it will be pronounced fifty years later, which is not the way it ought to be pronounced in July 1937. Whatever is going to happen to me, thinks Icyk, if not only Chaim Bialik but even Fejga informs me that the days of my language are numbered? The way it ought to sound is Gensze, Gensze. From Gąś, Goose. O Gensze Goose, your days are numbered; sentence has been passed. "I was on Gęsia Street only last Tuesday."

Whereupon Icyk grabs the brass bell with the wooden handle that hangs motionless for a moment in Fejga's palm, Fejga being doubtless somewhat awed by the historical perspectives in store for Gęsia Street. Then he shakes the bell and calls out very loud for all to hear: "It's time for lunch. The soup is getting cold."

The foolish mole hiding beneath the trampled molehill by the jasmine bush hears Icyk's shout and the sound of the bell. Terrified by this unfamiliar noise, it scurries away, burrowing deep into the earth.

FROM the steps leading down to Antoni's* one could see the Swiss Valley. No, that's wrong, for Antoni lived on the ground floor. To see the valley one had to walk past his front door and ascend to the mezzanine. There was also a good view from the large window of the room when we sat on the sofa, Antoni with his back to the valley, I sideways and enjoying a half-view. Also from the kitchen, where the best prospect was to be had by standing next to the refrigerator. I think that there was—there naturally still is—a small balcony with access from the kitchen. From there the view was magnificent.

I always associated Antoni with the Swiss Valley; indeed I still do, though perhaps I should associate him with Niecała Street, Wierzbowa Street, and the Saxon Garden, the places he identified with himself. But in the days when he used to saunter down Niecała Street, I was not yet born. In my mind's eye I see Antoni, his long white scarf winding and unwinding around his neck, as he makes rocking turns on the ice rink in the valley. Then his pince-nez catches the light as he rises to greet a petite and very pretty young

* A Polish Jew of leftist sympathies, Antoni Słonimski (1895–1976) was an influential poet, reviewer, and columnist of the interwar period, a rationalist and pacifist. In communist Poland he became a kind of moral exemplar and father figure for political dissidents. His wife, Janka, was a well-known graphic artist.

woman just entering through the white gate of the café on Chopin Street. The young lady is Janka. I see him too in the mid-fifties strolling through the valley, which has in the meantime turned into a ruin. I can see all that. Yet I don't even know if Antoni knew how to skate, or if he frequented the café in the valley before the war—indeed there may have been no café there at all—or if he went walking there in the fifties. He seemed to prefer exercising in the Botanic Garden and Łazienki Park. But for as long as I live Antoni will be skating in the Swiss Valley. That is where, as a young poet in a pince-nez, he will court Janeczka and other ladies.

Antoni treated me rather condescendingly, which is the best way to treat a much younger colleague. When I was successful, he liked me more. When things went badly, he liked me less. That I felt to be fair: let junior colleagues be esteemed in relation to their endeavors. The age difference between us was too great for us ever to discuss matters of principle, and there was never any question of his confiding in me. Yet I felt that Antoni had his secrets, the sort he would confide in no one, and about which nothing, or next to nothing, is to be elicited from his poetry, his newspaper columns, his comedies and novels.

Despite the even greater age gap between them, it is not impossible that Antoni confided in Adaś.* This dawned on me the very first time I met Adaś at Antoni and Janka's. That is the man, I thought at the time, who knows what

* Adam Michnik, currently editor of *Gazeta Wyborcza*, formerly a member of KOR, and also of Jewish origin, was expelled from Warsaw University in 1968, after which he worked as Słonimski's private secretary.

no one else knows about Antoni. I then provoked Adaś into a furious rage, not that that is difficult. He thumped his fist on the desk—there was a bookcase behind him, the one in Janka's room—and he shouted with his characteristic stutter: "I am a man of the left." From which I gathered that I am a man of the right. But the appellation left me cold at the time, for even as I watched Adaś insulting a man of the right, myself, in the most abusive language, I was devoured by jealousy. What do I care about left or right? I thought. He knows Antoni's secret, the one that I shall never discover. But I may have been mistaken. Antoni may well have confided in no one, not even Adaś. And what do I mean by Antoni's secret?

In *My Journey to Russia*, the book he wrote in 1932—my God, fifty-five years have gone by since he went to Russia—we read as follows: "Behind the stage of our life, concealed in the wings, great factories of suffering are at work that will visit us one day." A very odd remark for Antoni that clearly does not fit in with the rest of his thought. Factories of suffering at work, unknown suffering in store for us, some calamity brewing that we can do nothing to prevent, for it is ineluctable. Sometimes I feel that Antoni's secret lies hidden here. You will discover nothing from his poetry, because he masked himself so cleverly.

That is his great strength, the ability to create a persona. Even his best postwar text, the story "What It Was Really Like," in which he reveals most about himself, divulges next to nothing about his secret, even though it is the underlying theme or subtext. Antoni shrugs his shoulders, sentimentally pensive; an ironic smile invests what was meant to be sentimental with a slightly different dimension. Think what you like. I have my secrets, it's none of your business. That is Antoni in a nutshell. But I should like to know the real Antoni, and what the real Antoni actually thought about his own future and that of humanity. In 1932, in 1942, and in the years immediately before his death. So I appeal to Janka for help. "You ask him," I say, "he must surely tell you." Alternatively, in this warm February or cool March day in 1987, I drag Antoni out to the Swiss Valley for a walk and fire questions at him as we trudge through the crunching snow or slushy mud.

"Tell me, Antos," I say. During his lifetime I'd never have dreamt of taking such a liberty, and even after our *Bruderschaft* I always used to think of him as "old Pan Antoni" or "old Pan Antos," for that was how he signed postcards and books. That is presumably how he saw himself, so I felt I ought to conform. Yet, even though I never called him Antos, now that he is all forbearance I have no difficulty in being cheeky: "Tell me, Antos, what was it really like? What did you really think when you saw Stalin stepping out onto the platform in Red Square? 'Despite rumors about illness, the dictator of Russia looks like a bull. He is stalwart, sturdy, and dusky-faced.' And what did you think ten years later when he had Ehrlich and Alter murdered? And when the Allies refused to believe what was happening in Warsaw? But I am not asking about Stalin and Churchill and Roosevelt; they're irrelevant here.

I want to know what you thought at the time about our condition on this planet. And about our future prospects here on earth."

"I dislike provocateurs," says Antoni. "And you, my dear, are trying hard to provoke me."

"That's exactly why I have lured you on this walk to the valley," I say. "You dislike provocateurs, but everyone knows how easy it is to provoke you. After your journey to Russia and later too, did you continue to believe in the prospects of human reason, whose faithful acolyte you were? Did you believe it could somehow counteract the factories of suffering?"

"Did I ever tell you about my great-grandfather?" Antoni asks. "He was called Abraham Sztern and he came from Hrubieszów."

"I know."

"Well, listen," says Antoni. "My great-grandfather invented a calculating machine and when Staszic found out he had him made a member of the Society of Friends of the Sciences."

"You can tell me some other day about Abraham Sztern and his machine for deriving square roots. Now you must tell me the truth. Though perhaps I'll begin by telling you what I think now in 1987 about the book you wrote after your journey to Soviet Russia. Everyone knows how you used to lap up praise, so despite the slight change in your existential situation you probably still do. Listen carefully, because I intend to praise you. To my mind it is your best book, and I doubt if you ever wrote a better thing in your life. You saw everything in Soviet Russia that one could see and should see, things that sundry globe-trotting idiots from England and France were incapable of seeing. Progressive idiots. Even when they saw the poverty, hunger, lawlessness, and terror—and that wasn't very often—they failed to distinguish the cause from the effect. The basic significance of these data eluded their grasp. You saw deeper. Not just the children without milk, eggs, or butter. Not just the homeless loaded by the Main Political Administration onto trains—'wagonized' as you coined it—and deported to a destination beyond the Urals. Not just the camps, executions, and psychiatric hospitals worse than prisons. Some of your remarks are incredibly perceptive: 'The ghoul of the revolution was the executioner from the Tcherezvychayka. Now the ghoul is the bored official.' Who, back in 1932, knew that government officials had come to stay, and that they would be the ghouls of our era? That's something we discovered here only in the sixties. If not later. It would therefore seem that we read you superficially, dismissively even, for which I humbly beg your pardon."

"A writer," says Antoni, leaping over a puddle, "must be prepared for that, and it's hardly worth getting uptight about." And Antoni takes a flying leap over the next puddle, as lissome and light-footed as if the Almighty Himself had given him a hand—and who knows, perhaps He did. "Continue your praise."

"Anything to oblige," I say. "Even if you had seen no more than you saw, it would still be phenomenal. But you went further, you pinpointed the reason behind ghoulish, bored officialdom. Behind the egg shortage and Stalin's bullish health, behind the wagonization of the homeless, and the camps on the Solovetski Islands, you detected the presence of the all-powerful state. The state was all that mattered, all that provided meaning. And you identified it. Everything, but everything, is from the state and for the state. Now let me quote you."

"Let me quote myself," says Antoni, "I always enjoy that. 'A crime against the state is proof of incurable criminality.' 'The only lawgiver and master of life or death is the state.' I also wrote, though I don't remember exactly how I phrased it, that the all-powerful state controls every detail in the life of every one of its citizens."

"Please don't think," I say, leaping heavily, a million times more heavily than Antoni, over a puddle—hardly to be wondered at, since I now weigh a billion times more than he does—"please don't think that I am lavishing praise simply because you were smart enough to see in Soviet Russia what others failed to see, and understand what others could not or would not understand at the time. If that were the case, if you had observed no more than you observed, your book would be merely a historical document. But your book is different, it lives."

"How beautifully you put it," says Antoni. "If my book lives, it follows that I too am somehow alive."

"Your book lives," I say, "and deserves to be read because it encapsulates the drama of nineteenth-century reason, which, when transposed into the twentieth century, can no longer cope with the unforeseen events of our age. It endeavors to control them. But they are incommensurate, uncontrollable. Reason tries to understand—that's the drama of it."

"You're talking utter garbage," says Antoni. "Reason can achieve anything. You fail to realize its full power, my dear."

"All right, all right," I say, falling into a puddle and spattering mud all over Antoni's gray English-wool trousers. "I'll come back to that in a moment. Now we're talking about your trip to Soviet Russia in 1932, when you saw everything there was to be seen and everything our progressive Western globe-trotting cretins failed to see: the horrendous omnipotence of the state and the horrendous helplessness of the human being vis-à-vis that omnipotence. The individual is negligible. You once considered Mayakovski to be a perfectly good poet."

"He was a perfectly good poet," says Antoni. He is beginning to get angry with me, for he has definitely sensed by now what I am driving at and how I propose to corner him. "Perfectly good. Besides, everyone has the right to make mistakes."

"All right, all right," I say. "We'll talk about Mayakovski some other time, or preferably never. Let's get back to the subject. Projected into the twentieth century, nineteenth-century reason can neither accept nor comprehend that a human being, an individual, a sacred entity, is powerless beyond appeal. Reason will not accept that the omnipotent state can wagonize and deport a person beyond the Urals whenever it wants. Reason wants to explain and come to terms with the wagonizing; it must, so it seeks some justification. This is where the drama begins, by which I mean reason's devious subterfuges, so faithfully transcribed in your books—and that is its chief merit in our eyes. Reason says: 'Fair enough, wagonizing is going on and will most likely continue. Fair enough, a pound of butter costs around forty rubles—namely, the monthly wages of someone who therefore eats no butter. But,' horrified reason then asks, 'perhaps this serves an ultimate goal? Perhaps it is necessary and inevitable. It may make more sense in the future. For if the suffering serves no purpose, what is its point and what is its sense? Reason is a sensible being, and it would like everything to make sense.

"Now let me give you a few quotations from *My Journey to Russia*. 'In many respects Russia now leads the civilized world. Some fully completed fragments cleverly complement the building of socialism. A delightful vista peers through the mist.' 'Today the whole world is ailing. . . . Here in Russia the patient lies on the operating table. He is undergoing surgery without anesthesia. If the operation succeeds, he will bring health and incalculable new vigor to the world.' 'Marxism appeals to reason . . . it believes that the evil in Russia does not stem from the change in political system, but is rooted in the human being. This strikes me as a highly pertinent diagnosis. It explains the tragic and difficult situation of the Soviet government when trying to impose socialism on one hundred and sixty million simple people.' Meanwhile the homeless are being packed into wagons. Excellent."

"What is excellent?" asks Antoni, plumping heavily into

the dirty melting snow. "What are you going on about now?"

"I refer to your account of the mishap that befell nineteenth-century reason when it failed to make head or tail of the situation, yet persevered in its endeavors. To return to the beginning of our conversation, Antoni, I mean to your secret. When reason suffered that tragedy, you as its faithful acolyte had to try to salvage it. You could not desert it, you could not simply say let's give reason a wide berth, because reason is so stupid and clueless. That I understand. When terror reduced reason to a state of imbecility, you, the faithful acolyte, continued to serve; that's what the English call lip service. But my guess is that you served reluctantly. You knew by then that reason can achieve nothing. So where is the truth? Remember your sentence about the factories of suffering at work behind the scenes. Just what were you trying to tell us?"

"Frankly," says Antoni, "I believed in human reason. I consider it to be victorious even today. You mark my words, my dear, we'll see it crowned with glory yet."

"When the homeless were wagonized in the Moscow stations," I ask, "did you still believe reason would be victorious one day?"

"I did."

"And when Hitler staged the Kristallnacht," I ask, "did you believe then?"

"I did."

"And when the Germans did what they did in Poland? And when Stalin murdered Ehrlich and Alter? And when

Szmul Zygielbojm committed suicide? And when Roosevelt and Churchill did nothing to save Polish Jews even though they could? You still believed that reason wields some power and can, if nothing else, grasp the meaning of it all? I've always thought of you as a wise man, Antos. So please, please spare me all this nonsense."

"It's not polite," says Antoni, "to abuse elderly gentlemen. You may take such liberties in thirty years, because by then you'll be my senior. But for now you just listen to me. I know exactly what you're driving at and why you have dragged me out on this walk through the mud. You aren't remotely interested in the book about my journey to Russia, though it's nice of you to praise me, because everyone likes to be praised. Nor are you remotely interested in the adventures of nineteenth- or twentieth-century reason; that's simply not your scene, they're interesting in their own right, nothing more. But deep down you couldn't give a damn if reason is intelligent or otherwise. Am I right, my dear?"

"As always, Antoni."

"All you really want, all that really interests you, is to ferret out my secret. Though not the one you asked about. My thoughts about the human condition and reason's prospects for the future are well known to you. That's not what you're after, is it, my dear? You're after a much bigger secret altogether. Right?"

"Of course, Antoni."

"But I don't intend to tell you," says Antoni. "Adaś doesn't know it either; it was hardly an appropriate topic to discuss with him. He was too young, and I didn't want to demoralize him. Only Janka knows, but you'd better not ask her, she is sworn to secrecy. As I found your company not unpleasant, and there were times when I even liked you in a halfhearted sort of way, I'll tell you something vaguely relevant to my secret and to the sentence in *My Journey to Russia* about factories of suffering. Anyway, you can make your own mind up about that. Listen. We can judge God's intentions toward us only on the basis of creation, as that is the only source of reason's knowledge: we don't know where those great factories of future suffering are located. Now tell me, my dear, what if you write a poem that doesn't work? Does that ever happen to you?"

"Naturally," I say, "it happens to all of us."

"Precisely," says Antoni. "And when you write a bad poem, do you like it? Do you feel well disposed toward it? Or do you tear it up and throw it in the fire?"

"I tear it up," I say, "into tiny pieces. So that no one can read it if the wind blows it out of the garbage can."

"You've taken the words out of my mouth," says Antoni. "I guess it's the same with us humans in that we haven't turned out too well for God. Like a second-rate poem that's misfired. Anyway, you draw your own conclusions."

This is all pure fiction. Only the snow mixed with rain is real, a grayish curtain that engulfs the Swiss Valley and then drifts apart again. As I stand by the low wall on Chopin Street gazing at the ground-floor windows of the house on Rose Alley, I try to penetrate Antoni's secret. But then I think perhaps Antoni had no secret to hide.

Maybe I am wrong in thinking that he had some bond with his Polish or his Jewish God. When he mentions his grandfather and great-grandfather in *Warsaw Memoirs* (1957), he refers to "barren commentaries of an old, oft distorted and incompetently translated book," to "obscure Talmudism" and "the circle of obscurantism" in which "youthful victims of Talmudism" lived. For Antoni, the Jewish God would appear to belong to a sphere of customs or tradition of which, to judge by these epithets, he was not overfond. If Antoni had no secret, what do I want to ferret out of him during our walk in the valley? Perhaps I am an obscure Talmudist, uncircumcised Christian that I am, studying in my clumsy, unproductive manner within the orbit of an obscure Book.

The kitchen door opens onto the small balcony. Antoni appears in his gray Stetson. How sensible, I think, to put his hat on before going out; otherwise he might catch a cold in this snow and rain. Antoni removes his hat and seems to be signaling to me to drop in. I run diagonally through the Swiss Valley, slipping on the frozen crust of snow, getting trapped in the grayish curtain, leaping over muddy puddles. But when I reach the balcony there is no one there. A voice can be heard, but I don't know where it comes from.

"Come up here, my dear. I want to tell you something."

The Final Station: Umschlagplatz

✤

A HANDSOME man in glasses, aged about thirty, of very Jewish looks, the good looks of the Jewish intelligentsia. He was an agronomist, but if one didn't know, one might take him for a journalist, scholar, or writer. A prominent nose, long neck, deep brow. He wears a suit of dark, probably navy, light-striped material. The photograph is taken in profile. The branch of a fruit tree in the background, covered with minute leaves or large buds, tells us it is early spring. The year is easily established. The small girl in the arms of the spectacled man looks about two, and we know she was born in 1940. So the photo was taken in the early spring of 1942. On one of those cool spring days when the air itself gives a foretaste of things to come. The man wears a suit, the girl—her name was Athalie, but her parents called her Alusia and Aluśka —wears a warm coat with a hood, white stockings, and laced-up boots. She clings to the man's neck with one arm, and holds a toy bucket in the other. Chubby cheeks, large eyes, distinctly outlined eyebrows. She will, she would, grow up to be a beautiful woman. She appears to be smiling at us, but she is of course smiling at the photographer, presumably her mother, Anna Perechodnik, née Nusfald, whom the man in the glasses called Anka. Anna Perechodnik was the joint proprietor of the Oasis cinema in Otwock. The cinema did quite well, and just before the war Anna Perechodnik, together with her brothers, decided to build a second cinema. But the mayor of Otwock refused to grant them building permits, probably because two of the three, or even all three, cinemas in Otwock belonged to Jews, and the mayor, who disliked Jews, did not want another Jewish cinema in town.

The man holding Alusia in his arms is Calel Perechodnik, who at the time the photograph was taken was a policeman in the Otwock ghetto. Previously, on the strength of Wiktor Kulerski's article, I wrongly gave his name as Celek. In 1943 or 1944, while in hiding in Warsaw, Calel Perechodnik wrote his memoirs, a copy of which his brother, now apparently living in Canada, deposited in the archives of the Jewish Historical Institute. The staff there told me it is the only account of events in the Otwock ghetto known to them. The photograph of Calel Perechodnik, Alusia, and the vernal sprig is now filed with the diary, and the folder contains one other photograph of Calel. The bilingual caption in Polish and in French suggests this was his passport photo: Calel Perechodnik studied agronomy in France. When he returned to Otwock, Mr. and Mrs. Perechodnik began to consider the possibility of leaving for Palestine. They were fairly wealthy people, and they toyed with the idea of buying some land there, so that Calel could put the specialist knowledge he had acquired in France to practical use. But they never left.

"Why, Pan Calel?" I ask, looking at the photo with the bilingual wording. "Jews here were being beaten up at the university and thrown out of the blue-and-yellow trains and their windows were being smashed. So why didn't you both leave? You could now be living in Tel Aviv.

Your grandson would be exactly the age you were in 1942. Your grandson in glasses, deep brow, thin neck. And the same nice smile as you have."

"In the first place," says Calel, "we were really doing quite well for ourselves. Anka was the co-proprietor of the Oasis, and I ran a building firm. We were citizens of the Republic, and although the radical nationalists had plans for depriving us of our citizenship, we felt it was our Republic too. Second, Jews were being thrown out of trains and beaten up at the university during the period of my studies in France, so I never witnessed it myself, I knew it only from hearsay. And I obviously couldn't anticipate that the Germans would kill us all."

Thanks to Calel Perechodnik's diary, I can now rectify some of the information I gave earlier. When the extermination began in Otwock, the Jewish policemen (see Leokadia Schmidt) did not throw their caps at the feet of the Germans, and they were not shot. It is not true, as Abraham Lewin writes in his *Diary of the Warsaw Ghetto*, that the Germans carried out the extermination of Otwock "with the help of five hundred Jewish policemen from Warsaw," or that the Otwock Jews were herded to Warsaw on foot. The ghetto in Otwock was surrounded by a fence, not by barbed wire. There may also not have been two ghettos in Otwock, the town ghetto and the sanitary ghetto—this I had taken from Adolf Berman's story. Or at least Calel Perechodnik does not mention it. His account is so detailed that had there been two ghettos, he could not have failed to mention that fact.

As for the date, the extermination did not take place on

August 20, as one might deduce from Wiktor Kulerski's article, or on August 21, as I had concluded from Adolf Berman's story. Karl Brandt (Perechodnik gives the form "Brand") arrived in Otwock for the first time on Tuesday, August 18. He then asked for the plan of the Otwock ghetto and issued orders for the demolition of all its brick houses. The Jews were to use the material from the rubble to "wall in the ghetto" within the next twenty-four hours. This order was not executed, because it was obviously not feasible. It appears that Brandt merely supervised the extermination in Otwock, as Calel Perechodnik suggests it was directed personally by an SS man named Lipner, without, however, telling us anything about him. We are not even sure that his name was Lipner. This is how it appears most of the time in the diary, but in one place the letters "sz" (Lipszer? Liszner?) have been penciled in above. Operations began in the morning of August 19. "At seven o'clock in the morning I happen to be in the marketplace when the first carload of Ukrainians drives in through the Karczew barrier. The first shots are fired. I quickly run home just as a truck rolls up from the direction of Warszawska Street, followed by the limousines of SS dignitaries." One of these cars is doubtless a small black Opel often seen on the streets of the Warsaw ghetto. I assume that Brandt, Hoefle, Mende, Klostermeier, or someone of that ilk was inside it.

Now for a few extracts from the diary of Calel Perechodnik. I prefer not to add any commentary of my own, so I shall first explain a couple of points. The commander of the Jewish police in Otwock was named Kronenberg.

On August 19 the Otwock Jews were herded into the square outside a carpentry workshop enclosed by barbed wire. According to Perechodnik, there were about 8,000 of them in all. The Jewish policemen were promised that their wives and children would not be deported. But once the Jews from the Otwock Umschlagplatz had been loaded onto the freight cars by the Jewish policemen, the Germans no longer felt obliged to keep their word. They pushed the policemen out of the way and loaded the wives and children themselves. The train set off in the direction of Świder, Józefów, and Falenica. Executions began after the train had departed.

For the next few days the Jewish policemen were employed in cleaning up the ghetto and keeping an eye on the Jews who had gone into hiding or escaped to the forest and then been caught by the military police during their routine manhunts. Those who were caught were locked up in the Otwock jail and shot the next morning. Calel Perechodnik was among the cleaners and guards. His diary obviously ought to be published in toto. It contains several passages that are highly unfavorable to the Poles, and several passages that are highly unfavorable to the Jews, and it seems to me that most Poles and Jews prefer not to know the whole truth. Perechodnik, who fled to the east in September 1939 and returned several months later to Otwock, relates, for example, how the Jews behaved toward the Poles after the Soviet invasion on September 17. As a Jew from Otwock who considered himself to be a citizen of the Republic, he was truly amazed by the comportment of his fellow countrymen from the eastern borderland; he just couldn't understand. Unpleasant reading. Otwock, 1942:

"In the whole of Otwock only one woman keeps her wits about her, Kronenberg's wife, Tola. She orders her father-in-law to join the lineup, while she mans the telephone at the police station. Her husband had previously given Major Brand two gold watches."

"I saw a young woman who only a minute before was bubbling with life and health. I saw her just as a Ukrainian hacked her living body to pieces with a spade. He had run out of bullets, so he grabbed a spade and chopped between her breasts until he had cut her body in half."

"The Germans meanwhile pull up some armchairs and sit drinking beer, smoking cigarettes, eating, and laughing. From time to time they fire a shot into the crowd to keep the people on the move. They also select some from the crowd and beat them with truncheons till they drop dead."

"I return to the Square. 'Doctor, write me a prescription for poison.' He takes out his fountain pen and notepad. He writes something in Latin, signs it, puts the date of August 19, 1942, adding the usual formula for poisons 'for Perechodnik.' I return to the fence and throw the slip over to a Pole, who returns a few minutes later and hands me ten tablets of Luminal. He does not ask for money. Did a stranger pay for me, or did the pharmacist refuse to take money? I return to the Square. How does the Luminal work? Does one need a large dose? Who knows? Someone says that three tablets are a lethal dose."

"I want to believe that the convoy of Otwock Jews reached Treblinka without delay by Thursday. Though some say that the Falenica transport, which arrived on Friday, was liquidated before Otwock."

"I walk past the houses. It is after midnight. Houses that only twenty-four hours ago were teeming with life now stand dark and empty. I have to step carefully in the darkness, for I keep stumbling over the corpses of acquaintances, friends, strangers too. I do not turn my flashlight on them; I do not want to recognize them or see the spattered brains and pools of blood. I reach my parents' house, open the gate. My aunt appears. Resignedly I hand her some bread, a bucket of water, and say softly, 'All Otwock has been deported. Anka and Aluśka may no longer be alive. Rachela has also been taken.' "

"I leave my summer coat at Wolfowicz's; it is too heavy to wear. I return an hour later. The whole apartment has been smashed up. The Poles have ransacked it from top to bottom. The entire ghetto is still surrounded by Polish scum. They keep jumping in over the fence, axing doors open, and plundering everything. Sometimes they stumble upon corpses that are still warm, but that doesn't deter them. People tussle over warm corpses to wrest away a pillow or a suit. We enter Grynhorn's home where we meet a Pole who has already packed everything into a sack. He is angry and surprised. What right has Grynhorn to obstruct him? However, he has no option but to drop the bag and escape over the fence."

"Just as well the pits don't have to be dug; the Jews prepared them in good time. Every villa has an antiaircraft shelter already dug out, though not in use, where the women mainly threw the household garbage and slops.

Now the corpses have to be quickly dragged over and thrown fully clothed on top of the garbage, buried in sand up to ground level, and it's all over. We work in silence. The corpse of an unknown woman is already lying in one of the shelters. We throw the body of my friend Mulik Noj on top of her, and the body of Fiołek, a well-known thief, on top of him. Through the fence on Szkolna Street, Poles stand staring at us. Watching the gravediggers."

"I greeted the arrival of the first military policeman with an infinite sense of relief. . . . The first military policeman did not come to carry out the sentence; he just slipped away from the general roundup before his other colleagues because it was not a lucrative business. The money found on the corpses went into the general kitty, so this gentleman preferred to abscond. He appears before the jail, and then: *'Alles Geld, Gold, mysen zi awegeben aznyt werd ir derszosyn.'* That magic word *derszosyn*, as if they weren't going to be killed within the hour regardless. They all rush up to him, hand over all their money, offer to work eighteen hours a day, anything so as not to be killed. They cry out to him: *'Unserer Got.'* "

"Individual shots continued to be fired; anyone who stirred was given the coup de grace. At this point the workmen standing on the side came up to the bodies, went through their pockets, and briskly threw the still-warm corpses of the earlier batch onto the garbage. Space was cleared; the next group of ten could come up."

"The next time I came back I recognized neither Kupiecka Street nor any of the other streets. Nearly all the Jewish houses had been sold to Poles for demolition. Entire streets had vanished. . . . Throughout the ghetto all one could hear was the crash of falling walls. All one could see was the rubble of houses and the bonfires at which the workmen were warming themselves. It was November by now and fairly cold. Just before the demolition of our house, some Poles had been knocking down a house where sacred Hebrew books had been stored in the attic. A huge number of them, which they stacked up in a great heap and set afire instead of burning wood, which cost almost fifty groszy a kilo. The books didn't give off much of a blaze, they smoldered, but did not burn."

Calel Perechodnik escorted his wife and daughter onto the Otwock Umschlagplatz but did not go with them because he was afraid of dying. He then felt that because he had not gone with them he ought to die. He lived for another two years. After the Warsaw Uprising he was hiding in a bunker which was probably discovered by the Germans. All we know is the date, October 28, 1944, nothing more. The copy of his diary deposited in the archives of the Jewish Historical Institute is catalogued: "Memoirs Section, No. 55."

IT is raining, but can one call it rain when it is barely a drizzle? It's the sort of fine rain that is fairly typical for the outskirts of Warsaw. The fine July rain, for we are in July, falls slantwise and shows no sign of abating in the immediate future. There is a gurgling in the gutters, but as it is only a light rain, the sound is intermittent, as the water gathers impetus before splashing down. Raindrops hang from the branches of the pine trees. A man in a gray hood flits past between the pines near Sara Fliegeltaub's house. But Icyk, who is lying on his bed beneath a camel-hair coverlet, cannot see him, so we don't know if it is friend or foe hiding under the gray hood. It is pleasant to doze beneath a camel-hair coverlet, a magnificent cream-and-beige plaid that is Icyk's only valuable possession, apart from his gold-nibbed Parker, also quite costly, and the somewhat depreciated and dilapidated Remington. It is pleasant indeed to doze beneath such a luxurious coverlet, while a fine July rain falls outside, and something gurgles and patters and drips, and a mysterious figure in a gray hood flits past between the pine trees.

It is pleasurable to doze, but that is not to say that sweet slumbers induce sweet dreams. As you sink a bit deeper into sleep, the pleasant gurgling seems to come from above, from high overhead, while lower down rustlings and whisperings and rumblings rise to the surface of the nightmare at the level of the bed. Something rustles and murmurs in the dream being dreamt beneath the camel-hair coverlet, and it doesn't bode well. To judge by those murmurs and rustlings, thinks Icyk, sinking ever deeper into their midst, the dream I am about to have will not be a pleasant one, and I'd prefer to wake and rise back to the surface where the gutter is all a-gurgle and raindrops hang from the pine needles. But I seem unable to bestir myself.

At this point Colonel Adam Koc appears in Icyk's dream. A small figure in mufti wearing wire-framed glasses, he emerges from the whisperings and rustlings, which means they originate not from him but from the surroundings. Icyk does not know Colonel Adam Koc personally. How could he? But in his dream Colonel Adam Koc knows Icyk exceedingly well. He knows that Icyk writes a daily column for *Der Moment*, and he has even read his novel about the adventures of the Jews who in 1665 set off on a journey to meet the Messiah known as Sabbatai Zevi. Although Icyk and Colonel Adam Koc are now quite deep down inside the abyss, and cannot hear the gurgling in the gutter and the raindrops tapping against the metal windowsill, Icyk knows why he is dreaming of the colonel. Only he is not sure if that knowledge comes to him from within or outside of his sleep. In other words, is Icyk totally ensconced in his slumbers or is some part of him standing outside the dream and observing Colonel Adam Koc from that vantage point? Icyk is dreaming of Colonel Adam Koc because before lunch, before this drizzle set in, the following conversation took place.

"A few days ago," said Jakub Wurzel, "an attempt was also made on the life of Salazar—I mean the Salazar who governs Portugal. So there may well be an assassination gang at work, acting on the instructions of some foreign power. I wouldn't be at all surprised if in a few days' time someone attempted to assassinate Marshal Voroshilov or General Göring, or even both at once." Here Jakub Wurzel gave Icyk a meaningful look, as if Icyk had carried out both attempts in person, and was planning to try his luck with Göring and Voroshilov within the next few days. He's a dark horse, that Icyk. "Someone must have a vested interest in starting a second world war; that's probably the reason behind it."

"In other words," said Szymon Warszawski, "a new Sarajevo. But there will be no war. Only a madman would launch a war right now. Say what you like about Hitler, but he doesn't look like a madman to me. Mustard gas is the best deterrent."

"But it was very bloody," said Sara Fliegeltaub. "Fejga was at the butcher's today and heard that pieces of Bieganek's body were later picked up from the porch and the pathway. Someone who was in Świdry that day and happened to be walking past Colonel Koc's villa told her."

"The foreign power you suspect of plotting these attempts, Mr. Jakub," Icyk said, "ought to hire more competent assassins. A terrorist who blows himself up with his own bomb is not a terrorist, he's a dolt. I wish Colonel Koc no harm, but that was not a professional job."

"At the butcher's," said Sara Fliegeltaub, "they also said that Bieganek is, or used to be, a communist."

"If he was a communist," said Jureczek Wasiutyński, "we must infer he was a Jew. They may not be saying that today, but you can be sure they'll be saying it tomorrow. It simply doesn't make sense. Why on earth are we waiting here when we have our own state, or at least a fair chance of achieving our own statehood." Jureczek Wasiutyński now gave Icyk a meaningful glance, as though Icyk was personally responsible for the fact that the English had stopped issuing certificates for Palestine. "I occasionally get the impression that some Jews like nothing better than a good pogrom."

"But if only pieces of his body were found," Icyk said, "it won't be possible to establish Bieganek's identity."

"It was a real massacre," repeated Sara Fliegeltaub. "But I can't understand who would want to kill Colonel Koc. He's such a decent man. A distinguished man."

"Of inconspicuous build, with a large bald spot," said Icyk. Judging by the meaningful glances now directed at him, this last remark had not gone down too well.

"I think I can explain," said Jakub Wurzel. "It was not really an attempt to assassinate Colonel Koc, but rather Marshal Rydz-Śmigły. In the political field, Colonel Koc is Marshal Rydz-Śmigły's second-in-command, so it was actually a warning to the marshal: your deputy's turn today, your turn tomorrow. Foreign powers thus give Rydz-Śmigły to understand that if he isn't prepared to negotiate with them, they'll have him disposed of."

"Someone of Colonel Koc's standing," said Sara Fliegeltaub, "surely shouldn't be living in Świdry Małe. With all those copses and undergrowth, it's most unsafe. The assassins could easily hide in the undergrowth."

"Nowadays, Pani Sara, nowhere is safe," said Jakub Wurzel. "Today in *Our Survey* I read about the wagon harnessed to two Percherons that collided with the Great Voivode Michael's automobile. Jeopardizing—how did they put it?—Polish-Romanian friendship with a long shaft pole. Now just try to imagine the scene. The heir to the Romanian throne is driving along Nowy Świat and is almost killed by a shaft pole on the corner of Jerusalem Avenue." Here Jakub Wurzel cast yet another meaningful glance at Icyk, as though Icyk had been the driver of the wagon that collided with the car of the heir to the Romanian throne, or even one of the two Percherons at the junction of Jerusalem Avenue and Nowy Świat. "We live in dangerous times. We should all be more aware, not only Voivode Michael and Colonel Koc."

"Please come in to lunch," said Sara Fliegeltaub. "Fejga, if you break that tureen, I don't know what your mother will do, because she'll never have enough money to pay for it. You really can't imagine what a stupid creature she is." Whereupon Sara Fliegeltaub gave Icyk a meaningful glance. Oh no, thought Icyk, it really is a bit much to receive so many meaningful looks in the course of one quite brief conversation. I should protest, because I cannot be held responsible for everything: the issuing of certificates, an assassination attempt in Świdry Małe, the traffic at the junction of Jerusalem Avenue and Nowy Świat, and the tureen of barley soup.

Sara Fliegeltaub's glance meant that Icyk was responsible for the fact that Fejga, who at that very moment was bringing a tureen of steaming barley soup into the dining room, stumbled and nearly fell flat on her face with it. Luckily the tureen was not broken, because by some miracle the girl recovered her equilibrium. Now Sara Fliegeltaub's meaningful glance at Icyk was fully warranted. If Fejga stumbled with the tureen on entering the dining room it was only because she had noticed Icyk peering uninhibitedly from the veranda at her exceptionally long legs. As she moved in the direction of the table, she was not concentrating as she ought on the tureen of barley soup but was pondering the lurking significance of Icyk's glance.

Could a clever guy like Icyk be in love with a silly girl like Fejga?

So if Colonel Koc availed himself of the fine rain falling over Otwock to appear to Icyk in a dream, it is the fault not of the soup tureen but of the bomb that the terrorist Bieganek in the pay of some foreign power failed to plant outside the villa in Świdry Małe. In the dream Icyk is not lying under his camel-hair coverlet; he is at the Castle in Warsaw. As Icyk has never visited the Castle, the room in which he converses with Colonel Koc has rather blurred contours, though it is presumably furnished with tapestries or hangings or suchlike.

"With all those copses and undergrowth," says Colonel Koc, "it's most unsafe. Leave this place, Icyk. Please, I beg you."

"But I can't leave," says Icyk, "because she doesn't want to leave with me. And I won't go without her." And he points at Fejga's long legs—nothing blurred about that—as their owner chances to bring a tureen of steaming barley soup into the room at the Castle.

"If you don't want to leave," says Marshal Rydz-Śmigły, standing next to Colonel Koc in a long cloak and four-cornered hat with silver galloon, "why did you try to ram the Great Voivode Michael with a shaft pole?"

"I didn't want to ram him," says Icyk. "The Percherons shied and the driver lost control."

"But who was the driver?" asks Colonel Koc.

"I was," Icyk admits. "But Fejga is also to blame, as she was riding with me." Icyk looks around the room in the hope that Marshal Rydz-Śmigły will spot Fejga's long legs. But Fejga and the tureen of barley soup have vanished into thin air.

"You'd better leave, Icyk," says Marshal Rydz-Śmigły. "If you leave, we'll hush up the incident with the shaft pole and come to some sort of deal with the Voivode. But if you stay, it will soon be public knowledge that you were in the pay of a foreign power."

"Then persuade her to leave too," says Icyk. "If she agrees, we'll leave together." But Marshal Rydz-Śmigły and Colonel Koc do not appear to understand, because Fejga is no longer in the room.

"Leave, Icyk," says Colonel Koc. "This is your last chance. Upon my officer's word of honor."

"If you have no money," says Marshal Rydz-Śmigły, "we'll pay for your certificate."

"But I love her," says Icyk. "It's such woody ground, I cannot leave the woman I love in the undergrowth."

"I sometimes get the impression," says Marshal Rydz-Śmigły, "that some Jews like nothing better than a good pogrom."

"The certificate," says Colonel Koc, "may be picked up from my villa in Świdry Małe tomorrow. You will leave for Palestine under the name of Bieganek. But the English will be duly informed and won't create difficulties. Upon my officer's word of honor."

Icyk is now sinking knee-deep in snow as he tries to escape. According to the logic of his dream, he is obliged to run away because his departure for Palestine under the name of Bieganek is a singularly dangerous undertaking. So Icyk sinks deep into the snow as he tries to dodge the two men who want to give him a certificate made out in Bieganek's name and who are now pursuing him in between the pine trees of the Białowieska Forest. If we were in Otwock or in Śródborów, thinks Icyk, wading through snowdrifts and weaving in between the pines, I could easily escape, because I know Otwock and Śródborów far better than Colonel Koc or Marshal Rydz-Śmigły does. But I've never been to the Białowieska Forest in my life before, and they go hunting there several times a year. They know the forest inside out, so I don't stand a chance and it won't be long before they catch me. What's more, I'm in my pajamas, and they've got their fur-lined jackets and fur caps. Heaven knows when Marshal Rydz-Śmigły and Colonel Koc found time to change clothes; it minimizes my chances and maximizes theirs.

Icyk would like to turn around and explain that there is absolutely no point in continuing the chase, for even if they capture him, he'll never leave for Palestine without Fejga. It would make better sense to set off in pursuit of Fejga, for, if she is near at hand and they manage to catch her, she might then be persuaded to leave. But Icyk cannot turn around because the dream tells him that he who runs away in his sleep has no right to turn around. Colonel Koc has just sprung up behind him, and his fingers, which may well be those of Marshal Rydz-Śmigły, are just about to grab the collar of the pajamas that Icyk inadvertently slipped into after lunch, as he had not anticipated his forthcoming flight through the Białowieska Forest. It is most peculiar how the runaway Icyk keeps sinking knee-deep in snow, while his pursuer Colonel Koc not only does not sink but actually bounces up from the snow as from a trampoline. Just as his fingers begin to tighten their grip on the pajama collar, Icyk falls into a snowdrift, swallows a mouthful of snow, chokes—and pulls the camel-hair coverlet off his head.

The gutter is still a-gurgling; raindrops patter against the metal ledge. The rain, or rather the drizzle, is still slanting down, and shows no sign of shifting away from Otwock. Chaja sits at the table gazing out of the window and smoking a cigarette in a very long silver holder.

"Was I screaming?" asks Icyk.

"I would imagine you were," says Chaja. "Do you know what time it is? It will soon be time for high tea. Fejga is setting the table."

"That Fejga is a character," says Icyk. "I could put her into a story. Do you know what I was dreaming?"

"Am I supposed to guess?" asks Chaja, still gazing out of the window. By the looks of it she is not overwhelmingly interested in Icyk's dreams. "You were screaming, so it must have been a nightmare."

"Or a prophetic vision," says Icyk. "I dreamed of Colonel Adam Koc. It was obviously because of that bomb attack. He asked me when you and I plan to leave."

"I called Chaim Sandler," says Chaja. "He said he might have a part for me in Urke Nachalnik's *Nacht menszn.* He wants to stage it next season on Bielańska Street. Under the circumstances you can hardly expect me to leave. Nachalnik lives somewhere near here. You could go and tell him about me. Ask him to discuss me with Sandler. But say nothing for the time being. Listen. I do love that gurgling sound in the gutters. I could listen to it for hours."

"Then you can listen without me," says Icyk, pulling the camel-hair coverlet over his head in despair.

The rain, a fine drizzle, has stopped. The sky overhead is pale blue, or rather blue-white, as a white, whitish, barely white mist drifts high above the tops of the pines. Hania and I have parked the red Renault next to the school building at the corner of Narutowicz Street and Poniatowski Street, and we wade through a mixture of gray sand and pine needles toward the small square at November 11 Street. After passing a slag heap and a car dump, we have to turn left, then right. Then we'll find some rusty fencing to our right, and behind it stacks of bricks, also prefabricated doors and windows beneath a metal roof. An electric outlet is secured to a pine tree: a house is under construction. To the left we'll find more rusty fencing, on the other side of which a woman hangs her wash on a line stretched between two pines: pink slips and blue panties beneath a blue-white sky. If a fine drizzle sets in again—the whitish mist bodes no good—the woman's underwear will get a second laundering.

"It wouldn't be easy to hide here," says Hania as we pass the woman hanging out her laundry.

"You could hide in that gray house," I say. "Or in the sheds behind those pines over there."

"Those sheds probably didn't exist at the time," says Hania. "They look as though they're postwar. Besides, there were terrible penalties involved."

"If they'd hidden in those sheds," I say, "no one would have been responsible; it's a kind of no-man's-land."

"But even if the sheds were there," says Hania, "they must have been used for breeding rabbits or storing coal. Then the owner could easily be traced."

The wind rises and disturbs the sheets of roof metal that are held in place by bricks. The white-and-blue sky is covered by white-and-gray clouds. When the wind increases, the metal sheets flap and clatter.

"No," says Hania. "There is nowhere here to hide. Look at those pines. Now if there were thick forest around. But you can see everything through those pines."

"You could always spend a day or two in the juniper bushes," I say. "Only you'd have to lie flat on the ground. Then no one would see you, not even from the fence. Unless they came with dogs; then you wouldn't stand a chance."

The clouds have turned dark gray. We head back to the red Renault parked by the school. Again there is a fine flurry of drizzle above Otwock. In the vicinity of Sara Fliegeltaub's boardinghouse a man in a gray hood flits past between the pines.

IT all happened between Otwock and Karczew. It was recorded in one of the Jewish diaries, from which we must infer that one of the Jews, male or female, managed to escape. The diary was not published and I have not succeeded in tracing it. I was told about it by someone who had read it, but my informant may well have muddled or distorted the facts. So I shall be as succinct as possible and omit some minor details. Somewhere between Otwock and Karczew. A copse, a road, fields. There are also peat bogs between Otwock and Karczew. So perhaps there was a peat bog. It was August or September 1942, so if it was a field it was stubble or ripe wheat.

During a roundup or most likely by pure chance, a military policeman on horseback came across a group of Jews. Were there women and children among them? I do not know. Without dismounting, the policeman killed two Jews. He would then have proceeded to kill the rest, but he ran out of ammunition. He was probably infringing regulations by patrolling the area with only two cartridges in his belt. But he may have fired all his shots half an hour before. A boy was loafing around nearby, or happened to be passing. My informant did not mention his age. But it was a boy, a child. The policeman ordered the Jews to lie down on the ground—in the stubble or on the road, I do not know—and sent the boy to the police station in Otwock or Karczew to bring him ammunition.

The boy departed and was a long time returning. Perhaps he did not hurry, or perhaps it was a long way to the police station. The Jews were lying in the stubble or on the road. The policeman remained mounted. This went on for an hour and a half. The policeman was on horseback and helmeted (the photographs always show the mounted police wearing helmets), but he was unarmed. There were over a dozen Jews. An hour and a half later the boy delivered the ammunition. The policeman killed the Jews and rode off to Otwock or to Karczew. We must assume that once the boy had left, the Jew who described it all scrambled to his feet and made a beeline for the forest. The policeman then had to choose between pursuing the runaway or guarding the Jews on the road. A simple count told him that to kill over a dozen was better than killing one.

I am not sure we have the right to comment on such matters, but we could here quote the entry in Abraham Lewin's *Diary of the Warsaw Ghetto* for August 9, 1942: "The Jews go to the slaughter like sheep." Words to that effect crop up fairly often in stories of the Warsaw ghetto. I would put it differently, though. Abraham Lewin's cry is that of a Jew who cannot bear to see what is going on. And only a Jew who was compelled to witness it all has the right to make such a remark. It could be summarized more aptly in the following phrase: totalitarian regimes. They could have attacked the mounted policeman, they could even have killed him, but for some reason they preferred to wait passively for the boy to return with the ammunition. In exchange they were granted a one-and-a-half-hour reprieve.

THE most convenient way of shopping at Supersam is to turn from Union Square into Boy Street and park just about opposite the loading platform where the delivery trucks drive up. That is where I am now sitting with Mr. Hans-Ulrich in his white Opel, waiting for Hania as she stands in the rain in a mile-long line for a basket. She must be cursing the day she decided not to leave Poland, I think, because in Tel Aviv she would certainly not have to stand in a mile-long line. Though who knows. Having unforeseeably endowed the Jews with martial skills, God may have withdrawn their trading talents. If so, there are mile-long lines in Tel Aviv even now. A likely scenario. As Hania's reddish locks get drenched in the rain, they turn into reddish tufts and spirals and sidelocks that cling to her cheeks and neck. From the white Opel I cannot see them, but I can visualize them, a pastime I particularly relish.

"What happened then," says Mr. Hans-Ulrich. I promptly abandon the theme of the raindrops dripping down Hania's reddish tufts and start wondering how to translate Hans-Ulrich's second name. Could Mr. Hans-Ulrich be called Mr. Janek-Urszula? And when Mr. Hans-Ulrich thinks about himself, what does he call himself? Does he see himself as Hans-Ulrich or Janek-Urszula or as someone squeezed into the obscurity of that hyphen? This last hypothesis strikes me as the most plausible, because Mr. Hans-Ulrich, alias Mr. Janek, was born in a small township in the province of Opole. Over the past fifty-two years (he is my exact contemporary) Mr. Janek-Urszula has managed to be a citizen of the Third Reich, then a citizen of the Polish People's Republic, then a citizen of the German Democratic Republic, then a citizen of the Federal Republic, then a citizen of the Polish People's Republic again, then a citizen of the Federal Republic a second time around. Which state now claims Mr. Janek as its own I really do not know, and I am too embarrassed to ask, as

I'd be afraid of offending Mr. Janek. Seeing how much I like him, that is something I'd rather avoid.

In his Polish-German life, I think to myself, Mr. Janek must have accumulated some rich experiences, and if only he would commit them to paper for the benefit of Germans and Poles, his book would be a best-seller on both sides of the frontier. For the last few years I've been trying to persuade Mr. Janek to define himself in writing and tell us what it feels like to be both a German and a Pole at the same time. But Mr. Janek resists my blandishments and I'm frankly not surprised, as it can't be easy to be a German and a Pole at the same time. Both the Germans and the Poles have no doubt made life uncomfortable for him. One day, though, Mr. Janek yielded to my pressure and told me what it felt like in 1945, when the Russians entered the small township in the province of Opole where little Hans-Janek was born and little Hans-Janek was liberated. Or rather where Janek was allegedly liberated from Hans. But that is another story. Back to the present moment.

"What happened then," says Hans-Janek, "is as incomprehensible to me now as it was at the time. But who knows, the fact that I am two-in-one Hans and Janek may prevent me from understanding the character of my compatriots—my German compatriots, that is. At the time—I don't remember exactly when, but it was snowing, so it was winter, nearer the end than the beginning of 1945—the Russians issued a decree to the effect that all male inhabitants of our township were to report to Russian headquarters. An age limit was given, but I can't remember what it was—I was only ten and it didn't concern me. But it included all adult males, old and young alike, who lived in our township, and it specified that they should bring warm clothes, so you can make a pretty good guess what the destination was. And off they went, every single mother's son, except for one who decided not to toe the line and went and hid in a stove. Well, does that make sense to you?"

"Absolutely," I say. "I'd have hidden in a stove too. Or in the attic or behind a cupboard."

"I don't mean the one who hid in the stove," says Hans-Janek. "I mean the men who reported to headquarters. I agree, the guy in the stove behaved like an idiot, because he had no reason to hide. You see, the Russians didn't treat the Germans the way the Germans treated the Jews. Oh, I know they weren't exactly exuding the milk of human kindness: that can hardly surprise you. But they weren't carrying out raids or going around to people's houses dragging them out from under beds or out of closets. They just issued that decree and waited. Anyone who complied was deported. But no one would have been deported just for failing to comply; he would simply have been kicked out at some later date and landed in the American or English zone. I don't know how many of those who reported to headquarters ever returned. And I don't know where they went, probably to Siberia or some other camps. They could have ignored that decree. They could all have hidden in stoves and under beds. But no. They reported because the NKVD ordered them to, and when the police want you to do something you don't argue but do as you are told."

"If all those Germans had gone into hiding," I say, "the NKVD would surely have started a search or organized a roundup."

"Maybe," says Hans-Janek. "But they never even risked it. It never even entered their heads that it might be worth taking a risk so as not to die. I repeat, I couldn't understand then and I still can't understand now why they all reported. I agree with you that in their place I'd probably have hidden in a stove. From which we may conclude"—and Hans-Janek smiles to me, or maybe to himself, with a faintly ironical air—"that I'm more of a Pole than a German. But that's not my point, Pan Jarek. My point is that you are wrong in saying that the Jews went to the slaughterhouse like a herd of sheep. If anything, they went as a human flock. The Germans, English, Italians, or French would have gone to be slaughtered in just the same way. If the Gestapo or the NKVD or the Sûreté told them to. So it has nothing to do with their Jewish character and inclinations. It's something in human nature. Just issue the command and they line up in fours, and left, right, left, they dig trenches or go off to the gas chambers."

"If my memory serves me right," I say, "that was just before the Uprising. The Germans pasted up a *Bekanntmachung* in Warsaw ordering all men to go and dig antitank trenches. Several dozen reported, I think."

"Ah," says Hans-Janek, "you Poles! The Poles are a chosen nation. God elected them and said: Only you will disobey, only you will shout out in public that you couldn't give a fart for *Bekanntmachungs, prikaz'es*, and summonses, and get away with it."

"To be a chosen nation," I say, "what a lovely thought. At one time I derived ineffable gratification from the idea of belonging to a nation that had been chosen for some grand design. I mulled it over in my head with genuine delectation, as I tried to fathom the purpose for which God has elected the Poles and why He feels such fondness for them. But now I find it all rather comical, and I believe that we are all chosen, Jews, Poles, and Germans, and all other nations on the face of our earth. Only the purpose of our election is still not clear to me, for I do not know if we were chosen simply to exist or for some grander design. At times I think our election is one great miracle. Wouldn't it be marvelous if we had been chosen solely to co-participate and co-exist in existence.

"But other times I am assailed by the notion that we were elected for some utterly horrendous end and that we are marching toward it four abreast, as you put it, left, right, left. But when that idea comes into my head I don't even want to think it through, because I'd rather not know the finale. I'd rather not know who chose us for this calamity, or why. In this connection I remember something that harks back to what you told me about those Germans who were so naive or else so compliant that they all but volunteered for Siberia. Sometime in 1946 I was near your birthplace—in the Regained Territories, as they were then called."

"Did you ever visit my hometown?" asks Hans-Janek.

"No, never," I say. "But my grandmother, a highly enterprising lady whose estate had been divided, decided it would be safer to move out of central Poland for a time, as one never knew what might befall an ex-landowner on home ground. So Grandma went off to Cieplice, where she started up an inn in a house that had belonged to some Germans. Cieplice, you know, is near Jelenia Góra. In 1946 or 1947, I'm not sure, I spent my vacation there and I remember the Germans, probably no more than a handful of them, who hadn't yet left. They hung around with glum expressions on their faces and were exceedingly obliging toward the Poles. In fact, they were so obsequious and cringing it was unpleasant.

"But I was far more interested in the electric railroad—I think it had yellow cars—that ran between Jelenia Góra and Cieplice and I had great fun traveling on it. What I remember is not so much the train and the Germans as what was going on in my twelve-year-old head at the time. I am trying to clarify my thoughts about those Germans. In my considered opinion, the yellow railroad should have cars for Poles only—*nur für Polen*—whereas the Germans were all subpeople who ought to be annihilated, executed by firing squad or sent to the gas chambers, not for racist reasons, of course, but for their crimes. Don't forget that I was only eleven or twelve at the time. But even so, it's not a pleasant memory. I don't mean the Cieplice Germans, whom I now think of with compassion, even though they were responsible for what happened. I mean the twelve-year-old boy who wanted to travel in a car only for Poles."

"It's just as well you were only twelve at the time," says Hans-Janek.

"I simply wanted to make the point," I say, "that the idea of standing people against a wall and shooting at them with a machine gun can be quite compelling for a teenage boy, who may feel that the option offered by history is legitimate and self-evident. A group of people need to be annihilated, so annihilated it shall be. There's nothing repellent or even strange about it, because it is human to annihilate. Or something like that. I imagine it wasn't only twelve-year-olds who thought like that at the time."

"Those Germans of mine," says Hans-Janek, "who reported in so docile a fashion also seem to have felt it was all self-evident and that to oppose anything so natural and self-evident would be a sign of stupidity or even madness, evidence that the brave defaulter was not quite right in his head."

"The comparison may be inept," I say, "but while she stands in that mile-long line over there, Hania appears to have accepted its legitimacy. Otherwise she would surely start screaming outside the Supersam at the top of her voice that by any normal standards the line system is intolerable. How easily we assent to history's options."

"If you don't open the trunk," says Hania, thumping her elbow against the windshield of the white Opel, her arms laden with plastic bags full of groceries, "I'll drop everything. Have some pity for a woman."

"Don't count on that," I say as I lower the car window and look at her lovely tresses dripping with rainwater. "No one shall ever again show pity for another. Mercy has long since vanished from the face of the earth."

✣

"If you'd like," I say, "I'll tell you the dream I had early this morning."

"No, thank you," says Hania. "There is something vaguely obscene about telling your dreams. Like going out into the street in your pajama bottoms."

"But it was the sort of dream I simply have to tell," I say. "I dreamed of Antoni, and when Antoni comes into a dream, it is always worth telling. Just listen. We were in Jelonki, at the Friendship project, by the wooden houses where the workmen who built the Palace of Culture used to live. Why can't it be called the Joseph Stalin project, like the Palace he gave us? Our entire planet ought to be named after Joseph Stalin. But let's stick to Friendship, what difference is there anyway? So we were at the Friendship project. I think it was the garden of the greenhouse with the glazed veranda, where we attended the performance of the Domestic Theater, but I can't swear to it, and I wasn't sure in my dream either—somehow it was the same and not the same.

"At any rate, a performance of the clandestine theater was due to take place, and you, me, Włodek, Jacek, Janusz, Pani Ola, and several other people were waiting for Antoni in the garden. Antoni was late and we were all very nervous; it was obvious that if he failed to turn up the performance wouldn't take place. Then Antoni suddenly appeared, though not in the garden between the greenhouses in Jelonki, but in Ursynów. In other words, my dream transported me from Jelonki to Ursynów. This also ties in with the clandestine theater, because after the show we gave Włodek a lift back to Ursynów. But in the dream I didn't even give him a lift. I don't think there's a bus or trolleybus depot in Ursynów; the trolleybus depot is in Piaseczno. But in my dream that big depot with dozens or even hundreds of buses and trolleybuses was there, in Ursynów, between the enormous gray blocks of the Imielin project or the Na Skraju project.

"Antoni emerged from behind the trolleybuses, dressed just the way we expect of him: Stetson and topcoat with a tweed jacket underneath. Everyone who'd been waiting for him in the Jelonki garden or the Ursynów depot ran up to him, or rather threw themselves upon him and began to embrace and hug and kiss him. It took me some time to force my way through the throng, but when I finally reached him and grabbed his elbow—someone had taken his other arm, the idea was to escort him ceremoniously past the wooden houses of Jelonki and the multistory buildings of the Na Skraju project—Antoni stroked my cheek and said in a pretty aloof tone of voice, 'Oh, so it's you, ducky.' That was nice, but at the same time unpleasant, because although Antoni was undoubtedly the real Antoni, he was also indisputably dead. Antoni dead and buried, and we all of us knew it.

"As he walked out of the trolleybus depot, Antoni said he couldn't attend the performance, but I can't remember his exact words, so I'll give you only the general gist of what he said. 'I can't come to the show, as I am so old and tired. Make my excuses to the actors. Tell them I am very tired and am going to rest.' The dream didn't say where Antoni proposed to take his nap, whether at the Ursynów depot, in his apartment on Rose Alley, or in one of the houses of the Friendship project in Jelonki. Do you remember the young actress who played three different parts? The one in the green dungarees. He was particularly anxious to excuse himself to her. I had to explain to her that Antoni couldn't see her because he was feeling so tired. And there my dream ended. In a garden in Jelonki or amid the trolleybuses in Ursynów. Antoni goes off to bed, and I go to excuse him to a young actress."

"But what does your dream mean?" asks Hania.

"Nothing," I say. "Some dreams mean something, others mean nothing. They're not obliged to mean anything."

"But something tells me your dream has a meaning," says Hania.

"No, it doesn't," I say. "I dreamed of Antoni. That is all. It is comforting, but meaningless."

"Antoni ought to appear in dreams in his own Warsaw," says Hania. "In the Swiss Valley or the Saxon Garden. Or even on Ujazdów Avenue, between Chopin Street and Three Crosses Square. But you dreamed of him in Ursynów and Jelonki. There must be a reason for that. But I don't know what."

The Final Station: Umschlagplatz

A FEW more facts about Warsaw's Umschlagplatz, which I found in *Recollections of the Warsaw Ghetto* by Henryk Makower. The author, a doctor in the Jewish police, visited Umschlagplatz on numerous occasions, as his cap and armband allowed him to move around quite freely. How many exits were there from Umschlagplatz? From Władysław Szpilman's *Death of a City* I concluded that there might have been exits other than the main exit, or rather entrance, next to the two cement posts. Henryk Makower confirms my thesis: "We went off in the opposite direction and through the Transferstelle to Umschlag." The Transferstelle gate is clearly the entrance from Dzika Street. Having been escorted onto Umschlagplatz via the Transferstelle gate after his failed escape from the ghetto in January 1943, Makower walked out through a doorway or wicker gate situated on the far side of the tracks: "We walk around the side of the hospital and out of the Umschlag zone into an unknown street, though I know it is the right direction for Danilowiczowska Street." Makower then found himself in the Schupo police station on Bonifraterska Street. So he could only have gone along Pokorna Street or Żoliborska Street. This exit from Umschlagplatz, which is not mentioned elsewhere, must have been situated in the wall or fence that enclosed Umschlagplatz from the eastern side, or perhaps in the vicinity of the Old Archives building, on the southeast corner to the rear.

There was also a prison on Umschlagplatz. Makower mentions it twice. "She was caught by the Germans and is now in prison on Umschlag." Also: "He became ward head of the prison department on Umschlag." No other source refers to this prison, or prison hospital, and we have no way of establishing its location. Was it in the building of the children's hospital, in a hut, or in the Old Archives? Makower's diary further complicates the issue of the number of buildings on Umschlagplatz. I had previously added up five buildings, though I was not sure. Makower gives the impression that the only building was that of the children's hospital. He makes several references to a hospital where he worked during the great extermination, when he was also ward head in the infectious diseases unit of the Berson and Bauman Hospital. He likewise mentions the Old Archives building, the place where they waited to be loaded into the freight cars. Elsewhere he hints that there could have been a single building. "Almost all the rooms and corridors were covered with a slimy mud, a mixture of urine, excrement, and dust. People waded through this ooze just as they did later on in the second half of the building, which was reserved exclusively for the Umschlag." The "second half of the building" clearly refers to the Old Archives, implying that there was one building divided into two parts. The number of stories is also puzzling; likewise the public baths. In Makower's diary one scene takes place on the fourth floor of the children's hospital: "When I arrived at Umschlag, even before the hospital was transferred there, I was told that several doctors were staying in a separate room on the fourth floor." Leokadia Schmidt's book gives us no clues regarding the baths, which must have been in the hospital building. Makower mentions Mrs. Jaszuńska, the wife of the director of the communal post, whom he managed to hide in the hospital. "The orderly pushed his group into the baths just near there. But Mrs. Jaszuńska could not tolerate the nervous tension. She had a hysterical fit and started screaming. The Germans ran into the baths and shot everyone." But the baths could have been a separate building. Perhaps the orderly steered the group he was going to lead out of Umschlag to the baths only after he had left the hospital building.

In the last days of the great extermination, the first half of September 1942, Umschlagplatz appears to have been surrounded, at least on the south side, by a cordon of SS men. Was the cordon on Stawki Street, on Niska Street, or farther afield? It is hard to say. Referring to the group of people he led out of the hospital on the last day of the extermination, Saturday, September 12, Makower simply writes: "A moment later we were on the other side of the SS cordon." It occurs to me that the cordon of SS men may have been the obstacle that previously made escape from Umschlagplatz impossible for anyone who landed in the zone that in a sense both belonged and did not belong to Umschlagplatz—namely, the pavement outside the front entrance of the hospital or the iron gate of the Old Archives building, the section of street where Szmerling used to sit in the middle of the roadway. To get this far even during Szmerling's absence was not synonymous with escape. But I don't think there was a cordon of SS men, or even of Latvians or Ukrainians, standing continuously on or near Stawki Street between July 22 and September 12. There must have been barbed wire or fencing, and Makower refers only to the last day or days of the extermination.

I am also not quite clear what Makower meant when he mentioned the exit or exits from Umschlagplatz: did he mean the main exit, the wooden gateway, or some other passageways situated farther away, say where the cordon was? He mentions the exit twice. About the doctors who left Umschlagplatz on September 12: "Without a care for us, the hospital management together with the sly old fox of Umschlag, the plumber Dulder, walked over to the exit where an ambulance was waiting." Earlier, he mentions the children he attempted to take away from the hospital on Umschlagplatz by cart: "The cart set off; I walked alongside. When it reached the bend leading to the exit, a leather-jacketed SS man drew up on a motorcycle. He glanced at the cartload of children and shouted: *Nieder mit dem Scheiss*. (This doesn't need translation.) "The bend leading to the exit": does he mean the junction of Stawki Street and Dzika Street? of Niska Street and Dzika Street? of Niska Street and Zamenhof Street? If so, then the exit had nothing to do with the main entrance, the one with the sentinel, and it was situated beyond Umschlagplatz. The children returned to the hospital and were loaded onto the trucks.

To these notes from Henryk Makower's diary I should like to append a few excerpts from a report in one of the April issues of the Warsaw daily *Trybuna Ludu* in 1987, entitled "Lack of Privacy in the Stawki Project." It relates the day-to-day problems of the Stawki project residents. "Situated at the common boundary of three districts, City Center, Wola, and Żoliborz, the Stawki project consists of three irregular blocks built by the sectional method and set around a courtyard that serves as playground and relaxation area to create the impression of a harmonious whole. It was initially planned as the first of a far larger block of buildings along Stawki Street. At present a considerable section of the area scheduled for construction is taken over by a Polish Motor Transport base, whose administrators emphasized its exclusive rights only a couple of years ago by erecting a strong metal barrier." "It is a misconception that sites in the City Center equipped with technical infrastructure should be used as a parking lot. If a deadline for evacuating the Polish Motor Transport base and the Urban Transport Establishment depot cannot be given forthwith, care should at least be taken to ensure better neighborhood relations." "The project is caught between several forces: the Polish Motor Transport base on one side, the Urban Transport Establishment depot on the other, the delivery depot of the House of Books and garages of the Metropolitan Administration opposite, and, for good measure, the busy traffic of Buczek Street. This was to be further supplemented by a car wash, the Old Town Local Housing Authority workshops, and a consignment warehouse for Western cars. Thanks to the concerted efforts of the residents' association and the project management these plans were never carried out." "Considered to be on a par with Służew nad Dolinką Street for its attractively designed balconies and hanging gardens, the project was almost from the onset struck by the common malady of burst central heating and water pipes, initially outside the buildings, then inside. Ten years later the hot-and-cold-water system at 15 Inflancka Street had to be replaced. Work on this building is currently being completed, but its neighbor is already due for repairs, and elbows and couplings cannot be had for love or money." Now where does one find these blocks built in sections, this playground and Polish Motor Transport Base, the intriguingly designed balconies and sites equipped with infrastructure? In the Stawki project. Where is that project? Between Dzika Street and Stawki Street. What was there before? We do not know. Pipes burst. There is a shortage of elbows and couplings. How very disagreeable.

—It all began in Przytyk—someone says—when Jewish stalls were knocked over in the market. It went on for several days and two Jews and one goy were killed.

—In Przytyk—says a second—it all began when a peasant was beaten up for trying to buy bread from a picketed Jewish bakery. That's how it all began. Seven people were killed. I remember perfectly, because I'd just finished my first year in high school.

—What really happened—says a third—is that the Jews arrested a visiting bishop. Of course, they didn't arrest him—why should they?—but that was the rumor spread by the National Radicals. So that's how it all began. There were lots of victims, but I don't remember how many.

—It's no problem to verify the number of victims—I say—but it won't be so easy to check on the bishop, the peasant who wanted to buy a loaf of bread, and the Jewish stalls in the marketplace. After fifty years it may be impossible to discover what triggered it.

—They had two swords—someone says—entwined with a sort of snake which they wore in their lapels. It was called the Small Swords of Chrobry.

—I remember perfectly—says another—because after the brawl in the theater I was locked up in the same cell. I naturally didn't let on that I had shouted, "Shut the mouths of the Obwiepol," in the theater. It was one against a dozen; they'd have lynched me. In the cell they produced the badges they had hidden from the police and pinned them to their lapels. The sword was about one and a half inches long with a kind of wreath effect. A laurel wreath. It was called Chrobry's Sword.

—They pushed their sidelocks behind their ears of course—someone says. Some of them had long, beautifully groomed sidelocks hanging behind their ears. That was the fashion.

—I never saw that—says another. And I should know because I often went to Parysowski Square. They may wear their sidelocks behind their ears in New York now, but in Warsaw they never did. Be careful, you don't know much about it, you could make a stupid mistake.

—In those days there were fewer buses in Warsaw. The

ones that departed from Casimir the Great Square were red like the trolleys.

—You mean yellow and red. I often took the C line from the Main Station to Muranowski Square.

—The Great Synagogue had a green dome, like a patina of verdigris.

—It had a bronze dome that glittered.

—But surely it was gray. We can always check on the photos.

—If there are color photos, of course we can—I say. But—oh, Lord—they're black and white.

—There was definitely an ice rink there, so your Antoni can go skating. But I don't remember a café. Though wait a minute, there was a low building on Ujazdów Avenue opposite the Swiss Valley.

—Of course there was no café. On the avenue side there was a large building in the Secession style, with a sort of small palace behind it.

—The café was surely on a terrace.

—The entrance was from Ujazdów Avenue.

—More likely from Chopin Street. There was a low fence.

—The fence was green.

—The fence was white.

—Lord God Almighty, what do You say to that?

The Final Station: Umschlagplatz

✥

—FEJGA—says Icyk as he lies on his bed in his pale blue pajamas contemplating Fejga's elegant legs. Fejga is cleaning his room. In view of her reluctance to clean the guest rooms and her dislike of household chores in general, the event should be regarded as noteworthy. In Sara Fliegeltaub's boardinghouse it could happen only to Icyk, for whom Fejga has a soft spot. Icyk's intuition tells him that Fejga's favor has a certain special nuance or undertone which might qualify as erotic and which gives Icyk a genuine sense of pleasure, for it is gratifying to hear her announce: I'll go and clean your room now, sir. This could be interpreted as a promise or encouragement not to be detected in her voice when she makes the same declaration of intent on the threshold of Jakub Wurzel's or Szymon Warszawski's room. It is gratifying to think that in connection with this chore Fejga entertains her own nebulous hopes and experiences a little thrill of apprehension, warranted by the fact that I, Icyk, am staring quite uninhibitedly at her exquisite legs. —Fejga—says Icyk—you have the most exquisite legs. I must immortalize them. It is intolerable that your legs should slip into oblivion among a myriad other legs. —The way you stare at me when I'm doing your room—says Fejga—makes me feel quite ashamed. I can't concentrate on my work.

—How do you know I'm staring at you—asks Icyk—when your back is turned?

—Oh, I can tell—says Fejga, climbing up on a chair, then onto the windowsill to wipe the panes. —Which—thinks Icyk—look perfectly clean to me. I must therefore conclude that she climbed up onto the ledge so as to let me study her legs in a better light and from a more advantageous perspective, for they are even longer when seen from below. —So please let me get on. Because I still have work to do in the kitchen and Pani Sara will be mad at me for chatting with you here, and I haven't peeled the potatoes for lunch yet.

—Did you know, Fejga—says Icyk—that thousands and thousands of legs have been consigned to oblivion? Though they long to be resurrected, they cannot be. So unless I immortalize your legs, in fifty or a hundred years from now they'll be confused with thousands of other anonymous legs. Then no one will ever know what your legs were like and why they were different from other legs. I feel this is absolutely crucial. In a hundred years people will want to know. They'll resent our not having perpetuated all that deserved to be. That goes for your knees and ankles too.

—You're really something—says Fejga, placing a stool on the windowsill. —From which I must infer—thinks Icyk—that she wants to wipe the curtain rail above the window, or else show me her legs in yet another light and from an even more advantageous perspective. —Then Fejga climbs onto the stool and her legs appear to Icyk in a startlingly vertical perspective that ends in a darkness, filling the onlooker with a delectable sensation of weakness or pressure in the pit of his stomach. —If Pani Sara heard you she wouldn't let me clean your room anymore. Then you'd have to clean it yourself.

—That is why I feel obliged to paint your legs—says Icyk. Lest I be accused of neglecting my duty toward future generations. Icyk contemplates the long slim legs covered with a delicate down that traps the light against the jasmine-green background of Mrs. Sara Fliegeltaub's garden. —Though I could—Icyk thinks—enhance them further, begging the forgiveness of future generations. For they'd look marvelous in seamed stockings and high-heeled shoes. The darker triangle of the stocking ending just above the ankle where the seam begins. Quite marvelous.

—I didn't know you were a painter—says Fejga. But you're fooling me. You think I can't hear you writing on that machine there?

—I'll paint your legs in words—says Icyk. It's not the same, but they'll lose nothing by it. I don't, however, propose to explain to you why, as you wouldn't understand. We'd have to indulge in various philosophical speculations.

—Is it difficult—Fejga asks, standing on tiptoe to wipe the curtain rail, the stool below her seen against the jasmine-green background—to write on that machine?

—Be careful, don't fall—says Icyk. If you'd like, I'll teach you. —But to enhance those legs—he thinks—to dress them in high- or medium-heeled shoes would be foolish, for they are beautiful enough in their own right and need no embellishment. Moreover, they'd gain nothing from the treatment, because that which is beautified falls into oblivion. And quite rightly too, though the reason escapes me. And by dressing her legs in seamed stockings and putting them in medium- or high-heeled shoes, I would betray everything—her legs, my vocation, future generations, and God too, if God exists. So let them remain as they are, in felt slippers against a jasmine-green background. For the benefit of future generations, and to avoid any misunderstanding, the slippers were pale brown, with a darker, dark-brownish checkered pattern. Fejga's mother had recently bought them at the Karczew market. The stall owner was named Fogelman. Motek Fogelman.

—Fejga—says Sara Fliegeltaub, striding into Icyk's room and peering a trifle suspiciously at Fejga, or rather at the pair of long legs teetering on tiptoe. Fejga. How many times must I tell you? The potatoes. Do you want my dear guests to go without lunch today?

—Just finished—says Fejga, descending from the stool onto the sill, thence to the floor. In the process, the hem of her skirt catches against the sill. Were it not for the presence of Sara Fliegeltaub, who has me under observation, I could now survey her legs, Fejga's of course, not Sara's, from yet another perspective and—how shall I put it?—in a different light, the light of the whole. But nothing comes of it. Fejga pulls down her skirt and marches out of Icyk's room with the stool, the rag, and the broom. In passing, she smiles a strange sort of smile, but as her back is turned, I can't see it, Icyk can't see it, we don't see it. This is purely my conjecture. Another hypothesis is that she smiles at the thought of her legs being painted and immortalized. A third option is that she smiles because she cannot fully grasp the meaning of "painting" and "immortalizing." I assume that Fejga was illiterate, and even if she knew how to read, she was unlikely to have applied this skill to the perusal of books. She did, however, go to the Miramare and Oasis cinemas, so "to paint" and "to immortalize" might suggest to her the image of long slender legs on the screen of the Miramare. That is the association she would make, her own ravishing legs on the screen of the Miramare or the Oasis cinema. On high or medium heels. Marlene Dietrich in black stockings. Greta Garbo in a silver fur coat. But I prefer her in her brown felt slippers. That era had its great stars and prima donnas. For me, Fejga in her felt slippers was the greatest. Wherever she is now, I think she will be pleased to have been thus immortalized: Greta's silver fur, Marlene's black stockings, a pair of felt slippers from the Karczew market.

—Dear Mr. Icyk—says Sara Fliegeltaub—it is no business of mine. My dear guests may, of course, flirt with the servants if they so choose. But please be circumspect. As you know, my boardinghouse enjoys an excellent reputation in Warsaw.

—Fejga—says Icyk, sitting bolt upright, as it is hardly proper for him to lounge in bed in Pani Sara's presence. Fejga is such a pretty creature, Pani Sara, that I can make no promises. If you don't want me to flirt with her, you had better hire some frump in her place whom I'll be sure to kick out before she spoils my humor with her ugliness.

—I know she is a gem—says Sara Fliegeltaub. And I enjoy having such a charming creature to help me in the kitchen. Old women tend to dislike beautiful young women. But I find it actually cheers me up. If such pretty young things come into the world, it means that Someone up there wants them to be. Someone had the notion. It is a kind of proof. If you'd like, I'll tell you a story about pretty young things. But you're probably going for a walk with Miss Chaja.

—Not at all—says Icyk. I'd love to hear. Just let me put my smoking jacket on, I feel awkward talking to you in my pajamas.

—I went to Warsaw with Fejga—says Sara Fliegeltaub, planting herself on the chair by the window, the one I sit on when typing. In writing, I am anxious to be concise, accurate, and faithful to the truth I venture to call the truth of existence, the truth of our existence here in Otwock in the Warsaw region. To be exact, as the chair is by the window, instead of Fejga Rozenblat's felt slippers I now behold the somewhat disheveled hair of Sara Fliegeltaub against the jasmine-green background. The thought crosses my mind that the straggly yellow-and-black hair, through which yellow-and-pink patches of scalp are clearly visible, should also be painted and immortalized. For it is not true that some things are more worthy of immortality than others, or that certain objects are more beautiful and others more ugly. Fejga's legs and Sara's hair are a good case in point. Through the improbable and unprecedented fact of creation, all existence is beautiful and deserves to be perpetuated. It cries out for immortality. That craving is the only truth of our existence here on earth, the only thing on earth worth reckoning with, and the only commandment the would-be writer or *sofer* should obey.

—We were talking about pretty young things—says Sara Fliegeltaub. Well, it was about a year ago, sometime in the spring of last year, Fejga and I traveled to Warsaw together. I had a heavy package with me and needed her help. It must have been June, as it ties in with what happened at Corpus Christi. It all started with the altar in Warszawska Street. Now that was a most unpleasant incident.

—In Warsaw—says Icyk—it all seems to have started with the Polish Telegraph Agency communiqué about three communist Jews who snatched the icon of the Virgin Mary from a woman in Bielańska Street and trampled on it. The next day PAT withdrew the report, so it must have been some National Radical affair. Though who knows. That's the sort of thing communists would do. They have the weirdest ideas. It could be in their interests to provoke anti-Semitic disturbances.

—In Otwock—says Sara Fliegeltaub—it all started when a lunatic on the run from Zofiówka set fire to the altar on Warszawska Street. But I wouldn't be surprised if they did it themselves so as to incriminate us. That's when it all began in earnest, and the men with the Chrobry Swords came down from Warsaw and started smashing windows and throwing people out of trains. That's when Fejga and I took the train to Warsaw. Though perhaps we went earlier. I have a vague feeling the defenestrations took place in April and May. Once my brother-in-law ran the full length of the train to escape from them. Luckily it was just before Michalin, so he jumped out at Michalin and walked the rest of the way to Józefów.

—You should never have taken the train—says Icyk. Why on earth did you?

—I'm telling you, sir—says Sara Fliegeltaub. I had a heavy package. You can't tell people not to take the train, it's not right. The train is for everyone, that's what I think. Well then, we'd just passed Miedzeszyn when four hooligans entered our compartment. I call them hooligans because of how they behaved. They were students. Three of them had Bordeaux caps—you know the type—with embroidery on the crowns. Well, and then it all started. First one thing, then another. "It stinks of herring in here. I'd ban those herring-mongers from using our Polish railways." "Do we have to inhale that Jewish stench. We could do with someone like Hitler to sweep out the Jewish garbage." Oh, and various other obscenities which I would spare you, sir, though as a writer you ought to know. "Little Jewesses have it letter-slot style, why don't we check." That's what the bareheaded one said. And one of the students said, "I find them repulsive. I'd be nauseated to have a little Jewess." Fejga is young still, so there was no harm in their calling her a little Jewess. But imagine saying that about a mature lady. I mean, it wasn't polite.

—They say the same about me—says Icyk. They call me that little Jew boy. Sometimes highly cultured people, even my friends. That little Jew boy thinks. That little Jew boy wrote. That's the way those Polacks are.

But Icyk could hardly have said "Polack" in a conversation with Sara Fliegeltaub in 1937, as the word wasn't used in those days. —I'm sure I can't have used that word at the time—Icyk said to Hania in New York in 1977 when he told her of Pani Sara's adventure in the yellow-and-blue train. Not that I felt it to be inappropriate, for then as now there were plenty of Polacks among the Poles. I simply didn't know the word. I was more likely to have heard the Russian version: Paliachok, Poliachyshka.

—One often hears that word in Warsaw today—said Hania. The Poles refer to the Poles as "those Polacks."

—An ugly word—said Icyk. Now that they have no more Jews they abuse themselves instead.

—At the time I was afraid they'd throw us out of the train—says Pani Sara—so I was counting the stations. Michalin, Józefów, then Świder, where we could get out. I think it was just before Józefów that two of them sat down close to Fejga, and even though the one by the door had such an aversion for Jewesses, I was afraid something might happen. I don't know what I'd have done then. I'd probably have pushed Fejga out and leaped onto the track after her. But to open those automatic doors when the train's moving you need a strong man. So I don't know how it would all have ended. After Józefów the one by the door, who was more sensible, though he was still a hooligan for all that, said, "It doesn't make sense. If that tribe"—those were his very words: that tribe—"if that tribe crucified Jesus, then why does God allow them to beget such beautiful creatures?" He gave Fejga another look and added, "Such exquisite beauty." And the one sitting next to her said, "But as a punishment they have it letter-slot style." Then Fejga burst out sobbing, but that's the wrong word, she wasn't just having a good cry, she was bawling, howling. My Fejga, as you know, is not clever. She is pretty, but she is not clever. I mean, she's as thick as two little blocks. But stupid as she is, when those hooligans started blaspheming, she realized they were no longer insulting her personally, but someone else. I think that's why she burst into tears. They must have realized that too, you know. They looked ashamed and slipped off to another compartment. One of them turned back in the doorway and said, "Stupid Jewish cow," to Fejga, as though she had offended him by howling like that. As a result, we weren't pushed out of the train.

—As a result of what?—asks Icyk.

—I don't know—says Sara Fliegeltaub. Her terrible caterwauling, I expect. Or thanks to God. But I must go. She is so stupid she doesn't even know how many potatoes to peel for lunch. You are a serious gentleman, so may I appeal to you not to demoralize the servants. I ought not to tell you, but yesterday she said to Luba . . . oh, but I really can't repeat it.

—Said what?—Icyk insists. What did she say?

—She said you were in love with her.

And Pani Sara stalks out to check how many potatoes Fejga has peeled while sitting on the steps of the side entrance, a blue enameled saucepan at her feet. In pulling on his socks, for it is time to take a stroll, Icyk concludes that the sentence Fejga uttered yesterday over the blue enamel pot, blue outside, white in—namely, "Mr. Icyk is in love with me"—should be recognized as a quasi-truth or even an absolute truth, because he, Icyk, truly is in love with Fejga Rozenblat. It is not, I guess, the sort of love to which

Fejga privately aspires, yet for lack of an appropriate and accurate word to define what I feel when I think of Fejga, she, Fejga, and I, Icyk, are entitled to say we are dealing with love: "Mr. Icyk is in love with me" and "I love thee, Fejga Rozenblat." Because I, Icyk, am undoubtedly in love with Fejga Rozenblat, and with Mrs. Sara Fliegeltaub and Chaja Gelechter (in every conceivable meaning of the word with Chaja), likewise with Jakub Wurzel and lame Szlojmele. Each individual existence, and every desire contained therein, craves our love, which should therefore be fully bestowed. But—Icyk pursues his train of thought while fixing his suspenders—I am being carried away. The love I have for every single existence and the pity I feel for every desire, my love and my pity that would willingly immortalize every existence and every desire, will presently include the hooligan on the yellow-and-blue train who called Fejga a stupid Jewish cow. That would be logical and consistent, but it would also be going too far. The hooligan on the train should be immortalized for sure, but not with a view to giving him pleasure. Fejga is another matter. For all her stupidity, she deserves every imaginable pleasure, so I shall probably tell her, or at least give her to understand, that I am in love with her. That will undoubtedly please her very much. As she doesn't understand what it is all about, she is unlikely to find the immortalizing process a pleasant one. Though who knows. Fifty years from now, she may be quite pleased when someone tells her I have immortalized her. By then she'll be—how old is she now? eighteen, I guess—by then she'll be sixty-eight.

It may give her pleasure then. After all, the reason I have written all this is to give you pleasure, Fejga Rozenblat.

A BLUE envelope, the type favored by state institutions, inscribed: "Warsaw Ghetto Umschlagplatz," with the catalogue notation: "Inw. 1426." It contains a photograph. The staff of the archives of the Jewish Historical Institute told me it is the only photograph of Umschlagplatz in their collections. I've already mentioned seeing a photo of Jews being loaded into freight cars. In albums published both in Poland and in Israel I later found several more photos of a loading platform, freight cars, Jews with bundles. The photo in the blue envelope, however, presents a fragment of the actual Umschlagplatz. Yet I cannot be sure. The photograph has not been described, and can be identified only by the caption on the rather new-looking envelope. Someone quite recently decided that it was a photograph of Umschlagplatz. For all I know, he made a mistake, and it may represent another part of the Warsaw ghetto. It may have been taken during the great selection that was started on September 6, 1942, in the area between Gęsia Street, Zamenhof Street, Lubecki Street, and Stawki Street (according to Marek Edelman in *The Ghetto Fights*, because here too opinions diverge).

The photograph shows a wall to the right, and people with bundles by the wall who are either standing or walking, more likely walking. To the left is a house with ground-floor windows, something resembling shutters, and people outside. If these are shutters, this is not a photo of Umschlagplatz, for there is no evidence that the hospital or the Old Archives building had shutters. The ten or so figures outside the house are clearly Jewish policemen with armbands; their caps are a different shape from those of the Germans and the dark blue policemen. A friend who was in the ghetto told me the Jewish policemen wore two bands on the same arm, one with the Star of David, which I remember from wartime Warsaw, and a police one. But I have never read this in any of the printed sources, and the people in the photo have only one band apiece, so I don't know where the truth lies.

There is a roadway paved with cobblestones between the wall and the house, but no sidewalk. There is a gas lamp in the background where the wall joins the house (but this depends on the angle of the camera; the wall was certainly parallel to the house). In the middle of the roadway, also parallel to the wall and the house with the shutters, there is a gutter with something flowing along it. A man stands above the gutter with his legs apart, though perhaps he is striding across the gutter. He may be identified as a Jewish or a dark blue policeman. As he faces the photographer, we see his cap frontways, so we can't tell if it is a Polish or a Jewish cap.

Pan Michał, who escaped from the ghetto after the second extermination in January 1943, explained: "Depending on their rank they had from one to five studs on their caps. One with a lot of studs put me in touch with a very elegant SS officer, who led my parents out of the ghetto. It cost us a small fortune. He was wearing—the SS man, I mean—glossy white gloves." But the photographer was too far away, and even if the man straddling the gutter had a studded cap, we can't tell from the photo. Nor can we see the arm that ought to be wearing an armband. Nor does the uniform, if it is a uniform, enable us to identify him. Breeches and high boots.

The photo is slightly blurred, so we can't tell if it is the uniform of a dark blue policeman. The Jewish police wore no uniforms; their only distinguishing feature was a cap and armband. Yet they had their own fashion or style, by which I mean the light-colored coats and high boots they are usually wearing in photos. Although the man above the gutter has no coat, I am almost sure he is a Jewish policeman. I remember the dark blue policemen quite well, conversing with the janitor outside the entrance to our house on Koszykowa Street. One once entered our apartment—I don't know why—and stood a while in the corridor, so I think I'd recognize a dark blue policeman even now. The instinct of a seven-year-old, something programmed in my consciousness, would tell me if the man astride the gutter was a dark blue policeman. I must therefore conclude he is a Jew.

Just one clue, which may yield nothing: the man is stout, fat even. Strongly built, a hefty fellow. If the photo was taken on Umschlagplatz, it may be Szmerling, a hunch further borne out by the place where he is standing. Perhaps it was pure coincidence that someone who chanced to be in the middle of the roadway happened to have his photograph taken. But the place where people invariably saw Szmerling sitting or standing was in the middle of the roadway, between a house and a wall. Does the photograph represent a fragment of Umschlagplatz or doesn't it? This presents a major problem, especially if this is the only photo ever taken there, or the only extant photo; there again I am not sure. But another question looms even larger when I look at the fat man arrested above the gutter by the camera lens: is it Szmerling or isn't it? And if it is Szmerling, what are we to infer from that photo?

I know almost nothing about Szmerling. Emanuel Ringelblum notes that the Germans called the commander of Umschlagplatz "the Jewish executioner." "On account of his resemblance to the Italian marshal" the Jews nicknamed him Balbo, which no one now associates with the marshal. If anything, Balbo conjures up some monster from legend or fairy tale. Ringelblum adds that Szmerling was "a criminal ogre" and "an ogre with a pointed beard and the face of a brigand." In his *Recollections of the Warsaw Ghetto*, Henryk Makower also mentions Szmerling's beard: "His brazen face with its well-groomed beard, his elongated, slightly hunched figure, drove me to a state of fury." There is no pointed, well-groomed beard to be seen in the putative photo of Umschlagplatz. Which does not mean the man astride the gutter is not Szmerling. The photo is blurred, the beard might have smudged on the plate.

Another portrait of Szmerling is to be found in *Martyrology and Extermination of the Warsaw Jews*, in which Henryk Rudnicki describes him as "a very handsome sadist." If we place the hulking brigand next to Lejkin, who became commander of the Jewish police after Szeryński's arrest, we have a criminal version of Laurel and Hardy. To quote from Ringelblum's *Notes from the Ghetto*, Lejkin was "a small man with a small body and small head." Henryk Makower describes him as follows: "Small, almost dwarfish, but sturdy, strong, a man with an iron hand. Everyone trembles in his presence. For the slightest misdemeanor he thrashes one's face with a riding crop. . . . The Germans liked Lejkin; they even included his photograph in *Der Völkischer Beobachter* with the flattering caption *Der kleine jüdische General.* That sounds a bit farfetched, but if it is true, it would be worthwhile locating that photo, for we know as much about the little Jewish general as we do about Szmerling—that is, next to nothing. Our knowledge about the illustrious bandits of the Warsaw ghetto —Lejkin, Szeryński, Szmerling, and Gancwajch—is best summarized in the epithets: criminal ogre, handsome sadist, face of a bandit, iron hand. One could see at a glance they were sadists, bandits, criminals, murderers. But did these criminals and murderers look the same as all other criminals and murderers? I want to know more.

"Szeryński," Pan Michał said, "was of middling height. I spoke to him several times, so I remember him quite well. The last time I saw him was after the assassination attempt; he had a head wound—or was it his hand?—and he went around with a bodyguard. When he passed me on the street he pointed to the man walking behind him and said, 'That is my *tyelochranitiel.*' "

"It's his face that interests me," I say. "Do you recall his face?"

"He was of middling height," Pan Michał said. "He dressed well. Unfortunately I don't recall his face."

Why am I suddenly so interested in the physiognomy of murderers? It was only after I'd started writing this book that I suddenly needed to know all about their faces, uniforms, and distinctions, the thickness of their fingers, the slant of their eyes, and the shape of their chins. Initially I couldn't grasp the reason for this bizarre curiosity of mine. The murderers of the Warsaw ghetto—the German nationals at least—are to be seen in numerous photos from that period, so curiosity can easily be satisfied. But they are mostly anonymous, and I am interested in criminals I know by name and can connect with a specific deed or action. The relation between body and behavior. So I cared little about the looks of some German soldier or military policeman who happened to be drafted with his unit to the ghetto; I was intrigued by Brandt, Mende, Hoefle, and Globocnik, also Szeryński, Szmerling, and Lejkin. My interest in the last two developed later; as I couldn't see Brandt, I guess I substituted Szmerling in the hope of tracking him down more easily. Before I asked Pan Michał about Szeryński and Szmerling, we discussed Karl Brandt. A couple of times. Since our first conversation left me none the wiser, I rather rudely decided to corner Pan Michał in the hope that he would remember better under the pressure of a second round.

"Forgive me"—this was during my first conversation with Pan Michał—"I really remember nothing. Even though Brandt was standing right next to me, even closer than you are now, almost touching me. I was typing out the names of bakers who'd been allocated numbers. Do you know what those numbers were? To receive a number during the September selection meant a short period of respite. I asked the bakers if I could add my father's name to the list, and they agreed. As I typed away I could think of only one thing, how to save both my parents, so I added my mother's name to the list, and this led to a god-awful row. The bakers ranted and raved, and said it was a rotten trick. They were obviously right, as there was a fixed quota and someone else had to be dropped from the list. Just then Brandt arrived on the scene. Doubtless he was waiting for the list of bakers, though I can't imagine why. He marched up to me and snatched it from my hands. He may even have torn it out of the typewriter, though I won't swear to it. Now, I know you won't believe me, but I have absolutely no recollection of what he looked like."

"Too bad," I said, "but I understand. At such close range you probably had a fifty-fifty chance of surviving."

"You don't understand a thing," said Pan Michał. "That's not the point. I wasn't interested in Brandt; he left me stone-cold. I was thinking only of how to save my parents. That's why I don't recall him."

"Now, I wouldn't like to press you"—this was during my second conversation with Pan Michał—"but some hidden imperative tells me I must see him with my own eyes. Perhaps a sudden flashback . . ."

"The episode with the bakers," Pan Michał then said, "took place in a large room, but I can't even tell you if it was a covered market or a factory. Anyway, it was on

Zamenhof Street, more or less where the Monument now stands, a stone's throw from what was then the headquarters of the Commune. It was on September 6 or 7, during the last selection, when the Germans ordered all survivors to report between Lubecki Street and Zamenhof Street."

"All the Germans from the Vernichtungskommando and from Department IV-B-4 must have been there too," I said.

"They were exceptionally cultured," said Pan Michał. "Boots polished to a shine, white gloves. They behaved like aristocrats who find it distasteful to consort with a lot of louse-ridden beggars."

"In my notes I have a sentence from Abraham Lewin's diary," I said. "Listen now. A young officer is beating Jews on the street—I don't know what with, a stick or a hunting crop. He shouts, 'I've lost three years of my life on account of you cursed and scabby Jews. Three years you've been plaguing us, you curs.' He obviously shouted in German, so I asked a competent linguist to translate it for me. In German it reads as follows: *Euretwegen, ihr verdammten räudigen Juden, hab ich drei Jahre meines lebens verloren, schon drei Jahre lang quält ihr uns, ihr Hunde.* A young officer. But it surely couldn't have been Brandt. Was Brandt young?

"I don't know," said Pan Michał. "They were very elegant, refined gentlemen—I mean the officers, not the low-grade military police."

"How about white gloves?" I asked. "Did Brandt also wear white gloves?"

Something about Brandt bothers me. I wish I knew the reason for my obsession with Brandt, Hoefle, and Mende. I am not attempting to create a portrait of Karl Brandt, so it is not for literary reasons. I abhor the man, but if I perpetuated him in literature I'd probably abhor myself. I am not interested for documentary purposes, as I have not been assigned by a commission for the prosecution of war criminals to collect or collate evidence which, now that he is almost certainly dead, would be neither here nor there. I do not even expect to decipher their motivation from the description of their physiognomies. A murderer's face as a rule tells us next to nothing about his inner self. The motives of Brandt & Co. are public knowledge, as the two great bandits of our century, Hitler and Stalin, both spelled out their criminal ideas in book form. I see no point in muddling the motivation issue by quoting Naphta from *The Magic Mountain*; this is the specialty of liberal intellectuals, more especially those who've not experienced the effects of criminal ideology on their own hides. The truth is much simpler: the motives of criminals are on the level of criminals.

Then why am I so eager to know all about Brandt, about his eyes, mouth, hair, fingers, his uniform too (the Germans punched their caps into a variety of shapes)? I shall hazard a guess. Brandt or Mende may arguably personify or embody the monstrous evil that appeared among mankind in the first half of our century. I don't know if monstrous is the right word, but I can think of no other. When I try to visualize it, I see a kind of plasma surging and swamping, swallowing and engulfing. The plasma is spiritual, of course, not corporeal. It permeated minds, manipulated them and caused their secret mutation, ingesting and mangling what had once been compassion, mercy, and love. It was clearly enunciated in the books of the great twentieth-century bandits, but it also had its human embodiment, if human is not a misnomer. That, I guess, is why I want to know more about Untersturmführer Karl Georg Brandt, head of Department IV-B-4 (Jewish Affairs) in the office of the commander of the Sicherheitspolizei and SD of the Warsaw District: the human incarnation of our century's spiritual plasma.

That plasma was staggeringly new. Those who came across it in 1942 or 1943 were probably too bewildered to understand the new phenomenon. Even if they had some inkling, they lacked the words to describe it, so they resorted to the terminology that had served to describe scoundrels, bandits, and criminals for centuries past. Szmerling is a case in point. "The face of a brigand," "a criminal ogre," "a very handsome sadist." These banal epithets only prove my point that contemporary eyewitnesses lacked an appropriate vocabulary to define the novelty. One might also speculate that when confronted with a mind-boggling and totally unprecedented case, an eyewitness may simply reject it, and in so doing hark back to the old linguistic stereotypes and classify it among the easily digestible notions of their empirical past.

Historical sources usually describe Brandt in much the same terms as Szmerling, thereby transforming the Untersturmführer into a conventional bandit or criminal. Noemi Szac-Wajnkrank (*Gone with the Fire*, Warsaw, 1947) saw him drive up in his car to the column in which she was walking to Umschlagplatz: "His bulging eyes flashed like lightning." In Władysław Szlengel's reportage entitled *What I Read to the Dead,*" Brandt is "blue in the face and fuming." Henryk Nowogródzki chanced to meet Brandt during the great extermination near the building at 19 Zamenhof Street, where the Commune was situated: "His face contorted into a sadistic smile," "liverish pouches under evil eyes," "a vein popping on his temple." Henryk Makower probably gives a more faithful and more realistic picture of the SS men in succinct portraits no more than a sentence long. Brandt: "a stout man with a butcher's face." Mende: "a nice-looking man with a mild face." And again Brandt: "Brandt's bloated, churlish snout, piercing passersby with his small gimlet eyes." But even Makower shows the Untersturmführer "toying with his riding crop" as he oversees an operation or selection. In other words, he behaves just the way we would expect a cynical murderer to behave. The validity of this evidence is, in any case, undermined: did Brandt have small gimlet eyes or big bulging ones?

So Brandt is blue with rage and smiling sadistically. Thus he is not there at all; he has been conventionalized. It may also be that the evil that arose in the first half of our century induced no external bodily changes. Man's inner mind was changed, but this was not reflected in his outer appearance. Brandt, then, was transformed internally (the plasma) without showing any outward and visible sign of the process. Perfectly ordinary, respectable people can also have bulging eyes and liverish pouches under the eyes.

When he wrote "A Moral Treatise" in 1947, Czesław Miłosz offered a different view—namely, that the "impact of avalanches" on ethical systems brings about changes in man's exterior looks: "The shape of their eyelid differs from the ordinary man's." He also mentions the "dull insect glint" in the eyes of the Gestapo. A perceptive remark, for those who embodied plasma were probably most easily recognized by their eyes, at least during the last war. Things have changed since then. In Adina Blady Szwajger's *Short History of the Berson and Bauman Hospital* we read: "A Gestapo officer walked in, he was straight out of a picture book. There were some really handsome men among them, but their eyes were lumps of ice." The officer with eyes of ice then pointed a pistol at Szwajger's head and said that "he didn't really want to, but *Befehl ist Befehl.*" He was only joking, and the shot was not fired.

I agree with Miłosz that plasma is, or may be, recognizable from its visible form. Perhaps it is all rather irrelevant who ultimately has what sort of face. Yet the question formulated thirty years ago by Miłosz—"How does one recognize them?"—has lost none of its cogency today. Our loathsome century is not yet over; the plasma continues to swamp and engulf us and shows no signs of abating. It is useful to know if one is dealing with a normal man or an embodiment of plasma. Detection is not easy, as the issue is often blurred and confused. Like the face of the man astride the gutter in the middle of the road in the photograph that may or may not represent a fragment of Umschlagplatz.

Jarosław M. Rymkiewicz

ON the basis of what I was told at the archives of the Jewish Historical Institute, I wrote that Calel Perechodnik's diary is probably the only eyewitness account of events in the Otwock ghetto. But I was wrong. I ought to have said that Perechodnik was arguably the only chronicler of the Otwock ghetto. But someone told me of another account written by an observer from the other side of the barbed wire (published in *Twórczość*, No. 1, January 1947), the well-known theatrical director Edmund Wierciński, who was living in Otwock in 1942 and presumably drafted his story in the same year under the title "Acacia Branches."

I have read numerous accounts of the history of Jews during the last war and I consider Wierciński's to be one of the most noteworthy, perhaps less for its actual contents than for its tone. In my opinion, Wierciński writes about the Jews in precisely the way a mere onlooker should, and that is the way the Poles should approach the subject. The style is sober and factual. Wierciński voices his pain and anger at his fellow countrymen who profited from the tragedy of the Jews, and here again his tone is appropriately unhistrionic. I assume that in fifty or a hundred years, when his theatrical work is all but forgotten, Wierciński will be remembered as the author of these pages. Yet "Acacia Branches" has been tucked away among old issues of *Twórczość* for the past forty years, during which time not many people can have read it. Wierciński's name does not even appear in the index of the famous book by Władysław Bartoszewski and Zofia Lewinówna, *This Man, My Compatriot.* To my mind, a document of such weight should at least be listed, if only to help us discover whether our attitudes have changed at all in forty years. The fact that it is not mentioned must surely mean something. Perhaps we genuinely don't want to remember—I don't mean what happened to our Jews, but what happened to us as onlookers. Perhaps it is ourselves we would rather forget about.

Wierciński's text sheds light on the question of the two ghettos in Otwock. "The Jews were driven out of the sanatoria and herded into the real ghetto." So there was a "real" ghetto (elsewhere he refers to "ghetto boundaries demarcated by barbed wire"), and there was the zone of the Jewish sanatoria, which in Wierciński's perception did not belong to the ghetto. That zone was not fenced off, or only partially so: "I unexpectedly found myself among attractive houses on undulating, woody ground. I was surprised to discover such a corner in this ugly small town." It would appear that until the day of the extermination both the Jews living in the sanatoria and those confined to the ghetto proper could move about fairly freely. The ghetto was wired in and closed, but crossing over to the other side of the wires does not seem to have involved any major risk.

The extermination, as we know, began on August 19. Calel Perechodnik saw the first car with Ukrainians by the Karczew barrier at 7 a.m. The chambermaid who brought

Wierciński his breakfast informed him that the Germans had entered the ghetto during the night: "At three o'clock the Gestapo began to evacuate the ghetto." "Acacia Branches" enables us to reconstruct the main events with a reasonable degree of precision. It was an exceptionally torrid day: "A cloudless sky, sun, the branches of the trees do not stir. A stifling, torrid day arose." Elsewhere: "The heat increased by the hour. The air was sultry, the sun crept lazily across the sky, languid, sweaty, and pale from its own heat." When Wierciński went to the station at two o'clock, the evacuation of the ghetto was still underway. Shots could be heard, and columns of Jews were tramping toward the Otwock Umschlagplatz. The train, fifty cars in all, was not yet ready. From the window of the blue-and-yellow train Wierciński sighted just one car sprinkled with lime as it stood on a side track. The roundup must have been over by then, for individual Jews were being escorted to the square in the vicinity of the station. In all likelihood they had been captured in the evacuated zones of the ghetto.

Wierciński describes the Otwock Umschlagplatz as seen from the window of the blue-and-yellow train: "A small square some two hundred meters from the station was filled with a crowd of Jews. They were sitting on the ground in a close quadrangle of equally drawn-up lines. They watched the train pass without stirring and in total silence. A little girl standing in front looked quite unconcerned; she held her hand out to her mother, who was sitting stock-still on the ground. In her other hand she had a doll. The sun radiated dense heat straight above the heads of the crowd. There was not a single tree in the entire square to provide the desired shade. . . . Nearer the track, in the shade of some pine trees, soldiers were sitting at their ease around a mahogany table. They gesticulated in a lively manner, laughed out loud, wiped the sweat from their red, sunburned faces, and quenched their thirst with frothing beer. Bottles littered the table and the withered grass around it."

The loading lasted through the afternoon and ended late in the evening. Wierciński returned to Otwock around seven. By then a train with fifty-two cars was waiting between the railroad station and Umschlagplatz. Two, the first and last, were passenger cars. The remainder, freight cars, were numbered with chalk from one to fifty. "Half the freight cars were still empty." Every now and again the engine shifted and the train moved a few meters. That meant another freight car had been loaded and the loading of the next was about to begin. Late in the evening, probably after the loading was completed, bonfires were lit around the train and sentries were posted. The loading took place in total silence, but when dusk fell, the people in the freight cars first began to whisper and then to shout for water. The sentries and bonfires were there to prevent water from being handed through the barbed-wire windows of the train. The train set off by night. Wierciński does not give the time. He simply writes that he went out into the garden, where he sat on a bench—moonlight, chirping crickets, and fragrant acacia—and heard the whistle of the locomotive and the rumble of freight cars trundling off into the distance.

"Acacia Branches" further relates what went on in Otwock over the next few days. Jews who had gone into hiding were rounded up, executions took place in the ghetto, the victims were buried. The ghetto was guarded by Jewish policemen, though not very efficiently, so this did not prevent the local Poles from looting what their Jewish neighbors had left behind. "People were dashing about with a furtive air. They lugged huge bundles on their backs. They were bent double beneath the burden of pillows, counterpanes, mattresses, and clothes wrapped up in sheets or colorful tablecloths. They carried all kinds of objects with them—lamps, crystal vases, plaster figurines, children's toys, old tattered suitcases and elegant leather ones. Streaming with sweat, their eyes darting nervously about, they looked like overladen ants salvaging the treasures of their devastated anthill." Wierciński has described several such scenes. He also chatted with the looters. When asked about the reason for this behavior, they said, "It's not really stealing." "It would be a shame if things were wasted." "It's all ours anyway. They exploited us." Someone did, however, say, "It's plain robbery." And another: "They have no shame."

But there is something more important than the scenes of looting by neighbors as the Jews traveled to their death, something that deserves to be indelibly engraved in our memories. Wierciński relates an incident in Otwock on the day of the extermination. The blue-and-yellow train which he had boarded passed the Otwock Umschlagplatz, the Jews squatting in rows and the Germans drinking beer at the mahogany table. It then crossed the bridge over the small river known as the Świder. It was, I remind you, a torrid day. "A few minutes later we were crossing the bridge over the river. Hundreds of women, men, and children were paddling in the shallow water in their colorful bathing suits and lounging on the beaches or in the shadow of the riverside trees. Groups of slender, pleasantly suntanned boys and girls stood around the ice-cream kiosks and the kvass stands. Though the passengers were exhausted by the stifling air even though the windows were open, their faces slowly began to look more cheerful. Someone cracked a joke; tentative laughter was heard." It might just be worth invoking an analogous scene, the traffic circle in Krasiński Square in April 1943, immortalized by Czesław Miłosz in his poem "Campo dei Fiori." Many people remember the traffic circle. It was a stone's throw from the ghetto wall. It was also photographed, though not when it was in operation. The beach on the Świder is less well known. But it also deserves to be remembered.

"Acacia Branches" also supplies some hard facts regarding the head of the Otwock Gestapo, who was named Schlicht and in Wierciński's story figures as Mr. S.: "Those who had been hiding in the neighborhood were also caught. The head of the local Gestapo, Mr. S., personally headed a column of captured runaways." Wierciński gives us a fairly concise description of Schlicht. Because of his much lower rank, this Otwock official can't really be compared with Brandt or Hoefle. By a sheer fluke, a fluke answering to the name of Wierciński, we know far more about him than about the other two. For this reason memory cannot be used as a method or tool for meting out justice: memory is not impartial. We knock at one door, another door opens. But it's good that something opens at least.

Wierciński described Schlicht as "a small figure in a greenish uniform"; he reminded Wierciński of a spider. An ash-gray face and yellowish teeth. "He was an inconspicuous man, slim and of low stature. He wore a black-rimmed cap, a greenish uniform with black SS tabs. He sported high black boots on his crooked legs and clenched a stout riding crop in his fist, which was covered with gingery fuzz." Schlicht rode around Otwock in a cart fitted with rubber tires. The cart, with a driver in mufti, was harnessed to a pair of white horses. Wierciński enables us to pin down the places most frequented by Schlicht. Schlicht's Otwock haunts are the railroad station, where he stands behind the ticket collector scrutinizing newcomers; the restaurant near the bazaar, where he stands on the steps inviting someone in; and the garden of a modern, yellow-and-cream-colored house. The best shot is of Schlicht in the garden feeding cabbage leaves to the white rabbits in the hutches. Before joining the SS, Schlicht was apparently a tailor in a small provincial town near Berlin, though we cannot be one hundred percent sure, as Wierciński may just have been repeating gossip overheard in Otwock.

The Final Station: Umschlagplatz

"OH, let's stop here," I say, and Hania turns into the rest area and parks her red Renault outside a modern thirties-style house. Two-storied and coated with yellow plaster, it is separated from the street by some fencing and a hedge. The acacia hedge looks as though it has recently been pruned back to the height of the fence. There is no one to be seen in the neat front garden. Only he is present; I can see him standing by the acacia hedge on a stool or ladder in his yellow-and-brown shirt. He has hitched up his sleeves and loosened the knot of his black tie. Brandishing his pruning shears, he trims the hedge. "I think that's his place."

"Whose place?" asks Hania.

"His place," I say, "a modern, two-story house with acacia bushes. Wierciński saw him standing in the window of a house just like that one. Somewhere near here there should be a statue of the Virgin Mary with the words 'Crown of the Sinful, Defense of the Sorrowful.' I'll go in and ask."

"Are you out of your mind?" says Hania. "You mean you'll ask them if Gestapo officer Schlicht lived here, or if they remember Gestapo officer Schlicht? They'll throw you out. Anyway, that acacia is barely ten or twelve years old. And the plaster is new too; it was applied two or three years ago. And even if he did live here, so what? Does it matter where he lived? In a house from which the Poles had been kicked out."

"But don't drive away yet," I say. "If I went in, I could imagine him walking down the stairs or sitting in the kitchen drinking tea. With his elbows on a blue-checkered oilcloth. When we arrived in Łódź in 1945 we moved into a house where the Łódź Gestapo had been living. There was also an oilcloth on the table in the kitchen. Blue checks and blue flowers."

"I can't figure you out," says Hania. "What are you driving at? What do you stand to gain by tracking down Schlicht?"

"I can't figure it myself," I say. "It's a kind of inner moral imperative, though its sense is not clear to me. Certain places I have to see and describe so my readers can see them too. But why they should be seen and described I really don't know. What earthly good will it do my readers to visualize the house where Gestapo officer Schlicht lived? I haven't the foggiest idea. This moral urge of mine tells me to look at places that are highly unpleasant, defiled or desecrated even. But I don't know why, so please don't ask, why I'm not interested in describing the site of Anielewicz's bunker on Miła Street or the sewage manhole where Marek Edelman and his colleagues from the Jewish Fighters Organization escaped from the ghetto in May 1943—I think it was at the corner of Twarda Street and Prosta Street. From a historian's angle it would be useful to describe those places as they were then and as they are now, almost half a century later. I'm less motivated by places where vaguely heroic deeds took place. Of course,

I'm still interested, but I'm happy to let someone else do the work for me.

"There is something exceedingly unpleasant and humiliating both about the places and about the sense of obligation that compels me to describe, concretize, and show to others the site near Otwock Station where freight cars sprinkled with lime were waiting, the Otwock Umschlagplatz where they sat in rows, and the mahogany table at which the German soldiers swigged beer. Also the gap in the fence through which their Polish neighbors carried counterpanes, pillows, lamps, and sugar bowls away from the ghetto."

"Then tell me," says Hania, driving her red Renault out into the road. The yellow house and neatly trimmed hedge are behind us now, and we head for the station, for the mahogany table and the fifty freight cars sprinkled with lime. "Tell me, have you worked out some sort of hierarchy? Give me an honest answer. What do you think is more important, the bunker at 18 Miła Street or the siding on Stawki Street? How do you see it?"

"The siding," I say, "the siding is definitely more important. But why?"

"That's how I see it too," says Hania. "Because what happened in Anielewicz's bunker was nothing new: it had happened time and time again in the past. But what happened on the siding was quite unprecedented."

"The imperative," I say, "could be summed up as follows: we must erect monuments worthy of our epoch. The loading ramp and the track between Dzika Street and Stawki Street. The path taken by the looters laden with counterpanes and pillows. The field track where they waited under the supervision of the mounted policeman for the boy to bring ammunition. The beach on the Świder where people sunbathed and ate ice cream while their neighbors were being murdered a stone's throw away. Unique monuments."

"Is there anything else you want to see?" asks Hania. "Or would you like to return to Warsaw?"

"You can stop outside the station," I say. "I want to find the spot where the Christian boy in the white socks stood. The high platform where I stood half a century ago."

One last extract from Edmund Wierciński concerns the period after the extermination of the Otwock ghetto. "For the next few days children's hideouts were to be seen in the neighboring woods. Small pits, dug out in the warm sand and covered over with acacia branches. Some passersby threw food on top of the branches, and the pit dwellers crept out by night to the nearby wells." Wierciński then describes the pink notices that were posted in the streets of Otwock. Signed *Der Kreishauptmann in Warschau*, they declared that sheltering Jews was a punishable offense and said that the police or military police must be informed of the whereabouts of any escapees. Wierciński comments, or rather is left wondering: "Did anyone inform the police, the military police and the criminal police, that the children who had unlawfully left the Jewish residential district were to be found hiding in small pits covered over with acacia branches?"

The Final Station: Umschlagplatz

✤

"HERE," says Jacek, parking his yellow Fiat motorcycle-with-sidecar on Dzika Street, between the gas station and the two-story, blue corrugated-metal shopping pavilion where a kitchenware store (plates and detergent), a haberdasher, a newsdealer, a bakery called Camargo, and a large supermarket are all to be found. Access to the shops on the second floor is via some stairs attached to the outside, but I have never been there. From a distance the pavilion looks fairly respectable, but a closer view reveals the flaws common to all such edifices in my country: something peeling, cracking, chipping.

"Let's inspect it from the front first, along Stawki Street," I say. "Then we'll look for the site of the ramp and the freight cars."

We walk down Stawki Street, past the building which once housed the children's hospital and now accommodates several trade schools and the administrative offices of the Polish Motor Transport base. A handsome building, most likely dating from the late twenties or early thirties, it has two entrances. The main entrance appears to be on the side, where the names of the schools are to be found. The old main entrance consists of a brownish-red plank door with two oblong windows—one of the panes has been shattered—though the door is undoubtedly postwar.

"That," I say, "is the entrance where the Jewish policemen stood on guard lest the Umschlagplatz detainees slip across from the Old Archives to the hospital building. But where in your opinion did the Archives stand? Where was the iron gate leading out into Stawki Street? It should be adjacent to the hospital. So was it on the side of the gas station or on the side of the Polish Motor Transport base?"

The gable windows of the hospital, which overlook the whole of the site occupied by Polish Motor Transport, must have been there since the beginning. Farther along there is a plastered brick wall covered with whitewash, and a watchman's cabin.

"Do you mean the building where they were detained?" asks Jacek. "It must have been more or less where the gas station is. And the commemorative plaque. That wall was probably there too; it looks like an old wall to me. Take a good look. The plaster is postwar, but those are old bricks."

"A forty-year wall has the right to look a hundred," I say. "They might have built it when they set up the base."

"Do you think those trolley tracks are postwar too?" says Jacek. "There were no trolleys going down Stawki Street during the war; the tracks could be prewar, though."

"I have a map of the prewar trolley service at home," I say. "We can easily check. It's a very nice map from 1938, with red trolleys and blue buses. But I have a hunch that the wall separating Umschlagplatz from the ghetto used to run where those tracks are now. The wall went along Stawki Street, about as far as the junction of Dzika Street and Zamenhof Street, then around the corner and farther on northward along Dzika Street."

"In other words, the boundary went down the middle of the roadway," says Jacek. "And Umschlagplatz was outside the ghetto."

"That much could be inferred from the plan of the ghetto in Kermisz's book about the 1943 Uprising," I say. "The description is in Hebrew, but I met a delightful Hebrew scholar, who translated it for me. Though actually the plan is pretty clear, and when one compares it with plans of Warsaw, it's not difficult to visualize the layout. But if the wall was a bit farther along, Szmerling would have sat where the tracks are now."

Jacek and I are not making much headway, because all the time we're talking I keep wanting to cry, a bizarre feeling for a man of fifty, and all I want to do is sit down in the middle of the roadway and hide my face in my hands. On the spot where Szmerling sat. Pull yourself together, imbecile. You're the wrong side of fifty and you are here to testify and describe how things look now.

"Please let us in," says Jacek to a diminutive woman with gray hair and a pale face who is on duty in the watchman's cabin of the Polish Motor Transport base. "The tracks could still be here. You know," he explains to the woman, "the siding and ramp where the Jews were packed into freight cars. We'd like to see if there's anything left."

"If I let you gentlemen in," the gray-haired woman says, "I'll lose my bonus. Go ask the technical director in that hut over there. Turn left in the corridor."

The hut is between the cabin and the hospital building. But the technical director is not there, so we are unable to visit the site of the base to investigate the state of the rails.

"You know," I say to the gray-haired woman as we are leaving, "this is where Jews were deported."

"I know," says the woman. "I'd have lost my bonus. But I think it was over there, by the gas station, or where those houses are."

"Those huts," says Jacek, as we walk the length of the hospital building toward the gas station, "look as though they were used as warehouses at the time."

"The railroad siding can't have been more than a dozen or so tracks," I say, "with the same number of ramps or platforms. The Transferstelle bureau may have been where the base and those huts are now. Goods were loaded, uniforms for the Wehrmacht, whatever the ghetto produced."

"I'll take a photo of the gas station and that plaque," says Jacek. "I want you to be in it. I have a feeling that the courtyard where they were detained was here."

"A bit farther along, I think, behind the hospital," I say. "There are several entrances there. The nurse to whom Leokadia Schmidt handed over her child stood in one of them. Look, there are bars in the windows. She mentions those bars."

"The bars are definitely prewar," says Jacek. "They make different ones now."

Jacek stands in the road at the corner of Stawki Street and Dzika Street, and I stand with my back to the gas station. I remove my hat, because I feel awkward standing here with my hat on. But then it occurs to me that in deference to the Jews I ought perhaps to keep it on. We are in the greatest synagogue in the world. My next thought is that the synagogue of the Jews does not belong exclusively to them. It is the communal synagogue of Jews, Christians, everyone. The contract that was negotiated here in July 1942, and canceled the covenant of several thousand years ago, concerns every single one of us. It was contracted with all of us. The dome of the synagogue consists of gray clouds that trail from the City Center in the direction of Zoliborz.

"Let's go that way," says Jacek. "That's where the two cement posts were. They were still there when I came with Marysia in the 1960s."

"So that's where the gate was," I say, "and the barbed wire and the sentry. That's where they were all herded. This is where Marek Edelman stood for six weeks. Exactly where you are standing now."

In the place where the posts, gate, sentry, and barbed wire used to be, a narrow passage, or rather a road, now connects the site of the gas station to the blue shopping pavilion. We are now standing to the rear of the pavilion. The road along which they were escorted is reserved for delivery vans. A van drives past the sentry and barbed wire and cement posts with cartons of macaroni, trays of pastries, plastic packages of "E" powder or Pollen powder. Those who volunteered received three kilos of bread and a kilo of jam. As I read in Abraham Lewin's *Diary of the Warsaw Ghetto*, Lola Kapelusz, the wife of the Łódź lawyer, went along twice with her small daughter who had eaten nothing for two days. She was sent away, as there was no room in the freight cars. Apparently the Germans once had to send Jewish policemen to disperse the crowd with batons as it pressed in at the gate. This went on for several days, then no more bread or jam was distributed, and the raids were resumed.

If one walks along the rear of the shopping pavilion, one comes out into a playground. To the south it is closed off by fencing; on the other side of this is a courtyard, or rather an athletic field shared by the professional schools. The blue pavilion is to the west, the rear wall of the hut belonging to the Polish Motor Transport base to the east. The playground has metal poles for swings. Sundry contraptions cobbled together from planks to resemble tents or huts, so children can play cops and robbers, cowboys and Indians, Germans and Poles. Or even that other game. They can play if they want. Though I'd be surprised if they did.

"It could have been here," says Jacek, as we cross the playground in the direction of the houses between Dzika Street and Inflancka Street. "The tracks and the ramp for loading the freight cars."

"I know Rudnicki's book is rather muddled," I say, "but he came here three times, and the road he calls 'the sandy way' seems to have been quite long."

"From here to the hospital building must be about two hundred meters," says Jacek, "or slightly more. So it could have been here."

"I have a hunch that the last selection took place here," I say. "This is where they wanted Korczak to return to the Commune to try to save the children."

"The proposal was made when he was still sitting by the yard wall with the children," says Jacek.

"The great gate mentioned by Leokadia Schmidt ought to be near here," I say, "maybe by this swing. You know the one I mean, it had the signboard with the words 'No entry under penalty of death.' But the gate could have been where the pavilion is now, next to the supermarket—I bet there's a long line for baskets there on Saturdays."

"I don't understand why these apartment buildings and this pavilion were erected here," says Jacek. "Why are these children playing on the swings? I mean, this is a site that will always be remembered, like Thermopylae or Verdun, but more so. A few hundred years from now when all has passed into oblivion, Umschlagplatz will not be forgotten. New nations will be born, surpassing even our wildest dreams, and their historians will want to find the gate with the words 'No entry under penalty of death.' Why on earth did they construct those dreadful apartment buildings here?"

"As far as I know," I say, "the Jews didn't object when the buildings were put up. They had previously agreed—in fact, they might even have suggested it themselves—that the Monument be situated between Zamenhof Street and Gęsia Street or Anielewicz Street. Where the last September concentration took place. Though by rights the Monument should stand here."

"If they didn't object," says Jacek, as we enter the square or piazza—I don't know what to call the site hemmed in by apartment buildings between Dzika Street and Inflancka Street—"if they didn't object, then it's probably okay by them. Because I can't imagine them not caring. They wanted houses to stand here, they wanted life to go on. As though they were afraid of an empty Umschlagplatz with nothing but ruined huts, tracks, and freight cars. Let's have some life. Then Umschlagplatz will slowly fade and slip into the past. That would be one way of explaining it."

"There's no harm in people living here," I say. "That is also a monument of sorts. Besides, look, it really is quite attractive."

Compared with Poland's predominantly dreary backyards, the site between the apartment buildings is quite neat and attractive. Protected by small fences of stained boards, the thujas look healthy. The parking lot and the stench of the cars' exhaust are on the other side of the buildings. The pathways are swept. The garbage cans, tin trolleys on wheels, are tucked away out of sight. If trees have memory, three or four trees will remember. Soon they will turn pleasantly green, which will no doubt cheer up the residents of the gray buildings. Perhaps those are the poplars which Marek Edelman mentions in his conversation with Hanna Krall: "The locomotive was where the poplars are."

"I'll tell you when the leaves come out," says Jacek. "I can't tell from the bark. But they look like poplars."

A girl in jeans is walking a cocker spaniel; it comes to sniff my legs. A woman in a red scarf leans over a high baby carriage. Two boys, aged nine or ten, scramble up the ridge between the poplars.

"Do you know what used to be here?" I ask them.

"No," says one.

"Oh yes," says the second. "The ghetto was here. And the sidings they deported the Jews from."

If a sociologist were to put the same question to the people now queueing for baskets outside the supermarket, buying pastries at Camargo, carrying soap from the kitchenware store, washing their cars, or walking the dog, the answer given by the two boys would probably represent the national average. But we'd better restrict our questionnaire to children. With adults you never know who you are talking to.

"Let's go back to Dzika Street," says Jacek, "I mean the old Dzika Street. Only one house has survived. I think it was on the Aryan side, but close to the wall. When I came with Marysia it hadn't been plastered. It looks different with the plaster, but you should see it."

A perfectly ordinary house. Three stories, quite respectable. It was restored over ten years ago; the yellowish plaster is cracked in places. The gutter has rusted and needs replacing. There is nothing more to be said about the last house of the old Dzika Street.

"Now just try to imagine someone living there at the time," says Jacek. "The woman opens the window and places a pillow on the sill on which to rest her elbows. She leans out and watches. Day after day. How many days did the great extermination last?"

"At least fifty," I say, "about fifty-four. But I don't know if onlookers were allowed. They may have fired shots at the windows."

"Maybe they did," says Jacek, "but then again maybe

they didn't. Propped on her elbows, she watches. The wall below bristles with pieces of broken glass. Beyond the wall the ramp and freight cars are waiting."

"What about us?" I say. "What are we doing? We are looking too. Walking about and observing. The ramp is here, the freight cars are there. Here are the cement posts, there is the gate."

"It's not the same," says Jacek. "We are observing the present-day scene. We perceive what happened then through the lens of the present."

"Old Hillel Cajtlin was apparently shot beside the freight cars," I say, as the yellow Fiat drives down Karmelicka Street in the direction of the Monument. "Before death they used to put on a special liturgical robe, so that's how he dressed before leaving. Do you know who he was?"

"No," says Jacek, "I can't say I've ever heard of him."

"A journalist and writer," I say. "He seems to have been an influential figure, much respected. He had two sons, Aron and Elchanan. Singer spoke of Aron with great affection when he received the Nobel Prize. They must have been friends. I have read some of his poetry in Polish translation. It's pretty good stuff."

"Singer is a good writer too," says Jacek, turning from Anielewicz Street into Marchlewski Street. "Very good, in fact."

"A *sofer*," I say.

"What does *sofer* mean?" asks Jacek.

"It's the only Hebrew word I know," I say, "except for the words everyone knows, like zaddik, heder, yeshiva, or mezuzah. *Sofer* means a writer. But also a scribe, someone who copies out the Torah. Before he starts he must be ritually purified, after which he is not allowed to make a single mistake. If he does, everything he has copied has to be discarded."

"That is obviously unattainable," says Jacek, "especially if one is to learn from one's mistakes. But it could serve as an ideal to emulate."

"Or a commitment," I say. "You vow to do everything in your power not to make a mistake. Let's go to my place. We'll check my map to see if there were trolley lines on Stawki Street before the war."

To these loose, unstructured documents and notes of mine that may one day provide the basis for compiling a brief guide to the Warsaw ghetto, I would like to append the register of houses in the Northern District that were not destroyed by the Germans. I walk through the ghetto listing the extant houses.

We are now standing on Sienna Street, between Marchlewski Street and the Palace of Culture. On the northern side of Sienna Street there is nothing. Four highly respectable prewar houses on the southern side were restored no more than two or three years ago, but I am not sure if they belonged to the ghetto. Several sources compare wartime Sienna Street with the Champs-Elysées. The Elysian

Fields of the Warsaw ghetto. It was the most beautiful and perhaps the only tree-lined street in the ghetto, where trees were a great rarity.

If you felt like taking a stroll beneath the trees you went to Sienna Street or to the cemetery, the one by Okopowa Street. The cemetery, the ghetto's only park or garden, was also a place for walks in spring or summer, or so Pan Michał told me. People brought their folding chairs. Here they sit on chairs beneath the trees. There they toss a sack of potatoes over the wall. Over there a black cart trundles by laden with naked bodies. I wonder what the Jews talked about as they sat among the gravestones. Probably the same things one chats about in any park or garden. If people went strolling down Sienna Street beneath the trees, the whole of Sienna Street, north and south sides alike, was inside the ghetto. Yet I know that Sienna Street was barricaded by a wall, or barbed wire or a fence. If so, its southern side could not have belonged to the ghetto. Thus those four houses were situated on the Aryan side, but when? Sienna Street may have been barricaded at the time of the great extermination, or just before or just after. I stand in the middle of Sienna Street and crane my neck to look at four houses that for some unknown reason were not destroyed forty-five years ago.

"I wonder if those houses have been listed by someone," I say, "because if so I'm wasting my time. After all, it is quite possible that a register already exists."

"What houses?" asks Hania.

"The houses that weren't destroyed," I say, "and are still standing there. They demolished everything, but they left a dozen or so houses unscathed. God alone knows why. There must have been some reason. I wonder how many houses we now have left in our ghetto."

"Several dozen, I would think," says Hania.

"Not that many," I say. "I'll list them, you count. There are four here. The building where Femina was. The one on Marchlewski Street, next to Femina, which they are renovating right now. And the one on Leszno Street, alias Świerczewski Avenue, where the Thirteen was."

"That makes seven," says Hania. "Plus those three on Krochmalna Street near the corner of Żelazna Street. And the one on Chłodna Street near the bridge, where the pharmacy is now. That makes eleven."

"Two houses on Karmelicka Street on the other side of Nowolipki," I say. "Three on Żelazna Street, where the Befehlsstelle SS used to be. The house at 2A Wolność Street. Number 19 Żelazna Street, where the maternity hospital is. The one on Ciepła Street by the Prosta-Świętokrzyska traffic circle. But I think it's two houses."

"Twenty all told," says Hania. "That's quite a lot. Oh, and the house on Miła Street, close to Anielewicz's bunker. And two or three houses on Leszno Street, behind the Law Courts before you get to Żelazna Street."

"Let's go down Nalewki Street," I say, "toward Muranowski Square, and then along Gęsia Street in the direction of Bonifraterska Street. But I don't think a single house has survived there. So what's the total?"

"Twenty-three or twenty-four," says Hania. "But don't forget the hospital between Sienna Street and Śliska Street, it's probably two separate buildings. And three more on

Śliska Street, opposite the hospital. And the house next to the Phoenix on Sienna Street."

"We should also include the factory buildings on Okopowa Street," I say, "and the houses on Próżna Street and Grzybowski Square, because that's where the greatest conglomeration was. Próżna Street was in the ghetto until July 1942. That amounts to forty or fifty houses, maybe more. That's all that has survived. But those fifty-odd houses should be divided into two categories, those that were partially burnt out and then rebuilt and those that survived intact. A dozen of those, twenty at the utmost."

"The entire ghetto could now fit into one small street," says Hania.

"It was already shrinking at the time," I say. "Its boundaries were constantly shifting. And it will continue to shrink as the houses gradually disappear. Most are in pitiful condition and will have to be demolished. There is a book by Zieman, the author of *The Cigarette Vendors of Three Crosses Square*. It is called *The Mobile Frontiers of the Warsaw Ghetto* or *The Changing Frontiers of the Warsaw Ghetto*, but it is in Yiddish or Hebrew. So the boundaries are still shifting and shrinking. One day the ghetto will be just one house. After which there will not be a single house left."

"By then the entire ghetto, or what remains of it, will be under the ground," says Hania. "But it still has a few decades to go, so we won't be there to see it."

"Thank goodness for that," I say. "I hope I don't live to see the last ghetto house covered over with earth. Let's go back to Śliska Street. It's only a few meters away."

"You can see Śliska Street from here," says Hania.

"There's nothing there. Apart from the three houses with annexes overlooking Prosta Street. Or Pańska Street."

"Hillel Cajtlin used to live on Śliska Street," I say. "I'm not sure if he went to Umschlagplatz himself or if he was escorted there. He took nothing with him; he left all his manuscripts at home. Later on, Ringelblum or another member of Oneg Szabat acting on Ringelblum's instructions apparently went around to Cajtlin's apartment to retrieve his manuscripts. But he found nothing. Cajtlin had probably stashed them in some hiding place or buried them in the cellar."

"Do you know where Cajtlin's house was?" asks Hania.

"No," I say. "We will walk past it without even knowing. But perhaps the place will know us. Perhaps it will know we are walking past and thinking about it."

"Have you heard," says Hania as we pass the place on Śliska Street where the charred manuscripts of Hillel Cajtlin hide behind charred bricks, "have you heard about the woman who knelt down on the pavement?"

"When?" I ask. "Now?"

"In the summer of '42," says Hania, "but not here, it has nothing to do with the ghetto. She knelt on New World Street. I read about her in Abraham Lewin's diary. I don't know where he got it from. He must have been told by someone who'd returned to the ghetto from the Aryan side. A military policeman shot a Jewish child on New World Street. And then this woman, a Christian eyewitness, knelt down on the pavement and began to pray out loud. I remember how Lewin phrased it. 'She prayed to God that He direct his sword against the murderers.' Can you visualize the scene? Somewhere on the corner of Warecka Street, near the delicatessen. Or under that archway we pass on our way to Alinka's. By the cheese store. She knelt and prayed to God to take action at last."

"To ask for God to intervene strikes me as utterly futile," I say. "If God observes such a scene He ought to know what to do without our telling Him. Besides, we shouldn't apply our notions of 'ought' or 'ought not' to God, because our concept of duty does not and cannot concern Him. God has no obligations toward us. If He is and sees, then He does what He wants and not what we think He ought to do. He would be a paltry sort of God if He obeyed us."

"And yet you pray to Him," says Hania. "In fact, you're praying right now that He direct your steps to the spot where Cajtlin's manuscripts are hidden."

"I am praying like the woman on New World Street," I say, "that He turn His sword against the murderers. That He allow me to touch those manuscripts. That He keep in His care those houses, the register of which I intend to present to Him. But the sense of my prayer is not clear to me. I am praying, but that does not mean I know why I am praying."

"But you think it might help. That you will be heard," says Hania.

"Heard by prayer. Perhaps that is the best way to put it. I pray because I think prayer has a sovereign power. But that's the wrong word; I don't think, I feel, I believe. Prayer is a kind of intent listening. That prayer be heard and fulfilled by prayer."

"In other words, the God to whom you pray is prayer," Hania says. "Or dwells in prayer. Do you remember what Rabbi Pinchas of Korzec said? Everyone will find the hidden God where he can: 'one in tears, another in prayer, yet another in songs of praise.' "

"Prayer is prayer," I say. "That is all we are allowed to know."

"I REALLY am delighted you decided to come at last," I say. "Hania will be delighted too, but she's not at home, she's just run out to the supermarket."

"I've put up at the Hotel Victoria," says Icyk. I am slightly taken aback by this phrase, it sounds kind of quaint. But then I realize that Icyk must have formulated it in his head before he even dialed our number, so as to intimate that in coming to Warsaw he has traveled a distance not of seven thousand kilometers but of half a century. He is a visitor from a different time, a different epoch, a different aeon even. Between 1939 and 1945 one aeon ended and another began, a notion that Icyk and I both find highly plausible. Question: can a man spend the first half of his life—in my case, the formative years—in one aeon, and the second half, or life's end, in a different aeon? "I've put up at the Victoria, it's no distance at all. I'll walk through the Saxon Garden and down Tłomackie Street, and have a look at our synagogue on the way."

"There's no Tłomackie Street now," I say. "When you come out of the Saxon Garden, Mr. Isaac, you must turn toward Dzierżhyński Square."

"I know it doesn't exist," Icyk interrupts me. "You don't have to teach me, my boy. I'll walk down Tłomackie Street, and you can catch the D in Kazimierz the Great Square and go to the terminus at the corner of Zamenhof Street and Gęsia Street. But coming from Filtrowa Street you'll find it more convenient to take an eight from the corner of Independence Avenue and September 6 Street, though it will take you longer. Via Graniczna Street and Iron Gate Square. Then you'll have to get off at the corner of Zamenhof Street and Muranowska Street."

"What a memory," I say.

"What else is there for me?" says Icyk. "Memory is all I have left, nothing more. So catch whatever you can from your place and let's say we'll meet in an hour's time at the junction of Niska Street and Stawki Street."

"Bus 157 goes that way now. Or I could take a fifteen and get out at Stawki Street."

"The fifteen used to go to Wilson Square," says Icyk. "In '38 or '39 Miss Lilka rented a bachelor apartment in Krasiński Square. But why should I tell you all this? We'll meet in an hour at the junction of Niska Street and Stawki Street. Then we'll walk along Gęsia Street or Miła Street to the cemetery and I'll show you, my boy, what it used to look like in those days, and you can show me what it looks like now. What you've been building there."

"Blocks of gray brick," I say. "Nothing out of the ordinary."

"I didn't expect anything out of the ordinary. If my hotel is anything to go by, Corbusiers are a bit scarce. Perhaps you should have kept the ruins."

"It is the City Center," I say. "Can you imagine mounds of pulverized brick in the very heart of the city, Mr. Isaac? An avalanche of burnt bricks. Now that would be a monument."

"What are you going on about, my boy," says Icyk. From his tone of voice I gather that he is offended or even wounded by my use of the word "monument." "What do you mean by monument? Can such things be commemorated by a monument? Either everything is a monument or nothing is a monument. See you in an hour's time. But be punctual, because it is unseemly that an old Jew should have to wait for a young goy."

"Do you know how old I am?" I ask. "I'm fifty-two."

"And do you know how old I am?" asks Icyk.

"Of course," I say, "as old as everyone."

"Well answered," says Icyk. "But you cribbed that from me. See you later."

"There's a gas station there now," I say. "Just on the corner of Dzika Street as you come out of Karmelicka Street. You can't miss it."

"See you by the gas station," says Icyk.

"Right," I say, "see you at Umschlagplatz."

But that is not what I said, nor what I would have said, in my telephone conversation with Icyk. That parting sentence is, as I feel it, indelicate and unacceptable, though I would be hard put to give a reason. I decided to record it here, as its very impropriety requires that I give it some thought. I sensed its indecorum the moment it entered my head. Why?

In the first place, its phonetic or grammatical form allows for it to be uttered in a rather offhand manner, which is obviously intolerable, as it slights the memory of those who walked through the gate at the junction of Stawki Street, Niska Street, and Dzika Street. Second, by uttering that phrase I include myself, albeit symbolically, in the circle of those who have passed through Umschlag. Someone who has not been through has no moral right to adopt this stance. Third and most important, "See you at Umschlagplatz" seems to contain a warning or premonition that it will all happen here again, that people will again sink to the same depths as the SS men and the Jewish policemen from Umschlagplatz once did. Brandt, Szeryński, Szmerling. It must be that evil foreboding I find so intolerable. Does that mean one should not air these theories? I do not know. My opinion varies on this point. Anyone who lives within a stone's throw of Umschlagplatz knows that everything is possible.

The phrase that might have concluded my telephone conversation with Icyk when he came back to Warsaw after almost half a century was never actually uttered. But not because I might have offended him. "Whatever are you thinking, my boy," and Icyk hangs up on me. Later, when Hania and I call him, he says he is very busy and cannot see us. Hania would never have forgiven me, and I would never have forgiven myself either. I don't know why Icyk would have reacted like that, but he would have repaid us in kind, no two ways about it. In such instances he was incredibly consistent, and whenever Icyk considered himself to have been slighted, the offending party could at best expect to be treated like foul stinking air for several years to come. Even then he had been let off lightly. For if Icyk imagined he had been slighted by someone, he was capable of flying right off the handle.

I remember an incident during Icyk's last visit to Warsaw. We were sitting at a table in the Ujazdowska Café, the one in Ujazdów Avenue, near the old Kripo headquarters. During our conversation, which inevitably centered on the destiny of Jews, Polish Jews and Jewish Poles, here in Warsaw, someone, never mind who, said, "The Jews did a lot of harm here." Icyk barely reacted, which surprised me somewhat. He merely removed his thin-wired glasses, held them level with his nose, and peered above the frames, tilting his head at that someone, who was not a Jew. His tone may have been a trifle aggressive, but there was nothing reprehensible in what he said. It was obvious from the general context that he did not mean all Jews, but those who had sided with the communists and had been busy in the late forties and early fifties tearing out nails and crushing fingers in drawers in the building on Koszykowa Street.

But Icyk did not appear to understand the intended reference. Or perhaps he understood and was offended by the implied generalization, for he considered that a Jew who becomes a communist ceases to be a Jew. The conversation moved on to the life of Jewish Poles in Jerusalem. "If I were a Polish Jew born in Warsaw, or even a Zionist or revisionist Jew in the manner of Jabotinsky," I said, "I still don't think I'd feel at ease there. I'd dream at night that I was levitating above the Saxon Garden, or, higher still, above the skyscraper in Napoleon Square." "What can you know about that, my boy," said Icyk, rising from the table. "I'm going to get another coffee." I didn't ask Icyk at the time, and now I regret it, what it was he thought I knew nothing about. Did he mean the Jerusalem dreams of a Warsaw-born Zionist Jew or levitation above the Saxon Garden?

When he saw that Icyk wanted another coffee, the man who had, pace Icyk, commented on the Jews working on Koszykowa Street promptly sprang to his feet: "Allow me the pleasure, Mr. Isaac. I'll get your coffee." And a minute later he returned from the counter with a cup of coffee and set it before Icyk. "They've run out of cream, it's turned sour." Icyk took five twenty-zloty metal coins out of his pocketbook and without a word placed them in a small stack before the man, who reacted the way one always reacts in such situations and pushed the twenty-zloty pieces back toward Icyk, saying, "Do be my guest, Mr. Isaac." Then Icyk picked up the twenty-zloty coins, smiled politely, and said, "The Jews, my boy, have done a lot of harm here." Whereupon he flung the five metal coins back at his antagonist. Although he was smiling so politely, that could best be described as a fit of temper.

I return to the phrase I never uttered in ending my conversation with Icyk, who had put up at the Victoria Hotel: "See you at Umschlagplatz." I never said it because I never had the chance. Icyk never made the journey to Warsaw, so our conversation never took place, it had to be invented.

Even as I write this book I am irritated by my tendency to fictionalize, though I try to keep these elements to a minimum. Ideally my book tells the common history of Poles and Jews as it really was, with no imaginary additives. To my mind no other book could properly testify to the past, or provide the restitution we Poles owe to our Polish Jews. But I am limited to a spiritual rather than a practical experience of Polish-Jewish life, and this prevents my writing an unfictionalized testimony. Who knows, my novel, in which authentic facts are mixed with fiction, may also be an act of restitution. That is how I conceived it, and that is the best that I can do.

In the case of my imaginary conversation with Icyk, I feel that fictionalizing is here justified. Both Hania and I were very anxious for Icyk to come to Warsaw. In anticipation of his visit I often imagined our first meeting at Okęcie airport, our ride from the airport to the hotel in the red Renault, our telephone conversation between the Staszic Colony and the Hotel Victoria, and Icyk's visit to Filtrowa Street. "That picture above your sofa of Prince Joseph leaping into the Elster," says Icyk, "I remember it at your aunt's place in Żoliborz fifty years ago, Hania." I remember how when Hania and I once set off for Otwock in the red Renault I even attempted to concretize these imaginings. For Hania's benefit I began to construct my first telephone conversation with Icyk: he'll say that, then I'll reply, and he will answer. At this point Hania did what she usually does in such circumstances: she let go of the steering wheel, which one day will end in some terrible accident, and said, "He'll never come." "Why?" "You'll never understand." So I can say that my conversation with Icyk is imaginary, but not imagined. I rehearsed it several times with myself and uttered the final phrase in a number of different versions that came into my head, including "See you at the gas station on the corner of Dzika Street."

That was probably the last sentence Icyk formulated in his apartment on the twenty-second floor as he pressed his left palm on the metal window frame in search of a suitable closing for his novel. The typescript was lying by his right hand on the desk, scribbled all over with crossings and red and green inky scrawls in the margins; Icyk was using at least three fountain pens at the time. In the process he realized that something was up with him.

But we are free to speculate that other thoughts then pressed into his brain. "Damn that pacemaker," Icyk reflected, "it's just plain American *Scheisse*. I must get it changed immediately. Or more likely my hour has struck." His right arm seems to have become detached below the elbow. "How odd," thinks Icyk, "that my right hand should come away from my body, and not the left, which is giving me pain as it slides down the metal frame, I don't know why." The severed hand now flies above the desk and sweeps off the pot of red ink, the typescript of the novel, and the fountain pen with the gold nib, the same Parker that fifty years previously had been placed on the blue notebook between the shed and the red-currant and white-currant bushes.

"I wonder," thinks Icyk as he attempts to arrest his runaway right hand with his left. This proves unfeasible, because when levitating just above floor level you cannot grasp a hand that's hovering high over a desktop. "I wonder if it is like passing from one room to the next, as that pupil of Rabbi Mendel of Worki claimed, or if Rabbi Mendel was right in saying that it is no more than moving over to another corner of the room. But where did I put that book of Buber's where I read about it? If only I could stop levitating for just one moment, I could look it up." Icyk's right hand, the detached one, was fluttering within close range of Buber's book, third shelf from the bottom, and could easily pull it down. But at the very instant his hand alighted near the book, my friend Icyk Mandelbaum ceased to levitate.

And now Arie Wilner, Abrasza Blum, Zysze Frydman, Menachem Kirszenbaum, Władysław Szlengel, Anna Natanblut, Szachno Zagan, Tobcia Dawidowicz, Paulina Braun, Abraham Gepner, Icchak Giterman, Szmul Brasł aw, Niuta Tajtelbaum—Szmul's overcoat is ripped at the seam and the wadding is falling out, and Niuta's sailor blouse is soiled with lime, but does it matter?—and also the slightly older generation: Włodzimierz Meden, Chaim and Lejb Dawidsohn, Józef Szpisman, Bronisław Mansperl, and Jecheskel Portnoj all walk up to greet Icyk and with their warm fingers they touch his forehead, cheeks, and beard—Icyk with a beard? They take his arm and escort him from the building of the Law Courts—that's the shortest way to our district—out onto Leszno Street. Arms still linked, they walk past the Befehlsstelle SS at 103 Żelazna Street, then turn back onto Leszno Street and head in the direction of Karmelicka Street. They pass the Femina revue at 35 Leszno Street, where the Jewish policemen's orchestra is giving a concert by acetylene-lamp light under the baton of Szymon Kataszek. Unless the nightingale of the ghetto, young Marysia Ajzensztadt, is on tonight. How beautiful she is, Marysia Ajzensztadt, and now she will be eighteen forever.

They turn from Leszno Street onto Karmelicka Street, not far from the headquarters of the Thirteen. But they won't go there. They continue down Karmelicka Street, past the wooden fence, behind which Big Schultz has his workshop. The entrance to the workshop is on the corner of Nowolipie Street. They walk past. They go in through the next gate, the one that shuts off the exit of Karmelicka Street. They proceed along Nowolipie Street between the houses where Big Schultz's workers live. They are close to the overhead gangway that leads via the attics from Nowolipie Street to Nowolipki Street, and even as far as Smocza Street, from the workshops of Hoffman and Schultz to Roerich's establishment. They turn onto Smocza Street and pass in front of the police sentry, the one on the corner of Nowolipki Street. Hard by is the house where, in 1950, cans and metal boxes containing the second part of Emanuel Ringelblum's archive were found amid the rubble. But instead of going that way, they follow Dzielna Street, Pawia Street, Gęsia Street. When they pass the sentinel at the exit of Gęsia Street into Okopowa Street, they are only a few yards from the iron gate. In the cemetery between Okopowa Street and Młynarska Street the chestnuts are in bloom, and it will be pleasant to stroll beneath their white cones. Unless only stumps are left standing, broken by bullets, blackened by fire. The gate opens and they enter the cemetery where our parents are buried.

"Don't take offense, my boy," says Icyk as we come out of the cemetery and walk slowly along Mordechaj Anielewicz Street, between the gray buildings, in the direction of the Monument. "I find it very pleasant walking with you, but that is not really what I have come here for. There's something I'd like to hear, and you'd be in the way."

"Forgive my indiscretion," I say, "but what is it you want to hear?"

"Frankly," says Icyk, "I'd like to hear lame Szlojmele's great aria as he moans and stutters in communion with the Powers. Do you remember lame Szlojmele?"

"Of course," I say. "But how do you think you'll manage that, Mr. Isaac?"

"I doubt if Szlojmele can still be heard," says Icyk, "but he is singing his aria somewhere, you mark my words. Either here or in Otwock. I might go there tomorrow. What is this street called?"

"Mordechaj Anielewicz. And that one is Karmelicka Street."

"Karmelicka Street," says Icyk, "imagine that. Now you go home and give Hania a kiss from me. I may call you this evening. But now I'll just go for a little stroll."

Jarosław M. Rymkiewicz

✤

THE photograph everyone knows: a boy in a peaked cap and knee-length socks, his hands raised. We do not know when it was taken. During the great extermination, in July or August 1942? Or during the Uprising in the ghetto, in April 1943? Or perhaps some other time. But not during the second extermination of January 1943, as the photo was taken in spring, summer, or autumn, though definitely not in winter.

It is hard to say if the boy is standing in a courtyard or outside a house entrance in the street, as all we can see is one corner of the gateway and its dark interior. The flaked-off plaster indicates the old and decrepit state of the block of apartment houses from which he has been dragged. So we are on Miła Street, Gęsia Street, or Wołynska Street rather than on Sienna Street or Grzybowska Street. But it could be elsewhere. Behind the boy with the raised arms is an oblong pit with something white, probably garbage, in it; it is a garbage pit. So we are in a backyard rather than a street. To the right stand four Germans, one in the gateway, three by the entrance, near the dilapidated corner and the cast-iron gutter. Two of their faces, three even in good reproductions, are clearly visible. I have pored over that photo for so long and so often that if I were now after forty-five years to meet one of those Germans in the street I'd identify him instantly.

One of the Germans holds an automatic pistol under his

arm, apparently aiming at the boy's back. The Germans all have helmets on; the one with the pistol sports motorcycling goggles. To the left there are several women, a few men, and about three children. All with their arms raised. The men are wearing caps. On the far left stands a small girl aged five or six. She is smaller than the boy in the knee socks and wears a kerchief on her head. She also has her arms raised, but as she is at the edge of the photo we can see only one hand above her kerchiefed head. I have counted twenty-three people in this photo, though the figures on the left are so huddled together that I may have miscounted: nineteen Jews and four Germans. I would like to draw your attention to the very pretty face of the woman on the left, probably the mother of the girl with the kerchief. She wears her hair to the side, and has prominent cheekbones, large eyes, and a large mouth. One can imagine her blushing beneath her pallor. On her raised arm she has a white armband, but the Star of David is not visible. After forty-five years I'd still recognize that woman in the street. But I obviously never will.

The boy in the center of the picture wears a short raincoat reaching just above his knees. He must have a sweater under his coat, but it is hard to tell, as the coat is buttoned up. His cap, tilted slightly askew, looks too big for him. Maybe it's his father's or his elder brother's? We have the boy's personal data: Artur Siemiątek, son of Leon and Sara née Dąb, born in Łowicz. Artur is my contemporary: we were both born in 1935. We stand side by side, he in this photo taken in the Warsaw ghetto, I in the photo taken on the high platform in Otwock. We may assume that both photographs were taken in the same month, mine a week or so earlier. We even seem to be wearing the same caps. Mine is of a lighter shade and also looks too big for my head. The boy is wearing knee-high socks, I'm wearing white ankle socks. On the platform in Otwock I am smiling nicely. The boy's face—the photo was taken by an SS sergeant—betrays nothing.

"You're tired," I say to Artur. "It must be very uncomfortable standing like that with your arms in the air. I know what we'll do. I'll lift my arms up now, and you put yours down. They may not notice. But wait, I've got a better idea. We'll both stand with our arms up."

ZBYSZEK and Adaś, the Adaś to whom Antoni would not confide his secret for fear of demoralizing him, have just received their American prizes. We are standing in a living room on Idzikowski Street in Warsaw and at the same time in New York or Paris. In honor of Zbyszek and Adaś we drink wine and eat salami and ham with rice in a sauce.

"Marek Edelman is here," says Hania. "He's standing over there. You can have a good look."

"Could you introduce me to Marek Edelman?" I ask Wiktor. "I've just written a book about the Warsaw ghetto in which I quote him. So it might be just as well if I made his acquaintance at last."

"Did you really say"—that is the first question I ask

Marek Edelman after being introduced by Wiktor—"in that interview did you really say that strength is all that counts? I mean the interview you gave to the guys from the opposition."

"My very words," says Marek Edelman. "Strength is all that counts, nothing else."

Then after I have asked him all the questions I wanted, though countless others remain to be asked, Marek Edelman says, "There are no more Jews in the world. This nation does not exist. It will never exist again."

"Then I will end my book on that statement of yours," I say, "if you agree."

"I agree," says Marek Edelman. "There are no Jews left. And there'll never be any Jews again."